A Tour of the Heart

ALSO BY MARIBETH CLEMENTE

The Riches of Paris:
A Shopping and Touring Guide

The Riches of France:
A Shopping and Touring Guide to the French Provinces

AS MARIBETH RICOUR DE BOURGIES

The Chic Shopper's Guide to Paris

A Tour

of the

Heart

A Seductive Cycling Trip
Through France

Maribeth Clemente

Cover art by Chandler Thayer
Cover design by Mark Eversman
Map by Lauren Metzger

ISBN-13: 978-1479134366
ISBN-10: 1479134368

September 2012

To Mary Ellen and Frank Clemente,
my parents, my wonderful mom and dad,
with deep gratitude for all the love, laughter and travel
you've nurtured in my life

CONTENTS

La France

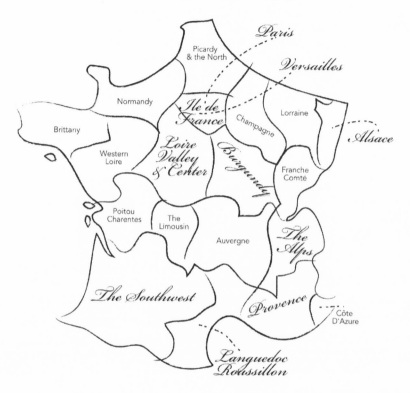

Paris

Versailles

Picardy & the North

Normandy

Brittany

Île de France

Champagne

Lorraine

Alsace

Western Loire

Loire Valley & Center

Burgundy

Franche Comté

Poitou Charentes

The Limousin

Auvergne

The Alps

The Southwest

Provence

Côte D'Azure

Languedoc Roussillon

PART ONE

Putting the Wheels in Motion

Even before marrying my Frenchman, I had established my own business, Chic Promenade, a shopping service that organized jaunts to Paris's lesser-known boutiques and arranged visits behind-the-scenes at the couture houses and other big designer names. Indeed, I spent eleven years soaking up French culture and fashion. With my husband, Stéphane, a professional photographer, we circulated in a high-stepping world filled with fascinating people at events such as cocktail parties at Cartier, art gallery openings and five-star hotel receptions.

But I was out of balance. And I didn't fully realize that until I moved back to the States and began a new life as a single woman. (How I hate the term divorcée.) It was time to reclaim myself, to figure out what kind of a woman I really was. That didn't mean shunning my fussy Parisian side or my French flair and *savoir faire*. But it meant becoming a little more real. We all need embellishments, traditions and a certain *style de vie*, but for me, there was too much emphasis on all that in France. I needed to figure out what else was important in my new life back in America.

I wanted to develop my other sides—especially my physical side. This didn't come as a conscious decision; it just happened. I found myself in my parents' garage, dusting off the Trek bicycle given to me by an old boyfriend (a not-so-subtle hint, I suppose) and began to ride. That was the beginning of my transformation from girly-girl to cycling enthusiast, a metamorphosis that seemed to lead quite naturally to my relationship with Peter—my polar opposite—who worked in the local bike shop. And eventually, to Peter's transformation and our own little "tour de France."

Almost a year after we began dating, and the morning of our departure for a six-week cycling tour in France, I headed home to my tiny, upstate New York apartment after rushing about to do some last-minute errands. I walked up the steep, narrow stairs of my old, historic building, juggling packages and hangers that felt like they were cutting into my hands. I trudged all the way to my top-floor apartment until finally I arrived at the landing. I paused outside the door, dropped my heavy load of dry cleaning, cat food and last-minute travel supplies and fumbled for my key. No noise emanated from within, so I wondered if Pete was inside. *I hope so*, I thought. *I hope he's finished his packing. Breathe*, I told myself. *You're almost there. You're on the good end of things. You'll soon be on the plane for Paris with a handsome guy you love, embarking on the adventure of a lifetime. Just breathe.*

"Hello," I practically sang out in a sweet, cheery voice.

"Hey, how's it going?" Pete called back.

"Ohhhhhhkay," I replied, feeling my jaw drop both from the drawn-out "oh" in OK and also the shock of the moment. I had made it all the way into my apartment and couldn't believe the scene before me.

Pete chuckled and gave me a wry smile. "Don't worry, I've got everything under control."

I stood there and surmised the situation as my bundles flopped at my feet. Mr. Kitty, my black-and-tan tabby, rubbed between my ankles and my pile of stuff. My eyes scanned the living and dining room area of my 600-square-foot Victorian apartment. It seemed like I was already assessing the damages. Pete had installed a large bike stand dangerously close to my eighteenth-century French armoire, the most important treasure that I brought back from France six years prior. His bike was clamped onto the stand; the front wheel was spun out at an angle, just inches from my piece of museum-quality furniture. He had laid out an array of tools and gear parts on an end table that was butted up against one of my other accent pieces; my precious flower-patterned chintz table skirts were fluffed out within perilous range. My off-white, shabby chic armchair wasn't much farther from Pete than the armoire.

I gasped. I probably should have counted to ten—or even twenty—but instead I blurted out, "What are you doing?"

"What does it look like I'm doing?" he bellowed back.

I could feel my heart accelerating and suddenly the romantic images of us—enjoying France together, pedaling through the countryside and sipping wine at a quaint hotel—whooshed before my eyes and then extinguished in one giant pouf.

Kitty rustled in the bags for his treats, purring intensely as he head-butted the sides of my legs.

Is this going to be our coup de grâce? I wondered in a flash as I looked around my prissy apartment, which had been transformed into a full-scale bike shop. Pete had more bike tools and accessories than many professional cycling teams and a good portion of them were strewn about my cozy abode amidst my cushy pillows and luxurious table coverings.

"Don't worry, it'll all be fine," Pete added in a much calmer voice.

"Ya think?" I practically hollered back.

He chuckled and then flashed one of his big, toothy smiles. I backed down. Finally I was able to breathe.

Fortunately Pete did not want his super slick (and pricey) road bike to tip over any more than I wanted my precious armoire to be scratched.

The best we could do was to laugh about it, regardless of all those greasy gears. Had I not been worried about getting messy, I would have given him a hug. I found his tall, brown-haired, brown-eyed and incredibly fit appearance irresistible. His large, expressive features sometimes made me melt. And in truth, his childlike, devil-may-care antics such as this one endeared him to me even more. Plus there was no time for a full on blowout. It was the eleventh hour, and the bikes needed to be packed.

I should have figured that it would take some doing to fit a six-foot-long bike into a four-foot-long bike box. The wheels, handlebars, pedals and seat all had to be removed. Helmets, water bottles and bike shoes needed to be tucked into the remaining spaces.

13

We were finally on our way. We left our charming little town of Saratoga Springs on a glorious end-of-summer day and breathed a sigh of relief that the dreadful task of packing was behind us. We would check everything in Albany, and, although we were changing planes in Boston, we would not have to deal with our cargo until Paris.

Pete barreled down the Northway (although we were headed south, this highway is still referred to as the Northway). I gripped the armrest of the car door but made a conscious effort not to ask him to slow down. Today his speed was warranted since we were running late. We always seemed to be late; that was something we had in common. I was sure that was a sign we'd be good travelers together.

"Whoa!" I found myself exclaiming as he darted in between two cars, switching lanes like a madman. I sensed his annoyance with me and decided once again to button it up. I didn't want another argument. No, the stakes were too high. No sense getting off on a bad footing.

I had taken many trips to France in the six years I had moved back to the States. But I had never gone with a man, I had never gone with a love. And this was to be a work trip to boot. I gazed out the window and admired the emerging array of marigold, burnt umber and rust amid the faded green of late summer. I took solace in the fact that I was trusting my gut, that my instinct was telling me to have faith in the process. I knew intuitively that I was meant to go on this journey with Pete. I just didn't know what the outcome would be for us–but oh, how I hoped it would be grand.

I wanted to live a fully satisfying love, whatever that meant to me—I was still trying to figure it out. I hadn't given up the hope— my heart's desire since I was a young girl—of having a child. Yes, Peter seemed to be a good candidate for that, especially since like attracts like—at least from a physical standpoint—and we were like, a not-so-negligible factor that drew me to him as a mate and lifelong partner. (I'm also tall, brown-haired and brown-eyed with large features, although not as fit.) Certainly I'd have a better sense of how we matched up after traveling with him for well over a month. *Or would I?*

My work goals for the trip seemed almost as nebulous as my relationship goals. I had already written three guidebooks on shopping and touring in France, but I knew this was a whole different project, something much more personalized, something that also had to do with cycling, my new passion. I approached the project with the idea that I was working on another guidebook but I knew there'd be more of a narrative, particularly with Peter along for the travels. Did I feel pressure to produce? Not really, I knew I would write something from the trip, I just wasn't sure of the format.

The various tourism offices (for regions as well as towns) knew I was a travel writer that delivered, so they were more than happy to roll out the red carpet and help me discover their land without me having to outlay much of my resources.

"What are you thinking about, sweetie?" Pete asked.

"Oh, not much. Just pondering the trip."

"You'll see, we'll have a good time. We'll have fun together in France."

"I'm sure we will—I have no doubt about that," I said in a reassuring tone as Pete sped off the exit for the airport terminal.

On the plane ride over, I asked Pete what his expectations were. "To enjoy myself and to be supportive of you," he said.

"Oh, that's sweet. For me, I really want to have a wonderful trip with you—the two of us together—*and* get into great shape. I can't wait to discover France with you," I added, as I gazed out the plane's window, already imagining myself on a bicycle zipping through the French countryside. I envisioned Pete and me riding alongside sunflower fields, vineyards and grazing muddy-brown cows. "I want to experience something significant every day. I want to feel the connectedness with nature in France that I've been feeling every time I head out on my bike in Saratoga."

"I know what you mean," Pete said.

The fading sky had become an impenetrable black. I closed the shade on the window and rolled over and leaned my head on Pete's shoulder, tucking the blanket in around my neck. *I want to feel my body morph into a stronger, more toned version of myself,* I thought. *I want to gain more confidence on every level. Yes, that's it. The bike is such a powerful instrument for achieving that.* My body began to relax for the first time all day. Romantic visions of how I wanted my travels with Pete to play out flooded my head and heart. *I want to have a fantastic time with him, and for the trip to have a really positive effect on our relationship. I've never done anything like this with anyone for such a long period of time—this is going to be a great test for me as well as for us.*

As Pete and I sat on the plane, holding hands, and toasting our travels with champagne, we glowed in the thought of all that lay before us. I said, "I just realized that we are headed to France for more than a month and that we're going to be cycling around some of the most beautiful countryside in the world."

"It seems almost surreal," responded Pete.

We arrived at Charles de Gaulle airport exhausted from a night without much sleep. The day was just beginning in Paris, and Pete was excited about absorbing the early morning activity of the city since it was his first time in France. Our plan was to taxi into Paris, pick up the car at Renault and drive off to Strasbourg in Alsace. Pete was apprehensive about how this was all going to come together, since he still had to reassemble the bikes before leaving Renault. I was confident it would all work out just fine.

Our taxi ride into the French capital provided a glimpse of Parisian life unlike most of what you see on TV and in movies. We cut through a small northern quadrant of Paris, primarily populated by working class people, including many emigrants from North Africa. It was early in the day, the hour in which shops are opening and people are rushing off to work. Awnings were being raised at the numerous Arab-run groceries of the neighborhood, outdoor displays of produce were uncovered and shop owners were standing at their thresholds greeting prospective customers. We saw people popping out of *boulangeries* with their still-warm croissants and baguettes and mothers taking their children by the hand to school nearby.

I looked at Pete taking in this vibrant scene and decided not to offer up any commentary. I'd have plenty of time to play tour guide throughout our travels.

We checked in at Renault and, while waiting for our car with the specially installed bike rack, Pete found a quiet corner where he could reassemble the bikes. All seemed to be going well until we learned that the car had arrived without a bike rack, although someone was hurriedly attempting to rectify that situation. It turned out to be quicker to have Pete take over, but by now he was understandably feeling overtaxed.

"This bike rack is bogus. I prefer fork mounts," he grumbled at me. "Am I supposed to climb Mt. Ventoux with that thing on my bike?" He was referring to some sort of a little widget that had to be affixed to each bike in order for them to be properly implanted in the rack. We were growing increasingly weary by the moment.

I was grateful that Pete did not blame me for these snafus. Overall I felt quite satisfied in how we handled the bike rack conflict, particularly since I imagined that it would set the tone for all other potential confrontations throughout our travels. I was proud of myself for letting Pete vent a bit about the rack without challenging him. As we finally drove off in our well-appointed sedan, I breathed a sigh of relief that we had both survived our first ripple and were still speaking to each other.

Our six-hour drive from Paris to Strasbourg on virtually no sleep was our next hurdle. Normally I stay in Paris for at least a few days before heading out to the provinces, but Pete and I had decided to continue on since our fair weather days were numbered. Thankfully, he was at the wheel, and would be responsible for all the driving throughout our trip. I was to be the navigator. Already, as we wended our way outside of Paris in search of *l'autoroute*, I could tell that Pete would be touchy about how I gave directions. Just as we were both on the verge of real crankiness, we stopped for a caffeine fix. I had been without caffeine for many months, but I knew that this was as good a time as any to artificially elevate my mood. It did the trick for both of us, which prompted much chattering about our trip thus far and our plans for the next few days. And as Pete pointed out while considering all the snappy little cars on the road, "The cycling is bound to be better here than in the States since we won't have to contend with so many SUVs."

"And I think the scenery will be pretty spectacular, too," I added.

Shifting Gears

Growing up with five brothers meant that I was destined to be either a tomboy or a priss. I became the latter and, with the exception of a few brief moments as a swim star, a short-lived presence on my eighth-grade volleyball team, and joining family jaunts to the local ski slopes, I was not a particularly athletic child. Gym class in both grade school and high school was pretty torturous for me. Mrs. Mosher, my grade school phys ed teacher, always called me Miss Butterfingers and to this day I am still totally inept at catching anything, even if it's tossed to me at pathetically close range.

Sports just weren't my thing, and back then, there weren't many special sports programs that encouraged young women to become physically active. Today girls are able to discover early on the empowering feelings that come with sports, whether they're highly competitive or not. I didn't get in touch with this power until the spring of 1999 when I took out my hybrid bike and made the decision to use it as more than just a means of transportation from one place to another. I decided that I needed to become a healthier person both physically and mentally, and instinctively I knew that more exercise was the key.

Cycling made sense to me at that point in my life. I was at an age at which many women have acquired an assured sense of self through a wholesome balance of mental, physical and spiritual attributes. I liked being outdoors but was already becoming bored with my fast walking routine that had comprised most of my exercise program in recent years. I was suddenly craving speed and felt anxious to break out of old ways of being and acting in slow mode. (My Dad prefers to refer to my slowness—a family trait of sorts—as being deliberate.)

My energy level had increased tenfold once I began riding my bike. And off the bike, I approached everything with a sense of confidence that I had never quite experienced. It was time to overcome old fears, and having to sometimes deal with speeding cars, weave in and out of traffic, or power up a steep hill helped me to do that, and more.

I was living in Saratoga Springs at that time, a very picturesque town in upstate New York, known best for its healing waters and thoroughbred horse racing. After having lived in this historic city for almost three years, I finally learned that the outlying area was also known for some of the best cycling in the United States. Indeed, with an abundance of country roads stretching out to scenic destinations such as horse farms, lakes, and the magnificent Saratoga Battlefields, the area resembles a bike rider's dream.

Serious cyclists don't pay much attention to the scenery but terrain does matter a whole lot. And that's a big reason why the cycling is so great in Saratoga. It's not the Alps or the Pyrenees, but there are a good number of hills that can whip you into shape. That's pretty much what happened to me during the summer of 1999. I'm still a long way away from super-jock status, and there are many parts of my body far too much like squeezably soft Charmin, but the discovery of cycling was a real turning point. It's the freedom I feel when riding the bike that I like the best. Each time out, it makes me feel like a kid again. Sometimes it's like meditation in motion; in fact, the first time I mounted a road bike (later that summer), I felt like I was doing yoga—one of my favorite practices—on a bicycle. Cycling does have that capacity to put the cyclist in an otherworldly state. (To me, it's like following the black lane down the pool when doing a long series of laps, something that still plunges me into a deep state of relaxation.) I'm sure that this near-feeling of transcendence is also part of the reason why the pros take it so far.

The summer of 1999 was also when Lance Armstrong won his first Tour de France, the world-renowned, three-week-long race considered to be the brass ring of professional cycling. In view of my newfound passion for cycling, and, being the Francophile that I am, I would gather snippets of information and brief updates at Blue Sky

Bicycles, the local bike shop in Saratoga, which served as my ultimate source for everything I needed to know (and buy) for this freshly adopted activity of mine.

I had lived eleven years in Paris, from 1984 to 1994 (plus my junior year abroad in 1982), and traveled there countless times after having moved back to the States in 1994. The life experiences I enjoyed in the City of Light—and the rest of France for that matter—shaped me into a Parisian sophisticate. Now it was time to be transformed into a biker girl. I was amazed by how well I took to Lycra. I outfitted myself in a bunch of double-reinforced, chamois-bottomed shorts and a whole collection of Crayola-colored tops. Add to that a space-age helmet, sunglasses that didn't remotely resemble anything I'd ever worn before, and clip-on bike shoes and their accompanying clipless pedals that took nearly two training courses to learn to use. I was slick! And each time I rode off on my bike, I felt like a million bucks.

However, even in my most fashion guilt-free moments, I couldn't help but wonder, *Where did all this come from?* After all, I had lived in France, a country whose national sport, by many accounts, is cycling. I can remember being out in the French countryside on Sundays—the day in France where you're likely to encounter groups of flashy cyclists on the roads—with my French husband, Stéphane. I'm embarrassed today when I think of how we sniggered at so many of those "little" Frenchmen that looked so silly in their tight Lycra shorts. And it was totally unthinkable that we'd ever watch any of the Tour de France, not to mention showing up on the Champs-Elysées for the finish. Watching the French Open was more than acceptable, but showing interest in the Tour was for the masses. It was part of those unwritten rules, so many of which exist in France—that people from this class do this, and others do that. Stéphane was from a noble family, and I followed suit—until, of course, I discovered the thrills of cycling and the Tour many years later.

My enthusiasm for cycling and my playful approach to bike fashion led me to purchase a bright yellow Tour de France jersey in the summer of 1999. The jersey was fun to wear but I'm not sure how many people around Saratoga "got it." Avid cycling fans in the know probably thought I was being too cocky for my ability. It was just the ticket, though, for that year's Christmas card. I had a friend take a picture of me wearing the jersey, perched on my beautiful Celeste-blue Bianchi, the road bike I had acquired by the end of that season. Fortunately, all my friends interpreted the picture on this homemade holiday card in the tongue-in-cheek spirit in which I intended it. And yet, it was also a way to introduce a brand new me.

Imagine the response that my card provoked among my European friends, all of whom knew me as not particularly athletic, let alone interested in the Tour de France. Their reactions were positive nonetheless, and I could tell that in addition to being rather amused by me, they were happy I was having fun.

In the span of six months, I had emerged as my own version of a jock. My carriage and manner of speaking still possessed the subtle refinements of a well-bred woman, but inside I felt more capable, less fragile and considerably more real. Appearances began to count less each day. I experienced growing internal strength and a more relaxed state of being that outweighed the benefits of external beauty. My emotional compass began to be influenced more by the sense of freedom and well-being achieved from a great ride rather than how put together I looked, how well I dressed, how my hair and makeup were done. In the five years since I had left France, I had devoted a lot of energy toward developing my spiritual side. Now my physical and mental dimensions were becoming better aligned as well. Cycling, and subsequently the Tour de France, became the vehicle of this transformation, but thankfully, I didn't question this metamorphosis. It just all felt right.

Much to my surprise, my burgeoning cycling interest eventually led me to love and romance. I met Peter Hazard (a great name for a guy, especially a cyclist) at Blue Sky Bicycles, the neighborhood shop where he worked and I shopped. Peter happened to be a Cat III cyclist, in addition to being a tall, slim, handsome man with chestnut-brown eyes and hair and the most terrific smile. (Cat III is a ranking in amateur cycling that includes categories I-V, with I being the highest, and V the lowest. Cat III represented an advanced level, since Cat I and Cat II cyclists sometimes race with the pros.)

Clad in a T-shirt and shorts, baring clean-shaven, exquisitely sculpted legs—the trademark of serious cyclists—I couldn't help looking at Peter as a sexy guy that summer. I was turned on by cycling, after all, and he had become an integral part of that whole package. Pete was always sweet and affable, but he didn't tug at my heartstrings, mostly because he didn't seem to have any romantic designs on me. He appeared to be too consumed with cycling—both his work at the shop and his own riding and racing—to have time for a woman.

It wasn't until my teenaged niece accompanied me to the bike shop one day, and picked up on some sparks that I had clearly missed, that I began to feel the flickering of a flame. "How about him, Aunt Bessie?" she cajoled with enough sincerity for me to give a potential romance with this man more consideration. "I think he really likes you."

"What makes you say that?" I queried.

"Didn't you see the way he looks at you?"

"No, I didn't notice."

Then suddenly I began to look at Peter with a different eye. Still, though, the season was winding down and I had already purchased just about everything I needed for my newfound passion, so I had fewer and fewer reasons to go by the shop.

At one point, though, I did suggest we take a bike ride together. He expressed interest but never called. Then one day he joined me at my early morning yoga class. He met me all sleepy-eyed and bed-headed in front of the studio with a big grin. As he stretched alongside of me, my attention was diverted away from my meditative poses to his long, strong legs (this time covered in black bike pants) and his beautiful back. His whole trim, athletic build became far more of a focal point during my yoga session than my third eye. *Isn't this interesting,* I thought, *a man who is health-oriented and physically active, clearly somewhat soulful, gentle, and not at all full of himself like so many men I have known.*

Peter surprised me a few weeks later with an out-of-the-blue phone call late one Friday night. We talked for two hours and, by the end of the conversation, I learned that there was much more about him that piqued my interest than his looks. We shared similar values and political views. Our visions of the world coincided more than they collided and, although he was kind of a jock and I often impossibly feminine, it appeared we had much in common. He was what the French would call *bien élevé*, or well raised, an expression that also conveyed that someone was well-bred. And that he was: Peter had Yankee roots that dated back to the colonists, he grew up in the tony town of Bedford, New York and summered in Nantucket. I don't mean to sound like a snob, but his background instilled in him a sort of *rafinement* similar to what I had become accustomed to in Paris. When he revealed that he enjoyed the History Channel, House & Garden Network and *Antiques Roadshow*, my heart jumped with anticipation of all that we could share together. My mind was thrown into fifth gear with thoughts of how a relationship with him would be—what maybe having a family with him would look like.

By Christmas 1999, our relationship had blossomed into a warm and fuzzy love affair. I discovered a kind and sensitive side to him beneath his sometimes rough-and-tumble exterior. I found him to be a very compassionate, caring and honest person. And the fact that he was three years younger than I was made me feel younger, too! His playfulness helped to lighten up my more serious side. Through him, I learned the importance of play, but at the same time I began to see him as very grounding for me. He was the most down-to-earth (and athletic) guy I had ever been with and being with him was very freeing. I no longer felt that I had to primp so much, and I enjoyed exploring a more relaxed and casual me.

At thirty-six, Peter had never been married. I assumed he must have commitment issues. I sensed he was hesitant to jump into a serious relationship, but the strong physical attraction we had for each other made it difficult to hold back. I began to trust my instincts more, which were telling me to have faith that it would all work out.

One of our major turning points occurred when we took a trip to New York City together for one of my book promotions. I'd had two books published on shopping and touring in France and had already begun to write my third. It was time for him to see me looking chic in a pink tailored suit, sporting heels and an array of fashion accessories, chatting about a favorite chocolate shop in Paris or explaining the rich history behind Provençal fabrics.

Peter was observing me for the first time in an entirely different light. He did not, however, appear intimidated by the sophisticated crowd of shoppers and travelers at the event. Instead he glowed with pride about what I had accomplished in my life before we'd met. Though it was not his normal milieu, he conducted himself beautifully and was very supportive of me. I was proud to be with someone who obviously cared so much. The idea of him being a manager in a bike shop without any grandiose plans for professional success didn't bother me, either.

By June 2000, the inevitable happened: I fell in love. (We had just passed the six-month mark, a significant notch for me in all relationships where I either am in love or decide to end it.) I could have listed many reasons not to be involved with Peter, but my heart won out and I allowed myself to fall for him. Falling in love to me is both a gift and a curse. The blessed part of it comes with the desire to open up my heart as wide as the gates of Versailles on the day of the king's outing. But once I've done this, I invest so much of myself into the relationship that energy is taken away from my own pursuits. I know that's not healthy, but isn't that what many women do?

I had my doubts that Peter would be able to bring the necessary elements to our relationship. He didn't seem like the go-getter type of guy that would commit himself toward making it work, but then again he appeared to have the potential for lifelong love. *Was he being aloof or just cautious? Or was it fear? Hmmmm.* My whole life felt different now. I once was married to a Frenchman (who as most Frenchmen do with women) showered me with affection and attention. We could spend days shopping and touring together and hours chatting about our creative pursuits. Now I was with a whole different type of man. Peter was clearly not interested in making me his number one priority; he still needed to carve out lots of time for bike riding (which was likely his way of achieving balance). He seemed determined not to give in to my already well-formed habits (and dare I say expectations), mostly those on the domestic front. My Frenchman would allocate all kinds of time to such mundane pleasures as selecting a ripe tomato, planning the meals for the upcoming week or working up a *plan de table* for the next dinner party. Peter wanted no part of such trivialities and it became evident that we'd share a different partnership than the one I had with my often doting French husband. I reminded myself that it was silly of me to expect the same attention to such frivolities from Peter—that just didn't come in a he-man package. No, it was up to me to adjust, and I thought I'd better learn how fast since I had already fallen in love with my swell, American guy.

My life was quite busy, at this point, since I was on a deadline for another book, *The Riches of Paris: A Shopping and Touring Guide*. Thank goodness I had a contract, or I might have been derailed from carrying out this project due to my budding relationship with Pete. Despite this added workload, we still spent a good amount of time together, and, by the end of July 2000, my love for him was growing right along with my love for cycling. It was fun for both of us to watch the Tour de France together on TV, and truly novel for me, since I had never shared a sporting interest with a man before. We would take the occasional ride together, too, but that was less of a thrill for Pete than for me since he still struggled with slowing himself down to my speed so that we could pedal side by side.

When we weren't consumed with cycling, we'd enjoy a good meal out or at my place and hang out and talk and play with Mr. Kitty.

I was living a highly contrasted existence that summer. I was working on a book that involved extensive writing about Paris's most celebrated and charming boutiques, cafés, restaurants, hotels and neighborhoods. A good part of my heart, though, was in the provinces following the Tour de France, and my thoughts typically drifted there every time I took a spin on my bike. I found myself recharged by describing the Tour de France boutique. I also enjoyed writing the description for a top cycling shop in Paris—not only was it a brisk change from all the honeys, handbags and bibelots, but it was also really fun to do.

I realized that I could truly embrace my interest in cycling without it detracting from my more feminine pursuits. I was more athletic but far from becoming a jock. My female side was still fully intact. I had just discovered a way to explore my male side a bit more. It all seemed like a pretty natural progression, and at times I would marvel at how easily I could slip from one facet of my persona to another. It seemed as though I was cultivating different parts of me while pruning back others. I still felt extremely comfortable in my femininity—in fact, probably even more so than ever. I was just growing another dimension of myself.

With each push of the pedal, I felt empowered. And it was largely thanks to the hours I spent on my bike each week that I was able to gain more confidence at my desk. I had allowed myself to be vulnerable much of my life. Vulnerability can be a good thing, because it allows you to open yourself to others and to new experiences. Too much of it, though, can be weakening. Cycling toughened me up.

So as my life alternated between the more feminine domain of shopping and touring and the male-dominated realm of cycling, it occurred to me that maybe there was a way I could bring these two worlds together. Being the Francophile that I am, interest in the Tour de France felt quite natural. I became consumed with the idea of actually cycling in France myself and the inclusion of Peter on such a trip seemed to be a given.

I was already familiar with the many terrific rural areas of France. I had scoured the provinces for *The Riches of France: A Shopping and Touring Guide to the French Provinces* and encountered a seemingly endless amount of country roads throughout. You can see many of these routes when you watch the Tour. And even when these roads are not blocked off for this internationally televised event, most of them don't see any more traffic than you'd encounter driving through the cornfields of Kansas. Almost overnight, it became my dream to ride Bella (the name I gave my bike) throughout the countryside of France.

It was already the end of July when this burning desire to cycle in France took hold of me, so I knew I'd have to act fast. I didn't hesitate for a moment when it came to broaching the subject with Peter. My enthusiasm was so electric that he could not help being caught up in the excitement. After just a moment's pause, Peter said yes, and I forged ahead without too much thought about what it might mean for Peter and me. And I had a vague sense that the trip could potentially strengthen—or test—our relationship.

Our plans began to take shape. The cycling trip represented a big turning point in our ten-month relationship. I expected the trip would result in another book, and this was a way to integrate Peter into my work—a big move, something I had never done to that degree with a man before. Such integration made the relationship more concrete; it represented more of a commitment. I was anxious to share an experience with him that I knew would probably be just as exciting (if not more so) as all the countless European cycling events he'd watched on TV in the many years he had actively followed the sport. And I knew that I probably could not—or at least did not want to—do it without him. He, after all, was the cyclist in this partnership; I was just the wannabe.

Spending such concentrated time living and traveling together in a foreign country would force us to be dependent on each other. This led us to wonder how we would get along for such a long stretch. (We had only gone away for five days together, once before.) We both felt a fair amount of uncertainty around that, so we began to proclaim (to each other and to others) that the trip would make us or break us. Certainly the trip was going to be the ultimate compatibility test. We felt very much in love, but neither of us seemed to be finding the harmony and togetherness we wanted. We butted heads about everything from making dinner to choosing a video at the movie rental store. But there was no conflict over our lovemaking, so it seemed that our soul connection was stronger than our personalities.

Nevertheless, I was in a make it-or-break-it frame of mind, never having been a lover of that in-between, things-are-going-to-get-better state of relationships. I was at an age, too, that dictated that there was no wasting time. I had left France in 1994 heartbroken. I had experienced great personal loss from multiple miscarriages, the death of a brother and eventually the dissolution of my marriage to a man I had loved very much. But there was still hope. Peter appeared not to want to fritter away his time with someone he didn't see a future with either, but, being very male, was closed down about expressing it.

So we tried to talk as realistically as possible about our concerns, knowing full well that, one way or another, we both really wanted to head off to cycle in France anyway. We knew that Peter was going to be extremely dependent on me, something that I feared wouldn't sit very well with his self-reliant nature. In truth, it was to be my deal: my work, my program. I was the tour director by all accounts, something I'm sure delighted and annoyed travel companions (mostly my mother and a couple friends) in the past. Typically I keep a rigorous schedule of activities—of my own doing and also of ones imposed upon me by tourism organizations—which leaves some people reeling.

"This being France, there will be a big emphasis on food and wine and culture during the trip," I explained to Pete. "I do want your input though, so feel free to tell me what's most important to you."

"France is your beat, hun," he replied.

"Of course, but I'd like you to give me some ideas about what you want to do as well," I insisted.

"Well, I'd like to go see that car museum in Alsace, you know, the one I told you about," Pete said.

"The one in Mulhouse?" I asked.

"Yeah."

"OK, then let's make Alsace one of our regions. I love Alsace," I continued. "Plus I've never been to Mulhouse. They have two museums there, one wallpaper museum and one textile museum I'd like to see." I noticed a suspicious look on Pete's face after this last remark and quickly added, "Don't worry though, I'll reserve plenty of time for the car museum."

I knew France, French culture and the French mentality extremely well and was fluent in French. This, along with the fact that I was our official tour leader and that much would be paid for through my work, put me in a more dominant position. Cycling, however, was Pete's expertise, so I was counting on this to help our balance of power.

So our plans progressed. I listened to the chatter in my head that questioned, *What will this trip do for the relationship as well as what will this relationship do for the trip?* I was the most feminine of all the women he had ever been with and he was definitely the most guy-like of the men I had known. I wondered how this would play out while traveling six weeks in France together.

Finally it became undeniable that the trip was a go. Poor guy— I don't think he had a clue about what he was headed for, especially with me as head tour guide. And, I suppose, I didn't exactly know what was in store for me, either.

We chose five regions to explore *à vélo*, or by bike. Although I would have liked to check out the cycling possibilities in each region of France, we knew that five was the absolute maximum we could handle during a six-week-long trip, particularly since we were spending time in Paris as well. We focused on the regions of Alsace, Burgundy, Provence, Languedoc-Roussillon and the Southwest, a grand swath of France that would allow us to experience a variety of terrain and landscapes. In addition, the last three regions were in the south, so we figured that here we would make out the best—weather-wise—for some nice fall riding.

Peter insisted we include some of the most renowned *étapes*, or stages, of the famous Tour de France bike race. (The Tour is actually made up of a prologue plus twenty stages, which take place during twenty-one days of racing. Each stage is like a separate race unto itself with a winner each day; however, it is the overall leader–and wearer of the famous yellow jersey—who has the lowest elapsed time for the prologue and all the stages combined.) Pete and I had pulled out the map of France countless times, circling our fingers to pinpoint the location of mythic climbs such as le Mont Ventoux, le Col du Tourmalet and le Col d'Aubisque. We had opted out of the Alps, but the Pyrenees were to be a major part of our stay in the Southwest. I, of course, had no intention of riding anything more than a big hill, but Peter was psyched about the idea of having the opportunity to tackle portions of the Tour's classic mountain stages.

At this point, though, Pete's biggest concern was what to do about bikes. I was determined to ride my own bike in France. He tried to convince me that if I just brought my seat, my pedals, my gear and all my favorite outfits, I would be fine. No way! This was all part of my dream; besides, renting decent road bikes anywhere in the world—even in France—is a major challenge. Most shops rent mountain bikes and hybrids, but road bikes are generally too specialized.

Once we secured our plane tickets, I investigated how to ship the bikes to France. We would fly into Paris and our bike tour was to begin the next day, in Alsace. Shipping prices to both Paris and Strasbourg (our first destination in Alsace)—by both Fed Ex and UPS—were well out of our range. Besides, I was feeling so possessive about Bella that I didn't want to let her out of my sight for more than a day's worth of travel. American Airlines came to the rescue. I learned that it would cost only an additional seventy-five dollars to carry the bike as cargo. Next we needed to procure two bike boxes, durable hard-sided cases specially designed for the transportation of bikes. The bike transportation problem seemed to have been solved; carrying it out would be another thing.

The only way to cover all these regions of France in a relatively short amount of time was to drive. It never crossed my mind to use our bikes as the primary mode of transportation. I wanted this trip to be really fun, not some kind of a bike race, and I wanted to leave lots of time for wining and dining, touring and relaxing on the side. It seemed that the best solution was to drive a car to all the major destinations and, from there, tour each area on our bikes. I contacted Renault Eurodrive, and they assured me that a brand-new Renault Laguna, replete with bike rack, would be awaiting us upon our arrival in Paris.

With our transportation problems solved and confirmations rolling in daily about hotel arrangements, Peter and I allowed ourselves to become excited about the trip. Now, as much as I plan ahead, I typically leave for a trip on one leg. There's always so much to do. This time proved even more challenging, since Peter is even more of a procrastinator than I. He had decided that not only was he going to leave his job just days before the trip, he was also going to leave his apartment.

We had agreed upon a somewhat temporary arrangement of him moving in with me for a variety of reasons. Since we were going to be away for so long and then after that Pete was planning to explore the West and do some skiing with friends in Bozeman, Montana, it just made sense for him to give up his place. He was at my apartment so much anyway that it seemed more logical to make it more of a full-time arrangement. It was more than apparent that our travel plans provided us with a convenient excuse to go a step further in our relationship, as well as with our living situation.

We didn't even talk openly about the meaning of his upcoming foray out West. I knew he had been itching to move to the wider, more open spaces of the Rocky Mountains for quite some time, and I was pondering it, too, but at this point neither of us was committing to making the move to the great American West together. This "minor detail" seemed to up the ante for a successful outcome to our trip. Would our France trip add more to our love or would it end up being our last hurrah? There was probably an undercurrent of fear that neither of us wanted to fully acknowledge.

A few days before this mega trip, I found myself over at Pete's wrapping up his kitchenware and helping him sort through years of clothing that should long ago have been given to Goodwill. A friend helped him move most of his belongings into a storage unit, and the rest was crammed into *chez moi*. There was not a smidgen of room left in my diminutive, Victorian era apartment. I had to take a deep breath and suck it up when I saw him debarking with his clothing and gear, all of which would have been accommodated far better in a large locker room than in my dainty abode. I had lots of table skirts, so we were able to stash quite a lot away from sight, items such as his five-foot-long hockey bag that we stuffed under my dining room table.

Pre-trip departures are often exceedingly stressful, but this was all a bit much. Even Kitty—my thirteen-year old, native French black-and-tan tabby—sensed there was a big change afoot. He spent time jumping from box to bag, then retreated for the next few days into his favorite hiding places. I felt overwhelmed by the mounting mess. It was Pete's plan to just leave everything in complete disorder, with the promise that he would deal with it when he returned, a week before me. I reluctantly accepted his assurance that he would put the apartment back into good order before I came home from France, but I still managed to instruct him on how I wanted him to organize all of this confusion.

So I did my best to ignore Pete's chaos and focused instead on my own stuff. I should have known to pack my bags way in advance to have them out of the way. Instead, I waited until the last minute and was forced to weave in and out of Pete's piles.

My mom stopped by a couple of days before our departure. She liked coming to Saratoga—just forty-five minutes from my parents' house—to get her hair done and to visit Mrs. London's, a famous bake shop that rivals Paris's most revered *pâtisseries/ boulangeries*. "Oh Bethie," she exclaimed as she side-stepped through my narrow entranceway and caught a glimpse at the shambles of my living and dining room area.

"I know, Mom—it looks awful, doesn't it?"

"You had a lot crammed in here before but now it looks like a moving company just unloaded a pile of stuff," my mom said, rolling her eyes and shaking her head. "I know you—you can't live like this," she added.

"C'mon, let's have a cup of tea," I said. We settled ourselves down at my small, wooden bistrot table, half covered with a table runner and a decorative tray, the same table that my ex-husband and I had carefully selected at the flea markets at Porte de Clignancourt on the outskirts of Paris. I fingered the dainty napkins that I had set out along with my colorful, flower-festooned service of faience, also from France. Here in this Old World, tile-floored kitchen, surrounded by my finery, I felt comforted. I braced myself for a bundle of cautionary words from my mother, even though she wasn't big on lecturing. "What kind of treats did you bring from Mrs. London's?" I asked.

"Elephant ears," she replied, clearly eager to try one.

"Oh, *palmiers*. They're your favorites."

"I know, that's why I got them," she laughed. "And I know you like them, too."

"I do," I replied. "I'm sure these are as good as the ones I'll soon have in France."

"You're lucky to be going. You're lucky to be setting out on such a nice trip with such a nice young man," my mom said.

"That's sweet of you to say, Mom. I didn't expect you to tell me that just now."

"I mean it. Good for you. It's such a romantic idea," she continued. "I think the logistics are a pain in the butt—you really don't have to bring your own bike and you don't have to travel around so much, you know. But you never do anything halfway, do you, my dear Bethie?"

"No, Mom, at least I try not to. Plus, this is a trip of a lifetime."

"I know. It's an adventure—I would have loved to have done something like that during my prime. Instead, I was busy making babies."

I weighed my mother's confession heavily in my mind and heart. We were so much alike that I often overlooked the big ways in which we were different. "Had I been able to have babies, I doubt I'd be going on a trip like this," I replied. "No, it wouldn't be happening. Sometimes I still can't believe all the pain I experienced in Paris when Stéphane and I were trying to have a child. So many miscarriages, so much hurt," I added, shaking my head. "And then when Phil died on the heels of all that suffering—it's no wonder I came back to the States. I just wanted to come home."

My Mom looked at me with tears welling up in her eyes. *What was she thinking?* I wondered. *Is she thinking that she was blessed with six children and that it's not fair I haven't been able to have even one? Was it fair that she lost a son? Should I not have brought up Phil? Talk of death and miscarriage—both such tremendous forms of loss—that's a sure way to put a damper on a conversation.* Plus, my mother had been with me during one of the miscarriages in Paris. I know she'll never forget how horrible that was for me. *And poor sweet Phil.* I began to feel choked up at the thought of it all. *Damn, I don't want to do this now. This is a happy time. I'm leaving for France on a wonderful trip.* I fought back my tears. Finally, after a long pause, my mother said, "There's still a chance it might happen."

I breathed deeply and said, "I know. I know, Mom. That's what I'm hoping for at least—I haven't given up hope. Maybe it *could* happen between Peter and me—who knows? Maybe the fact that I'm back living in the States leading a more active, healthy life. Maybe that'll make the difference."

My Mom took a sip of tea and then said, "Just try to focus on your trip right now. I know—one way or another—it will all work out for you. It really will."

I pushed my pink-painted chair back from the bistrot table and walked over to give her a hug. "Oh, Mom, you always say the right thing," I said as I burst into tears.

"Not always," my mom replied in an acerbic tone, characteristic of her occasional sharp tongue.

"The elephant ears are good, aren't they?" I blubbered, in an effort to add some sunshine to an otherwise heartbreaking exchange.

"They sure are," my mom said. "Nice and flaky."

Storybook Alsace

It was almost dark by the time we reached Strasbourg, exhausted but grateful we had arrived safe and sound. As soon as we pulled into town, we realized that Strasbourg was buzzing with bicycles, most of which were being used as a means of transportation by these environmentally aware townspeople.

By the time we checked into the Hôtel Hannong, a pleasant and conveniently located three-star establishment in the center of town, we were convinced that we had arrived in a city that takes bicycles seriously. Before we had to ask what to do with our bikes, they were whisked off to their *cave à vélo*, a specially designated area for bike storage.

Pete and I indulged ourselves with unpacking, since we knew this was the only hotel throughout the whole trip where we would stay for four consecutive nights. We planned to use Strasbourg as our base and take bike trips from there each day. After freshening up, we headed out for dinner to A la Tête de Lard, a typical Alsatian restaurant just a few steps from the hotel. The dinner was simple yet quintessentially Alsatian. We gobbled up a couple of *tartes flambées*, an Alsatian specialty consisting of a wafer-thin crust slathered with cream and little slices of *lardons* (similar to bacon) and onions. You have to eat it quickly because it cools off fast, but that was not a problem since our travels had made us ravenous. We ordered a *salade aux lardons* to accompany the meal and washed it all down with a quarter of a pitcher of Riesling.

Pete and I ambled the short distance back to our hotel arm in arm. We were satiated from our first dining experience in France but even more importantly, we felt flooded with happiness about how far we had traveled together both physically and emotionally. We had become a team within the past twenty-four hours and our sense of togetherness felt stronger than ever. Too bad we were so tired that back in our room, bleary-eyed fatigue put us into such a deep sleep that not even the effects of jet lag could disturb.

"Hello, I'm Christian, I'm going to be your guide for the next few days," said this blond, blue-eyed man from the regional tourist department that greeted us in the hotel lobby.

"That's perfect," I said. "Your English is excellent."

"Yes, and I love cycling."

"Well, we couldn't have asked for a better start than that— don't you think, Pete?"

"Yeah, that's great," Pete replied, although I sensed he was already questioning Christian's cycling ability since he'd showed up in a pair of flimsy track shorts—quite the contrast to the ultra padded pants Pete and I were wearing. *Hmmmm.*

We soon learned that one definitely doesn't have to look like an avid cyclist to be one. Christian knew his way extremely well around the bike paths of Strasbourg, of which there are many. I was a little shaky, at first, riding alongside the traffic in this bustling city, but it didn't take long before we reached a well-indicated and quiet path (one of countless that radiate out from the center of town). Pete had already snapped his fingers a few times at me and barked, "C'mon, c'mon pokey. Pedal!"

I can't believe he's bugging me right off, I thought. *Oh well, better to just ignore him.* I accelerated as much as I could and before long, we were all enjoying the peaceful landscapes along the river Ill. Thankfully I didn't dwell on Pete's remarks——the morning was too perfect for him to ruin it for me by being a jerk.

Swans and ducks completed the storybook picture on this stretch of bike path, which continued along another waterway known as the Canal de la Bruche. Built centuries ago for the transportation of wine and supplies, today the canal remains very sleepy, except for the presence of an occasional fisherman or a passing bicyclist. Picture-perfect views emerged: the postman pedaling down the path with his trappings of the day's deliveries; old stone houses originally built for the canal keepers, virtually all of which were punctuated by countless flower boxes spewing forth pink and red cascading geraniums; and, off in the distance, fairytale-like bell towers with hillside vineyards as their backdrop.

It was Tuesday, September 19, and the bright midday sun had burned off any remnants of a misty morning. It truly felt like summertime; we were doubly blessed. I was living a dream. I had not known such a flood of contentment for a long time. All was well and, thinking that, I gave a little ring of my bell. Pete and Christian turned and grinned, sweet smiles of affirmation that told me they were feeling pretty wonderful, too.

We had planned to have lunch in Molsheim, a historic town approximately sixteen miles southwest of Strasbourg. Before arriving there, however, we pulled off the bike path at Wolxheim, a village of wine growers who were well into the throes of their harvest. The heady smell of fermenting grapes hung thick in the air. A good number of the villagers were mobilized to help with the harvest and with the actual making of the wine. Tractors trundled about towing wagon loads full of ripe red grapes, a folksy rural scene that appeared locked in time. Drawn by the charming array of red-tile roofed houses painted in every shade of pink, from salmon to sandstone to flamingo to ochre, we took an extended tour around this village to take it all in.

"Are you hungry for lunch?" Christian asked.

"We're starving," Pete and I replied practically in unison. We ducked into a quaint restaurant and were served an onion *tarte* in a flash. Turkey in red pepper sauce accompanied by *spetzel* (a lightly fried, chewy pasta, typical of Alsace), and a *tarte aux quetsches* (a pie made with dark-red plums) soon followed. Our conversations ranged from light to serious.

"I love all the fairytale scenes we observed from Strasbourg to Molsheim," I said. "I've done the wine route in Alsace before but never felt *this* enchanted."

"When you're in a car, you say, 'oh, did you see that?'" Christian replied. "On a bike, you stop and look and observe the wine growers, then you smell the grapes that have already begun to ferment."

Pete and I nodded in agreement then listened intently as Christian spoke of the history that had shaped Alsace. "Under the reign of Louis XIV—around 1650—the region was French for the first time. In 1870, Alsace became German until the end of the first World War. During the second World War, Alsace was annexed. My grandmother was French, then German, then French," Christian continued. "We are lucky because no one died." Christian went on to say, "Having lived through these complex dynamics, it makes sense that the European parliament is based in Strasbourg."

"It sounds like this fusion of cultures gave birth to one distinct people, the Alsatians?" I ventured.

"Yes, many Alsatians speak-—or at least understand—some French and German. Alsatian is a dialect that closely resembles German; there is no written language," Christian replied.

"And it's because of the many German influences in the region that there's this charming Hansel and Gretel quality to all the homes and villages," I added. "Doesn't it look just out of a storybook, Pete?"

"Oh, yes," he answered with one of his wry smiles. I could tell he was half teasing me for being so captivated by our first half day of cycling in France. I knew he was loving it, too—he just wasn't one to gush.

"Let's stop here," Christian hollered, as he pulled into what appeared to be some sort of garage. We had left the bike path after Molsheim—after lunch—and set out on a more intrepid tour of the villages along Alsace's famed wine route. Here in Dorlisheim, it seemed like we were making an impromptu stop at a vintner's. "It's the first day of this winemaker's harvest," Christian declared.

We peeked in to see what was happening at the press. "Would you like some?" the vintner asked in French.

"It's fresh-squeezed grape juice," Christian said as he poured it right into Pete's empty water bottle and then did the same with mine. "It's cool to the taste since the just-pressed grapes still hold the chill of the night air." *Damn, all these French people are so poetic,* I thought.

"It's a little cloudy," the vintner explained. "The juice has not been completely filtered. Indeed, his nectar was churned up with all the richness of the earth. "With time and the right care, this yellowish liquid will turn into a fine Pinot Blanc," he added.
"Look, it's beginning to fizzle," Pete said to me a couple of hours later as we were softly pedaling along the route. "It's already beginning to change."

I took a sip of my water bottle and puckered my lips. "'Twas a delicious beverage that's now a tad sour," I said with an English accent and pursed lips.

"You're such a goofball," Pete said, shaking his head at me. We laughed and cruised forward.

We next stopped at Rosheim, a picturesque town made even more noteworthy by a prominent bell tower and one large Romanesque church. My eyes took a few seconds to adjust to the dimness of the interior, in contrast to the bright sunny day. I felt overwhelmed by the quiet grandeur of this sacred space. Erected during the twelfth century, the church of Saints Peter and Paul in Rosheim is known to be one of the finest examples of Romanesque architecture in Alsace. I would have stayed longer but I couldn't help but feel rather irreverent standing in church in my tight-fitting Lycra shorts.

Along the way we passed our first group of French cyclists, who seemed friendly as they waved by. There must have been about twenty of them in all, all sporting colorful team jerseys from one of the top European professional teams, Français des Jeux, as well as fancy shoes. Even though they were amateurs, they were smartly outfitted like pros. My enthusiasm about cycling in France grew by the minute. It felt like a different game over here. Even if cars did zoom by at breakneck speed, the drivers were respectful and pulled way out in the lane so as not to jolt the cyclists.

It was late afternoon by the time we reached Obernai, our final destination of the day. We were much too tired by this time to visit another storybook town, so we headed directly for the train station, where we had planned to take the train back to Strasbourg. As I pulled up to the quay, I checked my odometer for the day's total mileage. Twenty-nine miles—not bad for the first day out. The one-way train ticket back to Strasbourg was dirt-cheap; the bikes could travel for free. (Bike hooks are provided at the front of the train.) "It's wonderful how easy it is to discover Alsace by bike," I marveled.

"Yes, about thirty, medium-sized bike tours originate from Strasbourg," Christian said. "For most of them, there's always a train to hitch back—or you can take the train out and ride back."

"I bet some people don't even take the train," Pete added.

"Oh, yes, that's for the very serious cyclists," Christian said.

As we slumped down into our seats on the train, heavy from all the cycling and sightseeing we had accomplished that day, we were glad we'd opted for the less ambitious one-way tour of the region.

I think both Peter and I were secretly relieved to awaken to rain the next morning. It was not a hard, driving rain and certainly hard-core cyclists would have ventured out, but we were feeling pooped from the ride the day before—and still weary from jet lag.

"How about we do today's tour in my car rather than on our bikes?" Christian suggested when he called to update us with the day's plan.

"That sounds good to us, Christian," I replied. "We can probably get more sightseeing in that way."

I was thrilled that Pete liked this plan. It was nice to see him getting along with Christian so well and I was elated he was taking such a strong interest in the cultural and gastronomic aspects of our bike tour. True, we were only one day down but we were off to an exceptionally good start. I felt almost giddy about the companionship all of us shared.

We headed northwest of Strasbourg to Hochfelden to visit Mé-téor, one of the last family-owned *brasseries*, or breweries, in Alsace. "*Brasserie* refers to both the site of beer production and the site of beer consumption," Christian explained. "In this case it's both."

By the end of the visit here, I was grateful it had turned out to be a wet day. "I don't know how I would have had been able to pedal back after all the beer sampling we did here," I exclaimed as we walked out of the *brasserie*.

"You could always have taken a little nap in the car while Christian and I cycled around," Pete joked.

I smiled at him and wondered if that would have been his preference.

The handfuls of pretzels we consumed at the tasting weren't enough to satiate our hunger, and Christian suggested we drive off to Saverne for lunch. Saverne was farther west. We discovered that, had we cycled out there, it would have been nearly a forty-two-kilometer ride (about twenty-six miles) from Strasbourg. Beer tasting or not, it's nice to know that people usually have the option of taking the train back to Strasbourg wherever they are in the region.

The ride from Hochfelden to Saverne was one that Peter and I would have liked to have done on our bikes. We took mostly the *départementales*, routes far less traveled than the *nationales*, which are roads second in importance to *l'autoroute*, or the highway. The bucolic scenery lulled me into a near-sleepy reverie, partly induced by the beer I had consumed. I was registering an emotional postcard of this contented moment from my vantage point in the backseat as Pete chatted about the region with Christian. I was delighting in the camaraderie they shared up front and how we all were visiting this land together in such a convivial fashion. The countryside was hilly, perfect for cycling, and also ideal for growing hops, a flower with buds that are essential in the making of beer. We passed one hops field after another, and although much of the harvest had been done, we were still fascinated by the elaborate trellis system that coaxed the vines as high as twenty feet.

By now, hunger was creeping up on us and we were happy to hole ourselves up within the cozy interior of the Taverne Katz for another long, leisurely French lunch while the rain continued to fall outside. At this point, we were chilled, as well as famished, so we all decided to order some hot, hearty food. (As if you need an excuse in France.) "I think I'll have the *joues de porc aux carottes*," I said. "That's pork cheeks with carrots," I said to Pete with a little wink.

Christian nodded his approval and said, "Nice. I am cooking cheeks often."

The meal was made even better by our further *bonne entente.* Pete and I immensely enjoyed Christian's company and his colorful explanations about the region. As is the case with many French people, Christian's extensive knowledge on a vast number of subjects and his *culture générale,* or general cultural knowledge, was most impressive, as was his casual, unpretentious delivery. And to think we could have been stuck with a bore.

An added benefit from this unique threesome was that Pete and I were interacting flawlessly. It felt almost like having a chaperone along. With Christian present, both Pete and I were on our best behavior; there were absolutely no disagreements between us. Matters such as which direction to take, what to do next, or how long to stay in one place were no longer sources of contention.

Our lunch was topped off by a *tarte au fromage,* a sort of cheesecake, typical of the region, which also happened to be one of the specialties of this *winstub.* Some people think that *winstubs* are Alsatian wine bars but, once again, Christian clarified the meaning for us. "*Winstubs* originally served as showcases for the wine growers. They were places where they could have their clients taste the wines—food was just served as an accompaniment."

It was too dreary outside to fully appreciate the charm of this town, but I did make it a point to investigate Cristallerie Carabin, a crystal shop, and Muller-Oberling, a famous bakery, before leaving Saverne. The rain was easing up, so we decided to drive five kilometers up a mountain (quite a climb on a bike) outside of Saverne to le Haut Barr, a twelfth-century castle in ruin. Christian shared more of his knowledge and held us captive with his stories about twelfth-century life. I don't know whether I was more amazed with his stories, his command of the English language, or the fact that here I was thousands of miles away—mentally and physically—from the life that I had been leading back home in Saratoga, just a few days before. The French refer to that as *dépaysement,* or change of country or scenery, one of the many great benefits of travel. All I know is that on top of this almost eerily quiet corner of history, I felt a sense of serenity.

Pete and I had just enough time left in the day to check out some of the bike shops of Strasbourg. We plodded around, crisscrossing town, feeling overtired and cold, until we had checked out nearly every bike emporium in the city. I had wanted to have an overview of the retail bike scene in such an important French city, and Pete was vaguely interested in buying a saddle. (He was already regretting that he had left his ergonomically designed one at home.) We were disappointed with our findings overall and concurred that there is nothing like your favorite bike shop back home. Exceedingly weary by now and sullen from not having found exactly what we wanted on the bike retail scene in Strasbourg, we opted to dine on some Thai food in a restaurant around the corner from our hotel and then call it an early night.

Jet lag had finally settled in by the start of our third day in Strasbourg. So much so, in fact, that we just pulled the covers over our heads when we heard the little rat-ta-ta at the door signaling the arrival of our breakfast tray. I had traveled enough throughout Europe that I found it quite normal that a strange person should enter my room before I had even brushed my hair—as long as they were bringing me my breakfast. In fact, I think this is one of the best parts of staying in hotels in France. No matter how small and modest the establishment, chances are it will be more than equipped to bring you your croissants and coffee on a tray in the morning. The French expect this, and I had come to expect it as well. Pete at first found this arrangement—this rather bizarre yet most welcome intrusion on one's privacy—somewhat disconcerting. But because of his fatigue, he came to accept it. Shortly thereafter he was quick to check that I had properly filled out the little menu card that you hang on your doorknob the night before, the one that indicates your preferred breakfast choices for the next day. I smiled to myself about his newly adopted habit, this slight Europeanization of *mon américain*.

We spent most of the morning regrouping. After I caught up on office work—during which time Pete flipped through French television—we set out to explore the heart of Strasbourg by foot. We both liked how much the center of town is reserved almost exclusively for pedestrians. The sun shone brightly, and as lunchtime approached, the streets were animated with people hurriedly walking about in search of a quick sandwich or a purchase or two.

"Let's check out these shops," I said to Pete, as I dragged him into some fashion accessory boutiques. "I forgot to pack my black evening bag and my black dressy scarf—maybe I can find something here. I can't show up at Le Buerehiesel, one of the top restaurants in France, looking like a slouch."

"You're not going to buy them just for tonight, are you?" Pete queried.

"No, of course, not. I'll have plenty of occasions to use them throughout the trip. Don't worry—I'll be fast."

I completed the shopping most expediently—so fast, in fact, that Pete barely had time to complain. (It's easy to find what you want in France, with the choice selection of goods that even the smallest town provides.) We then bought a couple of sandwiches from a *croissanterie* and sat down to eat them on a city bench.

As usual, I enjoyed hearing some of Pete's observations. "Most of the bike tires are flat in this town. I don't mean a little low—they are really flat. Many people are riding on their rims."

I laughed and asked Pete "What do you think that means about the people? What does it say about the Alsatian or French culture?"

"I have no idea," Pete replied.

"Well, they were a war-torn region for a long time," I added. "Maybe it has something to do with frugality."

"I'd say it has more to do with stupidity," Pete quipped. "They're going to wear out their rims doing that."

Then with an air of disappointment, Pete commented about not having seen nearly as many beautiful women as he'd expected.

"It's only our third day in France," I said. "Wait until we get to Paris!"

"Yeah, but still, this is a big city and I'm surprised I haven't seen many attractive French women," Pete insisted.

"I do think, however, that French women know how to make the best of what they have, they know how to fix themselves up better than most American women," I said. "Look at their haircuts *and* their makeup—they're so much more natural than in the States. Plus, they dress with such flair."

Pete looked around at all the women bustling back and forth, pondering my remarks. Then he looked up at me and declared, "You're prettier than any of them." I was somewhat surprised by Pete's remark since he wasn't big on compliments. "As I've always said, my Bessie is beautiful inside and out," Pete continued in his coy manner, an endearing style that made him appear all the more sincere. "You're tall, slender, brown-haired and brown-eyed. You have a ski jump nose, a full mouth and a huge heart. And I love you."

"Whoa—I guess today's my lucky day! You're not usually so effusive," I teased.

"No, I just felt inspired to express certain feelings—that's all," Pete said with a shrug.

I smiled and gave Pete a smooch on the cheeks, careful not to show too much affection since he wasn't comfortable with PDA. "That's sweet, hun. Thanks," I added. "I love you, too."

We rushed back to the hotel in time for me to change into my bike clothes and meet Christian for a ride around town. Pete had decided to opt out, perhaps since he suspected that our tour might involve a fair amount of stopping and starting, something he didn't have patience for on a regular basis. That was fine with me, plus I thought that time apart—even when two people feel blissfully happy—is always beneficial to a relationship. We probably wouldn't have much of that in the weeks to come. Pete and I had been as inseparable as high-school sweethearts the past few days and I assumed this is how it would be throughout the upcoming weeks. I had never spent as much time traveling with anyone except my mother, and we have always been naturally compatible, particularly when it comes to travel and shopping. So far, Pete and I were faring well together, but I also sensed that we were in a honeymoon mode.

We kissed each other goodbye and I affectionately squeezed Pete's hand saying, "Just wait for tonight." It was to be our first grand—and hopefully very romantic—evening together in France.

"You have fun," Pete replied, and then added, "I'm looking forward to tonight, too."

As nice as the tour was through Strasbourg, I decided I'm not a city rider. I am not known to have steely nerves, and the little protection prayers I say every time I go out on my bike weren't enough to make me feel totally at ease. No matter how much I "wrapped myself in pink light," I kept feeling that I could be bumped from one minute to the next. I discovered how it felt to go through the infamous French roundabouts, those circular junctions where traffic must travel in the same direction around a central island. France has a ton of them and people power through them far faster than in the States. Imagine how I felt careening around these intersections on a bike. The key is to make sure you're in the correct lane; unfortunately that's not always possible, particularly when you're not sure where you're going.

I believe one should be ultra-quick, and an expert bike handler, in order to cruise alongside traffic and dart across busy intersections. I am neither, and riding through Strasbourg with Christian that day, I came to realize why I relax so completely on lone country roads and byways. I found myself happy that Pete wasn't along since I was sure that, with him present, the pace would have picked up considerably, and I would have felt even more nervous on my bike trying to keep up with him. Pete tends to push me, thinking that will help me to be less fearful; sometimes that's just what I need, other times that backfires. As it was, I was on a complete sensory overload and began to think how grounded the Strasbourgians must be to cycle so much around town. I had a good workout, though, having pedaled some twenty miles, just enough to feel deserving of the gastronomic feast that awaited me at Le Buerehiesel that evening.

Back at the room, Pete and I were content to find each other again after having been apart for the first time in a number of days. I found him lounging about in some much-needed downtime. "So how'd it go?" he asked as soon as I walked through the door.

"OK, I guess, but I actually felt pretty spooked much of the time," I answered.

"Why's that?"

"The traffic—the whole city scene—it was hair-raising," I admitted. "I hardly ride through the streets of Saratoga unless it's to find my way out of town. Here it's a big city—it's a whole other scene."

"I told you, hun, you gotta be more aggressive. You have to go for it—no one wants to run you over. You just have to find your own line."

"I know, but I don't like riding around cars anywhere."

"Yeah, but sometimes that can't be avoided. So you better get used to it. You just have to get into your zone," Pete insisted. And then he added almost as an afterthought, "Your poking along only makes matters worse."

He hit a sore spot with his poking comment, maybe because it rang so true. Pete studied me for a reaction.

I looked at him lounging on the bed in his black cycling warmups and wondered where I should go with this conversation. If I addressed my pokey behavior I sensed that our discussion would escalate and maybe end up in an argument. I felt like I was the only one allowed to bring up my slowness. No, instead I eyed his long, slim frame and smiled.

He laughed, stood up, wrapped his arms around me and gave me one of his big, grinning smiles. I laughed, too, maybe about my hopelessness, my seemingly unattainable quest in becoming a bona fide jock. *Would I forever remain in a quasi-fearful state?*

Now was not the time to dwell on anything negative. We fell onto the bed and rolled around in laughter. Thankfully, we still had time to snuggle before dinner. We were visiting one of the most romantic countries of Europe, and we wanted to be sure to incorporate that romance into our intimacy as well. It felt wonderful to have him there with me in France, and even better, I sensed that this closeness stemmed from a place that wasn't just about the locale we were visiting.

I had taken most of my trips abroad alone, but I had reached a point in my life where I really wanted to share my experiences with someone who meant a great deal to me. I hoped Pete was that person. I felt a wellspring of love for him. Our compatibility was still sometimes dicey, yet I was beginning to think that that was a male/female thing I'd find with every guy on the planet (yes, I even experienced some of that with my French husband). I was beginning to realize that the secret to real harmony was letting go. That's what I did with his pokey remark. As a wise friend once told me, "If you don't want a tug of war, let go of the rope."

The Parc de l'Orangerie, a magnificent park embellished with manicured gardens, a handful of stork nests and grand promenades, is the setting for Le Buerehiesel, the three-star Michelin restaurant, where Peter and I were going that night. We were sure it would rank among the gastronomic highlights of our tour de France.

With the main dining room of this famed establishment built as a sort of large glass atrium, the views from each of the tables are nothing less than enchanting, by day or night. We were seated at a choice table and informed that the chef, Monsieur Antoine Westermann, had prepared a special menu for us. This meant that we would be feasting on several of the chef's specialties; I looked forward to a memorable evening. Being a travel writer that struggles to make ends meet, the rewards for my hard work pay off handsomely from time to time.

For starters, Pete reveled in his lobster salad, while I felt dangerously indulgent with my *foie gras des Landes* (foie gras from the southwest of France), served with an array of figs, fig jam and fig jelly. The champagne we were nursing as an apéritif accompanied both dishes perfectly. After our plates had been imperceptibly cleared—with a whisk here and a quick brush there—little finger bowls were carefully positioned at each of our places.

"What could this be for?" I wondered out loud to Pete. And then after just the right amount of time had passed, we were served one of the chef's signature dishes: frog legs. "In all my years and visits in France, I've never tried them," I said to Pete after the waiter disappeared. "But here, I wouldn't dream of flinching."

Pete began to eat them enthusiastically. "They're delicious," he declared.

"I love this little accompaniment of ravioli with onion *confit* and watercress cream," I said as I savored their exquisite *cuisses de grenouilles*. "What a perfect marriage of flavors and textures."

By now, the sommelier had poured us an excellent Riesling, a 1993 Grand Cru from Josmeyer, with two very snappy turns of the wrist. "Look at how elegant he's dressed," I said to Pete after he walked away. "Did you notice he's even wearing French cuffs and a pocket square? You don't see that much in the States." Pete and I were beginning to feel like two very privileged players on one of the world's finest gastronomic stages. Here, grand-styled romance clearly reigned supreme.

I held my breath in anticipation when two servers wheeled out our main course, another one of the chef's signature dishes, *Poularde de Bresse à la Baeckeoffe*. An extraordinary presentation, this prized chicken, from the Bresse region of France, was cooked in a huge Alsatian ceramic tureen, encircled by a wide rim of pastry crust used as the sealant. One of the waiters deftly removed the lid and declared, "*Voilà.*" Then they both proceeded to expertly carve the bird with the sharpest, most skillfully executed gestures. This, too, seemed as though it had been rehearsed—or at least played out numerous times before. Pete and I remained quiet as we observed the servers' every move.

A garden bouquet of baby vegetables surrounded the chicken, and had I not been thinking about the eventual arrival of the cheese and dessert cart, I would most certainly have succumbed to seconds. I was glad to have saved my appetite for the Munster, the region's best-loved cheese, which was served with a rich, walnut bread and a glass of Gewurztraminer. The silver tray of sweets—miniature walnut *tartes*, *macarons*, meringues and a variety of other sugary confections—served with our "primary" desserts provoked a look of panic on Pete's face. "Don't worry," I said— "We're not expected to eat it all."

As is customary in fine restaurants in France, the chef usually says hello to his clients at this point in the meal, making sure they enjoyed their dining experience. Pete and I were thrilled to learn that this tall, fit-looking man was also an avid cyclist. "*Oui*, I need to clean out my head sometimes," Monsieur Westermann said, referring to the frequent cycling trips he takes to the nearby Vosges mountains and the Black Forest. "I cycle about 5,000 kilometers a year in France," he added.

As we "*bonsoir*"-ed our way out of the restaurant, I thought to myself, *I'd better go out pedaling tomorrow*. This was the first extravagant meal of our trip, and I knew it wouldn't be the last.

Both Pete and I were yearning to do one more bike ride like our first one in Alsace. But that possibility evaporated when we learned that we were expected in Mulhouse, a major Alsatian city a good two-hour drive south of Strasbourg, in time for lunch with a local dignitary. We had decided to add Mulhouse to our itinerary for two reasons: I had never been there and wanted to check it out, and Pete had read about their extraordinary car museum, which sounded like a must-see. We initially thought we'd be able to do some cycling around town, but after my city riding experience in Strasbourg, I had my doubts. We had heard, though, that the Tour de France had passed through Mulhouse that previous summer, so we still thought we might be hooked up with a good ride at some point over the weekend.

Our stay in the cosmopolitan city of Mulhouse was greatly enhanced by the gracious welcome extended to us by Jean-Pierre Walter, a dapper Frenchman who happened to be the deputy mayor. As a visiting *journaliste de l'Amérique*, I've had many meals throughout my travels in France with various official people. Peter and I met Monsieur Walter at Aux Caves du Vieux Couvent, a traditional brasserie, where he had arranged for the three of us to lunch. Monsieur Walter received us both as though we were visiting dignitaries. Despite the fact that he didn't speak more than a smattering of English, he exuded so much warmth and charm that we could hardly tell that any sort of language barrier existed. He and Peter communicated beautifully by the use of gestures, the exchange of a few words in French and English and by me serving as interpreter. Pete, a typically shy guy, was having a delightful time hobnobbing with one of the cognoscenti of Mulhouse.

Never had I met anyone as interesting and genuine as Monsieur Walter. Often, no matter how hard they try, the French cannot easily tone down the sense of formality that their rigid system of education (and often, family upbringing) imposes upon them. Basically, the French can be quite stiff—at least until you are able to break through that sometimes off-putting demeanor. Then they begin to seem more relaxed and open. Monsieur Walter was not at all stuffy and I felt relieved that Pete and I were lunching with such a charming man. (I can only imagine what it would have been like had the town's designated representative been a dreary, old functionary.)

As we feasted over *rollmops* (pickled herring and cream), onion *tarte*, wild boar in wine sauce, and *baerawecka* (a delicious sort of fruitcake-flavored ice cream), our conversations jumped from the history of Mulhouse (an independent republic until it became French, some two hundred years ago) to more philosophical matters. We learned about the importance of Mulhouse as a major industrial center, throughout the centuries and to this day. "By the end of the eighteenth century, Mulhouse was the primary textile supplier for all of Europe," Monsieur Walter explained. "It's thanks to all the wealthy industrialists that Mulhouse became such an important tourist destination in recent years," monsieur continued in French. "All these rich folk amassed huge collections of all sorts. Probably the biggest—and most popular—is the Collection Schlumpf. It's a colossal conglomeration of prized cars that today makes up Mulhouse's Musée National de l'Automobile."

Pete gestured to Monsieur Walter that that was where we planned to go. "Tell him, Bessie, tell him that's the main reason we came to Mulhouse."

Monsieur Walter understood the reason for Pete's excitement before I even translated what he said. We spent the next five minutes talking about the highlights of the Collection Schlumpf as Monsieur Walter raved to Peter about how much he'd be impressed by this world-renowned museum.

Pete smiled and nodded in agreement and even I became convinced that it was something I'd enjoy.

We also talked a lot about Monsieur Walter's official duties as deputy mayor, which require him to officiate over marriages. Monsieur Walter was off to marry some people after our lunch, in fact.

"I share in their happiness," Monsieur Walter said. "It's important to mark that moment. To be at the start of a couple is very significant."

"How true," I said, and I couldn't help feeling that if I married again, I'd love to have Monsieur Walter officiate.

"I once married seventeen couples in one day," he added.

"I'm sure you provided a vibrant and inspirational presence at each of the ceremonies," I replied, smiling.

We were sad to leave Monsieur Walter, but after all his debriefing about the amazing cultural richness of Mulhouse, we were anxious to go museum hopping. First stop was to the Musée Français du Chemin de Fer, or the French railroad museum. Here we ambled around an immense sort of railroad station looking at cars as splendiferous as the Imperial car of Napoleon III.

It was all so fascinating, we could have stayed another hour, but Pete expressed concern that we'd run out of time for Mulhouse's famous car museum. I'm the first to admit that I'm not a car person, so it's a huge compliment when I say that the Musée National de l'Automobile in Mulhouse is fabulous. Considered to be the largest and most modern automobile museum in the world, it reeled Pete in from the get-go with its spectacular collection of some four hundred exceptional automobiles, including over one hundred Bugattis, the crème de la crème of the collector's car. Pete was very appreciative that I was taking an interest, since it sometimes frustrates him that I don't share even a smidgen of his passion for any sort of motorized vehicle.

We had barely enough time to rush back to our place of lodging, the Hôtel du Parc, a handsome Art Déco establishment and indisputably the best hotel of Mulhouse, and quickly change for dinner. We were meeting another tourism official at La Poste, one of the most elegant restaurants of the city, and we had no time to spare. Much to our surprise, Monsieur Walter and his lovely wife were waiting for us at the restaurant for the apéritif. He had made it a special, out-of-the-way stop in between his official duties and a dinner engagement with friends. Along the way, he made a point to pick up an elegant-looking box of chocolates from Mulhouse's best-loved chocolatier and *patissier*, Carlos. I *was* beginning to feel like royalty. Pete and I were totally charmed by the kindness and generosity of all the Mulhouse officials.

We scurried about town the next day, visiting more museums and taking in more sites. The Musée de l'Impression sur Etoffes (M.I.E., or Textile Museum) particularly captivated me, but after just a half-hour, I could see Pete was becoming bored. Besides, we were longing for our bikes. This trip was supposed to be our own tour de France, and, by now, we were beginning to have a sense of just how much sightseeing and merry-making that entailed.

Beautiful Burgundy

We felt such great affection for Alsace that we were doubtful Burgundy would delight us nearly as much. As soon as we pulled off the highway from Mulhouse, though, and found ourselves in the thick of the lush, green countryside of *la Bourgogne*, we sensed right away that the cycling would be sweet. The terrain there was much hillier than I had expected, but this, of course, just made the bike riding more interesting. Summer had followed us to Burgundy, too, and the weather forecast for the upcoming days promised even more warmth and sun than during our stay in Alsace.

Geraniums, dahlias, petunias and pansies still bloomed in the large planters in front of the Hôtel de Bourgogne, the country inn in Cluny where Pete and I planned to stay for two nights. The garden terrace had just been closed for the season, but still this old, homey establishment was clearly intent on bringing the wonderful freshness of the outdoors in. The screen-less, wide-open doors and windows brought up many sentimental feelings for me toward my beloved France, and I remembered how much the way of life in this country is often both elegant and down-to-earth. We enjoyed a fine meal that evening at the inn, accompanied by a bit of Montagny 1er Cru and a Givry, two fine wines of Burgundy. Our sojourn in Burgundy was off to a good start.

We woke up on Monday, September 25 to chirping birds and a day that presented itself as much hotter than what we would have expected in this part of France at this time of year. Pete and I did a little twirl on our bikes around the hilly town of Cluny, a village named for the Benedictine Abbey founded here in the eleventh century. We decided not to visit the abbey just yet, since we were anxious to head out onto *La Voie Verte*, a scenic bike path that extends from Cluny to the Côte Chalonnaise. Once a railroad line, this forty-four kilometer (twenty-seven mile) stretch of perfect pavement allows cyclists to discover many of the most interesting villages, towns and sites of southern Burgundy. I felt confident, too, that the cycling would be doable for me, since the terrain was probably quite flat.

The first stretch was glorious. Peter and I were charmed by the picture-postcard views of the countryside. Eventually, though, even I became rather bored with the path, since it was so totally flat. We pulled off at one point to consult the user's guide of *La Voie Verte* that we had picked up at the hotel, and then realized that this explicitly marked "green way" also encourages cyclists to leave the route from time to time, to explore neighboring places of interest. "You take these turnoffs to access the climbs," Pete said. "There are thirteen loops, with varying degrees of difficulty."

"Let me see," I said as I took a look at the map. "Oh yeah, they call them *boucles*. The guide also indicates different sites along the way."

I could tell that Pete was eager to start climbing, which I understood. But still, there were visits to do in the area and a lovely lunch to be shared, so I hoped he could hold off until the afternoon to knock himself out. I mustered up all of my feminine charms to persuade him to wait to do the hills later on. "We've gone sixteen kilometers (ten miles) at this point, already," I said. "How about if we just stop here for a quick visit at the Musée du Vélo (Bicycle Museum)? Then we can have a nice picnic somewhere—and then we can have the whole afternoon for the climbs." I held my breath and waited for his response.

"All right, if you think that's important to your story," he finally mumbled.

"Oh, it is. I'm sure that museum traces the whole history of cycling. It's a must-see, I'm sure," I eplied. "C'mon," I said as I dismounted my bike and wrapped my arm around his shoulder. "I know you'll like it, too."

Set in an old farmhouse alongside the bike path, seemingly out in the middle of nowhere, we discovered what must be one of the richest collections of bicycles and bicycling memorabilia in the world. There was not a soul inside, so we had the two floors of the museum all to ourselves. Downstairs, the collection consisted of 5,000 different pieces of memorabilia, all of which had some kind of connection to bicycles or cycling. Many of the *objets* were emblazoned with cyclists or some sort of insignia that paid homage to local cycling clubs or similar types of organizations. As expected, the Tour de France collection was quite amusing, particularly the display of wine bottles of special vintages that were released to commemorate the Tour's great champions.

Old wool jerseys (no Lycra back then), signed by their famous owners, lined the stairwell leading to the main part of the collection upstairs. Here some 135 bikes trace the history of *le vélo* (the bicycle) since its creation. We learned, for example, that a German invented a sort of bicycle in 1818 that was propelled by pushing both feet. It wasn't until 1861 that a Frenchman, Monsieur Michaux, added pedals to this contraption, and hence, the velocipede (also known as the boneshaker), the precursor to the bicycle, was born. Highwheelers (bicycles with the big wheel in front) were in fashion in 1875 in France and elsewhere, but an Englishman is credited with having constructed the first modern bicycle, in 1887. As much as Pete does not like to dawdle in museums, on top of the fact that he was busting to cycle, he was very excited about what we had stumbled upon. There was even an example of the type of bike used at the first Tour de France, in 1903. It was all fascinating, and at the end of our tour, we had the pleasure of meeting Monsieur Grezaud, the passionate collector and cycling enthusiast, who had assembled this marvelous collection. "I started collecting when I was very young," he said, and after a bit of reflection added, "and I still cycle."

After our visit to the Bicycle Museum, we pedaled a kilometer into the village of Cormatin. The hotel had packed us a lunch for the road, so I hoped to fulfill a romantic notion of Pete and me partaking in our own special *déjeuner sur l'herbe*, or lunch on the grass, like the two lovers portrayed in Manet's celebrated painting of the same name. (Unlike the woman in the painting, however, I planned to keep my clothes on.) I didn't have much time to pick the right spot since I could already tell that Pete's patience was wearing thin. He became fidgety and his eyes flared, maybe because I was taking one minute too long in search of a nice, grassy area. All of a sudden he became irritable and said, "Let's do this fast." I didn't appreciate his crankiness and impatience, but was determined not to ruin the moment by making an issue out of his attitude.

We agreed upon a lovely bit of field on the hillside overlooking the expansive countryside and the little village of Cormatin, with its old church and bell tower perfectly positioned in the foreground. It was a Frenchman's *pique-nique*, far better than the tuna sandwiches that make up my standard picnic fare. Someone had lovingly wrapped chicken (with a side of homemade mayonnaise), tomato and rice salad and bread and cheese into a neat picnic package that we could have feasted upon for days. A local Burgundy was also provided and, as much as it complemented the meal perfectly, Pete and I vowed never again to drink wine while cycling.

We picked up four bottles of water at the local *pâtisserie* before continuing on, and wondered if they would be enough to quench our thirst throughout the whole afternoon.

"Do you want to visit the château in Cormatin?" I ventured.

"No, I think we've had enough downtime," Pete replied, through almost-clenched teeth. "And no more flat!"

It was easier for me to understand and accept Pete's gruffness here than the one he had sported just before lunch. If a guy is a major cyclist, yet so far on this bike tour he's only had one real day of cycling, I can easily comprehend his frustration. Even I felt like I really wanted to stretch my legs with a good ride, so I could only imagine his exasperation. The surrounding hillsides tempted him, and he was anxious to set out on some good climbs. I also wanted Pete to have a say in the program and I found it important for our balance of power that he have the opportunity to make some of the decisions in our itinerary, too.

We biked head on into the farmland, rolling across a country road that traversed glorious vineyards and countless farms that appeared locked in time, all near the Côte du Bray. The rustic views of stone houses the color of French bread, the richness of the soil and the beige and chestnut cows made me glad to be experiencing this beauty on a bicycle.

Just as I felt nearly lost in this bucolic symphony of sensations, Pete began to instruct me on gear shifting. "Big ring, small ring, shift down, shift up, pedal! Shift again, one more, no, higher, OK, lower——you're coming to a hill!"

"I *am* shifting!" I yelled back almost apologetically.

"Think downshift, smaller ring; upshift, bigger ring," Pete shouted for added emphasis.

"Does small mean easier, big mean harder?" I asked, feeling stupid, but wanting to be sure nonetheless. *Darn, how I get frustrated with myself. I hate how I freeze up whenever I have to do or think about anything mechanical. I get blocked.*

"Yeah, that's right," Pete said. "Just keep pedaling!"

I appreciated that he didn't take the opportunity to make fun of my lack of bike savvy. He knew that I had come so far——I've even been trained on how to change a tire. I'm not completely sure I could do it, but maybe I could in a pinch. I couldn't help thinking *do I really need to know all this?* With gear shifting, I just go by feeling, and when the pedaling is too hard or too easy, I shift in the direction that I know will make the pedaling harder or easier. Like much of my life, I ride on intuition and how it feels.

"All this big, small, up, down is confusing me even more," I yelled back to Pete. "Anyway, if ever I have my doubts, I just glance down at the gears." *Boy, I wonder what my life would have been like had I been given a toolbox when I was a child instead of a circus-sized collection of dolls and stuffed animals. My five brothers likely had toolboxes galore.*

Pete didn't understand why I couldn't get all this; why I possessed such a definite lack of enthusiasm for basic bike mechanics. I knew that he just wanted to help me improve my game; I valued his expertise about cycling enormously. But this lesson didn't go well, particularly since his timing for hard-line coaching was so off. Sensing that he felt unappreciated for this impromptu mentoring, I decided to give it my best effort and attempt to take Pete's many instructions.

When I finally felt like I was going at a relatively acceptable clip, Pete lowered the boom. "Listen, from now on, I am imposing a ten-mile-an-hour minimum."

"No way. I can do that on flats and, of course, downhill, but not on inclines. You knew what my riding ability was before this trip," I added defensively. That seemed to quiet him down considerably, and then for a while we just rode along, gazing at the beautiful scenery. The gap between Pete and me widened (both figuratively and literally) and what began as ten feet quickly turned into fifty. I knew I was slogging along but I couldn't go any faster. I regained my composure in the physical distance that helped to separate us emotionally. Soon he was almost out of view, which I thought was just fine since he obviously needed to stretch his legs and break away from me.

Suddenly he came flying back. I could tell by the look on his face that he was going to have some sort of fit. "Can't you go any faster? I have never seen anyone go so slowly on a bike in my life! I don't go as slow as you even on my slowest day."

I didn't dare yell back at him because by now, even to me, it seemed as though I was indeed riding with the brakes on. "I think there's a pretty strong headwind," I said. "And look, the road has been a false flat for as far back as we can see."

Fortunately, we only had a short distance to go before we found a fork in the road at the little village of Cortambert. "OK, so here, you take the high road and I'll take the low road and we meet where the two come back together," I said. He took off before I even finished my sentence.

Once he was out of sight, I couldn't help but breathe a sigh of relief. *Boy, can he be tough*, I thought to myself. *Hadn't he ever heard of positive reinforcement? Couldn't he see how much I was trying?* To me, our best times cycling together were when we'd just cruise along and enjoy the ride.

We met at the end of the ride, back toward Cluny. Pete was elated. "The cycling here is sick," he exclaimed. I'd had plenty of time to gaze out at the cows, to write in my journal, process my thoughts and catch my breath. I was relieved to see that Pete had released his pent-up energy and was ready to share a cozy dinner back at the inn. I made a mental note to give him more opportunities to break out on the bike, break away from me. But it was unclear how we could make that happen, since so far we seemed inseparable. Total mileage for the day was twenty-five miles.

As I prepared myself for another intimate evening, I couldn't help thinking that I had been challenged, both physically and emotionally, several times throughout the day. In a sudden reflective—if not insightful—moment, I began to think that maybe the key to our harmony could be found in a greater understanding of Pete and the way he thinks, acts and communicates overall. I promised myself to work on this, and also not to let Pete's blow-ups get the best of me.

We woke up tired the next day, partly because of the ride the day before, but mostly, I think, because we were having a lot of ongoing issues to manage. Pete was cranky when I woke him up which lead to a tiff right off (despite all my good intentions about understanding him from the day before). I was also on edge because I still hadn't figured out how to make my laptop work. (That was perhaps a blessing since it was foolish of me to think I'd find the time to write on this trip.)

So we had our reasons to be irritable, but we both lost all patience over our laundry situation. We thought we had planned it just right by doing a fair amount of hand wash—bike shorts, jerseys, socks, undies—in the bidet upon our arrival. That in itself was a merciless chore. But as much as I spent most of my free time shifting the laundry around so that it would dry properly, it still was not dry enough to be packed up by the time we were to leave that morning. So Pete and I took turns drying laundry with the hair dryer we had borrowed from the front desk. All the while we felt pressured to get a move on since we were told that an official photographer from the regional tourist board wanted to follow us around that day in his car. *Oh, great.*

The tourist department that helped me arrange this segment of the trip had asked us to change hotels again, largely so we could enjoy the "so-called" benefits of cycling to our next destination without worrying about our luggage. The owner of the auberge where we were to stay that night was to come by and pick up our bags, while someone else was going to take charge of the car. (*Quelle organisation.*) We were to do a one-nighter in another hotel just north of Cluny, at Saint-Boil. This way we could ride our bikes even farther north, up and alongside the bike path all the way to the new hotel. This was the first and only time in my life that I would use Bella for both transportation and recreation. The idea was a good one, but we were not in the best of pack-unpack moods.

A few skirmishes later, Pete and I were finally out the door and on our way to our designated meeting spot with Alain, the photographer. It was another beautiful, sunny day, but I felt rather out of sorts and somewhat disoriented. I didn't think it was only due to our conflicts. Pete and I rode for about two miles then I stopped and said, "I can't believe it—I forgot to put in my contacts in. No wonder everything looks so blurry. This has only happened to me a few times since I began wearing them decades ago. This is crazy!"

A wave of emotion came over me, and I broke down in tears. Pete stood there silent, realizing (thankfully) that the pressures of travel had finally overwhelmed me. "What a stupid idea to do this baggage transfer," I griped. "The whole thing discombobulated me— I never go out without my contacts. I feel so flustered," I said in a blubbering voice.

"C'mon, Bessie. It's not the end of the world," Pete said.

"But I always need something—I don't like to be separated from my stuff," I proclaimed. "I might not even be able to get to my luggage." Pete stood there holding his bike and mine, eyeing me.

"I'm sure you think I'm a kook," I said, choking on my words, half crying, half laughing.

"I know you're a kook," Pete replied, half joking.

I think I'm a nutcase myself, too, I thought to myself. *Here I am a grown woman, a professional travel writer, bawling in the middle of a scenic bike path. I feel even more ridiculous standing here in my skintight bike shorts sporting my Tour de France jersey. Ha! What the heck would Lance Armstrong think of this scene.*

As though he read my thoughts, Pete laid the bikes on the ground (no bike stands on our sleek bikes) and wrapped his arms around me.

"C'mon, you're just stressed out," he said.

"I know," I replied in one big heave. "You see, I told you there'd be a lot of imperatives and schedules to follow when touring with a travel writer."

"It's not so bad," he replied and hugged me tighter.

We chuckled some over the situation—although not too much since I still dreaded the idea of a day of riding with fuzzy vision. It was time to get back on our bikes, retrace our ride and attempt to locate my contacts.

With the passage of so much time, we weren't sure that our bags would still be at the hotel in Cluny if we chose to pedal back. We managed to set up another designated meeting spot with Alain, the photographer, for later on, rode back to the hotel, and dug out the lenses from the bottom of my suitcase, which we finally located at the back of the hotel's storage room.

Amazingly, my little crisis really seemed to have cleaned out a lot of mental clutter. "I feel much better," I said to Pete. "Who ever said that traveling is always fun?" I joked. Pete was doing better, too, and I think he was secretly relieved that he wasn't the only one who had let his emotions have the best of him that day. (He'd never apologized for his sour mood that morning but I learned to accept his actions as a sign of remorse.) As exciting as every day of travel had been so far, we still felt destabilized by the hectic pace and the out-of-the-regular-routine aspect of our days. Just waking up during the night and finding my way to the bathroom in so many different surroundings was already proving disorienting to me, and we still had many more weeks of travel ahead of us. Sometimes I thought I had no business being a travel writer since I find the familiarity of my fabric-adorned *chez moi* to be so comforting.

"We're not going to stop and do any visiting today," Pete said. "Besides, I don't like standing around in my bike shorts once I've done some riding."

"Fair enough," I replied. Here again it seemed reasonable to me that Pete take charge of the day. We had already lost a good amount of time and there wasn't one particular visit I was burning to do, so why not let him be the boss? I couldn't help but think, though, that I had heard no mention of his bike short discomfort when we cycled a full day in Alsace with Christian. We were finally off to experience another day of fantastic cycling. The pressure of meeting up with Alain eased up, too, since after our first brief encounter with him that morning at breakfast, we could tell he was a nice guy and had no intention of interfering with our cycling program.

The hills that Pete was busting to climb had somehow disappeared in this stretch of farmland, north of Cormatin. We rode long straightaways the likes of which you'd see in the Tour de France, passed through tight, wooded areas just when we needed a bit of shade from the day's heat, and lost ourselves in rambling fields where it seemed as though no cyclist had ever passed. Just when we were feeling way off-the-beaten-path, we encountered *un pépé*, an old man, in his vintage *deux chevaux* (an iconic French car) rounding the bend. After we exchanged a few directions, he asked about our nationality. "*Américains, très bien.*" The sweet ole gent then launched into old war stories and other anecdotes about the occasional encounters with Americans he'd had throughout his lifetime.

Once our americanophile friend put us on our way, we regained the route that we were to cycle on for our rendezvous with Alain. "I'll just wait on the side of the road for you and take some shots as I see you approaching,"Alain had explained. So throughout the afternoon, as we rounded each bend and mounted each hill, we expected to see Alain standing outside of his Citroën, waiting to take that full-action shot. We had gone about twenty miles and there was no sign of him.

"He probably thinks we lost him," Pete said.

"Oh, not to worry," I said. "We've done the best we could all day with all these time constraints."

And as we were feeling the most relaxed and drawing toward the end of our ride, we turned a corner and there was Alain. He had positioned himself at just the right angle to capture Pete and me in the foreground and the glorious landscape of Burgundy in the background. He clicked away in a rapid-fire manner as we came into view. I couldn't help wondering for how long he had maintained that camera-ready pose. He was obviously a real pro, though, and knew the importance of being in the right place at the right time. After another series of shots in a couple of other choice locations, he thanked us for our cooperation and bid us goodbye with promises to send some prints. By now, Pete was becoming quite impressed with *la politesse française*, or French politeness.

"He's a super nice guy," Pete exclaimed, not at all perturbed by having to pose in his bike shorts for twenty minutes.

"Yeah, he is," I added. "Most French people are pleasant, especially to Americans," I continued. "It's a misconception that they're unkind. They just have a different approach, a more formal way of interacting——until you get to know them at least."

"What did you say those pictures were for?" Pete asked.

"I have no idea, some kind of quasi-official photo to appear in a brochure or catalogue, showing that there was a visiting *journaliste américaine*," I told Pete with a wry smile. "Don't you know how important I am?" I said laughingly.

"Oh yeah, you're the Queen of France," he chuckled.

I always got a kick out of Pete calling me the Queen of France. That kind of teasing amused me so much more than comments about my speed.

"Maybe they'll mention something in the photo's caption about the Queen of France's—errrr, I mean *journaliste's*—handsome boyfriend," I teased.

"No, I don't think so," Pete answered. "C'mon, let's get going. We still have to pedal back to the hotel."

Our total for that day was twenty-three miles. Hot and sweaty from our ride, we checked into our hotel in Saint-Boil, the Auberge du Cheval Blanc, and were delighted to see our luggage waiting for us in our room. The baggage transfer was not such a bad idea after all; otherwise we would have needed to select a ride that would have looped back to the hotel we left from in the morning.

That evening at the auberge, Pete and I enjoyed a delicious meal filled with much discussion of the food and wine. Pete wanted to know more about the wine, so we took a few more swills of our Burgundy, and then talked about some of the characteristics of different French wines. I shared with him what I had learned from a wine course I had taken in Paris. He asked about the cheese we had been served—an Epoisses, a particularly strong cheese from the region. "Do you eat the cheese with or without the crust?" he asked.

"There are two schools of thought on that," I replied, "so, basically you can do what you want."

Not surprisingly, Pete ate the crust. I didn't.

By the time we left the restaurant, I could tell that Pete was really enjoying being in France and was making an effort to connect with the people and the culture. "*Bonne noir*," I heard him say as we left, a phrase that translates into good black instead of goodnight, or *bonne nuit*. As I attempted to conceal my giggles, I couldn't help but feel proud of him for so completely embracing *la vie française*.

Day three in Burgundy promised to be a good one since we were driving north toward the world's most prized vineyards, where each parcel of land is more valuable than the first. Near Saint-Boil, the grape picking was largely mechanical, but farther along the road toward Beaune, the task was carried out by hand with the same care that had been practiced for generations. Activity along the wine route (D981) from Saint-Boil to Beaune was at its peak at this time, and, as in Alsace, we were fortunate to catch it when the harvest was still in full swing. Trucks, tractors, trailers and carts of all shapes and sizes slowed our travels along the way, a welcome impediment that provided a colorful display of the region's plump, ripe harvest.

The signage along this tourist circuit read like the wine list from one of the world's finest restaurants. Puligny Montrachet, Meursault, Volnay and Pommard were just a handful of the villages we passed through in this most venerated part of Burgundy, known as the Côte d'Or, or the Gold Coast. Unlike the Médoc in Bordeaux, life is very discreet in the Côte d'Or; although the importance of the Burgundy châteaux rivals those of Bordeaux, here the châteaux (in the castle sense) are smaller in size and far fewer are open to the public. As we passed from one sleepy village to the next, Pete and I were itching to take to our bikes. We had considered finding a place to park and riding from there, but we thought it best to settle in at our next hotel first.

It was mid afternoon when we arrived at L'Hostellerie de Levernois, a grand establishment surrounded by manicured gardens and ten acres of unspoiled nature on the fringes of Beaune. The hotel was quiet, since our arrival marked that lull in the day between the bustling activity of the morning departures and the afternoon check-ins. We were tempted to loll the afternoon away in the tranquility of our luxurious room, and then delight in what the French commonly refer to as a *cinq à sept*, or five to seven, considered by many to be the most opportune time of day for making love. But the cycling beckoned.

All cleated up and ready to ride, we asked the woman at the front desk for directions to Nuits-Saint-Georges since we couldn't locate it on our map.

"It's only about fifteen kilometers, just head into Beaune, then take the *nationale* (a major roadway) for a bit, then follow the signs for the *Route des Grands Crus*," Madame informed us. The idea of taking the *nationale*—certainly a busy route, second only to *l'autoroute* in importance—worried me. But I decided it would be OK, since it was to be for a short stretch only. I did find it strange, however, that the markings madame had made were off the edges of our map. Still with just a slight shrug of our shoulders, Pete and I figured we'd find our way just fine.

"This will be perfect," I said. "This gives us enough time to take a good ride and then come back to the hotel and leisurely prepare for dinner."

Riding along *la nationale* proved to be harrowing. We didn't see a sign for the *Route des Grands Crus*, so when it became too nerve-wracking to tolerate any more vehicles peeling by us, we ducked into the vineyards and followed the signs for Savigny. Here we felt as if we had landed in the full splendor of the impeccably maintained vineyards of Burgundy. Enveloped in a golden light, radiant with all the richness of autumn, we stopped briefly to take a few photos and then continued on along the scenic route in what we hoped was the direction of Nuits-Saint-Georges. Eager to see if we were headed the right way, I stopped an elderly woman in front of the post office to ask for directions. "*Ça va être difficile. Ça monte,*" she said, meaning it's going to be difficult, it goes up.

From Savigny, the ride went well enough. We looked at each other and smiled, happy to have found a glorious route. Then the road slowly started to climb. Then climb more. And more. Eventually we found ourselves cutting straight up through the vineyards on a narrow road that wouldn't accommodate much more than a small tractor. My legs were burning and my heart felt like it might burst through my leopard-print jersey as the ride progressed.

"Good job," Pete called out to me. "Keep it going, you can do it," he rooted me on with words of encouragement that I needed now more than ever. I nodded my head in acknowledgement of his support.

The view was truly spectacular way up on top of the Hautes-Côtes de Beaune. The problem was, I couldn't really take it in or else I'd have to step off my bike. And I was determined not to do that. As the sweat stung my eyes and poured down my face, my main focus became the idea of reaching the top. I wanted to say that I didn't know that Burgundy vineyards grew so high up, that I was glad for Pete that we had come upon such an extraordinary climb, but I couldn't utter a word. I felt like I was going to explode, or at the very least, my bike was going to topple over, with me on it, permanently stuck in my clipless pedals. We passed a *viticulteur* (wine grower) who shouted encouragingly—in English—"Only ten more meters to go to the top." Just like when an enthusiastic fan cheers out to a cyclist at the Tour de France, I felt buoyed up. For a fleeting moment, I wondered how he knew I was American when Pete and I weren't talking. But then I shifted my thoughts back to the crest at the top of the enormous hill, my focal point.

I made it. My reward was a fabulous panoramic vista that I'm sure only the local wine folk and an occasional errant visitor are privileged enough to see. I felt on top of the world, geographically but especially mentally. This was far better than anything I had experienced on my bike in Saratoga. Pete shared in my triumphant feelings and commanded that I ring my bell, the very bell he had affixed onto Bella when we barely knew each other.

A sign indicated ten more kilometers to Nuits-Saint-Georges. Thank goodness it was mostly downhill, a spectacular descent that more than cooled me off from the grueling uphill climb. The town was a flurry of activity by the time we arrived. It was 6 p.m., the hour in France when people typically shop for food before the stores close for the day.

I was starved by now, totally depleted of all energy reserves after such a heroic effort. "You've bonked," declared Pete, which I took as a compliment. This was the first time in my life I had felt so wasted from such physical exertion, and Pete's recognition of this, with classic cyclist lingo, was like initiating me into a special club. I dashed into a *boulangerie* and bought the last two remaining croissants and a *pain au chocolat*. Pete looked as fresh and ready to go as if he had just been warming up, but at least he admitted that he was thirsty. We both chugged a quart of Tropicana, and I remember thinking that never had orange juice tasted so good.

"We better get a move on," Pete said rather anxiously.

"What do you mean?" I asked. "It took us so long to reach Nuits-Saint-Georges, and I want to explore this charming town."

"Are you kidding?" Pete cried. "It's going to be dark soon and we still have to head back."

"Ohhhhh, I guess I almost forgot about that," I admitted, rather sheepishly.

It was time to figure out which road to take back. I had thought that, having finally found Nuits-Saint-Georges, we would be able to pick the right road back to Beaune, the road we had apparently missed on the way out. Was I ever wrong! While stocking up on water from a grocer, I learned that there were actually three ways back, none of which sounded like easy routes. We could either go back the way we had come (out of the question) or ride alongside the *nationale* all the way back to Beaune (I didn't think so). The shopkeeper suggested that we take a little road that cuts through the vineyards, almost parallel to the *nationale*, from Nuits-Saint-Georges to Beaune. His suggestion sounded by far the best solution; the only real question was whether we could find the road on the way out of town. "Let's get a move on," Pete urged. "We have about twenty-five kilometers (sixteen miles) to go one way or another, and night will soon fall."

A mile or so out of town, just as we were about to zoom by the turnoff, I spotted it. "There, there to the left," I shouted to Pete. We found ourselves on a quiet little road that, once again, was reserved primarily for the wine workers. But just as our angst was subsiding and we were even beginning to feel proud of ourselves for having discovered such a pleasant route, the road turned into a gravelly mess. We followed it for a short distance, growing steadily more suspicious, and then the road came to an abrupt end. We were suddenly lost.

"We can either turn back," Pete said, "which would add on at least another six k (four miles) from what we've already done, or somehow find our way."

We persevered, crossing over train tracks and hauling our bikes over precarious terrain, and then zig-zagged through the alleys of the Burgundy vineyards in search of another access road that would lead us in the right direction. We repeated these types of maneuvers countless times, with absolutely no reassurance that once we found ourselves on a road, it would actually lead us someplace other than to another row of grape vines. The quest to return home had become increasingly unsettling, and we felt a mounting fear as the sun fell closer toward the horizon. We both have a good sense of direction, so we knew we were oriented in approximately the right way. We just needed to extricate ourselves from the labyrinth of roads that crisscrossed the vineyards.

By now I was so overcome with exhaustion that I didn't have much more pedaling in me. I had a secret plan, though. I decided that at the next village, I would hole myself up and sip a nice glass of Burgundy while Pete zoomed back to the hotel to pick up the car. The problem with this plan, however, was that we hadn't yet en-

countered a single village—not even a little bar in this middle of nowhere—where I could rest my weary bones.

I didn't tell Pete about my little scheme. It would have seemed
selfish, since here—out in the middle of nowhere—we were acting
like a team, we were unified in our mission to find our way back to
the hotel. We were so in sync that it worried me; our cooperation
seemed a real cause for alarm, especially since Pete seldom agrees so
much with me in these kinds of challenging situations.

Instead of fantasizing about my Burgundy café stop anymore, I
kept moving to show Pete how hard I was trying.

"Faster!" Pete yelled. "It'll be dark soon and we can't be stuck
out here when that happens."

"But I can't go any faster," I whined, nearly on the verge of
tears. And with that I felt him ride up alongside of me and put his
hand on my butt and push me along. "Hey!" I yelled.

"Hay is for horses," Pete said. "I'm going to help both of us get
back before dark."

Pete had tried numerous times before to do this sort of sidecar
action, but I had always bristled, out of fear that he would make me
swerve and crash on my bike. At that moment, though, I felt myself
relax and let him help me do the work. With Pete pushing me, I was
able to ride about twenty miles an hour, double what I had been riding on my own. I began to enjoy myself immensely. I was thrilled to
feel my legs pedaling at such a high cadence and was exhilarated by
the strong breeze blowing in my face.

"What's this called?" I asked.

"Pushing Bessie," he replied.

I could sense that he was proud of me. I knew he was happy
that I was able to let go and allow him to help me. He was my knight
in shining armor. I wanted to turn and look at him but I was petri-
fied to look over my shoulder at that speed. I sensed, though, that he
was definitely sporting one of his huge grins.

We both whizzed into Beaune——just as the sky became dark
with night. It was 8 p.m., the hour of our dinner reservation. We
asked for an extension of half an hour, and ran upstairs to dress.

We hurried down to dinner with our hearts still beating wildly from the adventurous ride. A smartly dressed *maître d'hôtel* greeted us, assuring us that our delay posed no problem at all, and invited us to sit in their lounge area for the apéritif. Pete and I toasted our exploit with perfectly-chilled glasses of champagne. "That was definitely a ride to go down in my bike history book," I declared, beaming with contentment over all that transpired.

"See, you can do more than you realize," Pete said.

"Now, now, no lecturing."

"No, really. Today proved that you have more in you than you think. You just have to push yourself more," he added.

"You mean you have to push me more," I joked.

Pete laughed in his shy-boy manner, not wanting to take extra credit for the heroic role he had played in our day's adventure. Instead he winked and appeared to relish his swill of champagne more than ever.

We commented to each other about the other guests. The crowd was quite chic, rather hip, totally international, and on the young side overall. Half of them looked like Hollywood mogul types. The ladies appeared stunning, most accessorized with fabulous jewelry and scarves. I was glad that I was feeling good in my short black skirt—better than usual, in fact, since my legs felt toned and sleek from the ride.

In the dining room, the crowd was equally as interesting, and Pete and I were happy to have been strategically placed for people watching. "I've never seen such a diverse group of people in a fancy French restaurant," I commented to Pete. "Wine connoisseurs must be an eclectic bunch. Half the men are in suits, half aren't, and look, one man is wearing jeans and a flannel shirt."

As the parade of specialty dishes began, however, our focus shifted to our table. The chef, once again, had selected a special menu for us as well as a sampling of wines from the region since my travel writer status elevated us to be treated as privileged guests of the house. A little *crème de persil* (parsley cream) was presented to open our appetites, a subtle beginning to what clearly was to be an extraordinary meal. Next, a plate framing two generous lobes of foie gras, accented by a little row of *fleur de sel de Guérande* and a little row of ground pepper from Les Landes, was placed in front of each of us. This simple marriage of ingredients was exceedingly pure, both visually and to the taste.

"This salt has been harvested near the medieval village of Guérande, in the Western Loire next to Brittany, since the seventh century," I explained to Pete. "I went there when I was researching *The Riches of France*. It's considered by most chefs to be the most flavorful salt in the world."

Immensely impressed by this little gastronomic debriefing, Pete offered his opinion, "The salt brings out the flavor of the foie gras really well."

"I can't believe it," I said to Pete. "I just realized that in less than a week I've had foie gras three times." I enjoyed every bit of the delicious dish, which was greatly enhanced by its accompanying Chablis Premier Cru, but I could only finish half of it.

"Do you have a problem with the foie gras?" the waiter asked.

"Oh, no, but if I eat it all, I won't be able to fit into my clothes," I said somewhat sheepishly, knowing that my comment would be reported back to the chef, and I would forever be remembered as *la journaliste américaine* that did not finish her foie gras. (The chef in a restaurant of such unparalleled quality is always apprised of these kinds of happenings.)

After a brusque exchange of worried looks, the headwaiter rushed over and smoothed everything over. "Ah, we will make a foie gras sandwich tomorrow for you to take on the road," he declared with a huge amount of professionalism that put me at ease.

When the sommelier poured us a Chassagne-Montrachet '97, I ascertained that the next course would most likely be from the sea. And with that, out came an outstanding roasted lobster. We were each served a half, delicately dressed with a rosemary cream sauce and skirted with little scoops of wild rice and ratatouille. After finishing the lobster, our appetites were satiated.

Even after all the calories I had surely burned during the afternoon's cycling, I had to unzip my skirt an inch to better enjoy the next course, a most fragrant-filled saddle of lamb, served with fresh baby vegetables. To accompany this course, the sommelier carefully poured Vosne-Romanée premier cru '93, a wine from just above Nuits-Saint-Georges. "This is an homage to your trek up to that part of Burgundy," the sommelier added with a twinkle in his eye. The wine was so delicious that we were pleased with ourselves for having bragged about our day's exploits to this friendly wine steward.

As we dined, we observed the pageantry of the large, busy dining room. Pete and I were particularly impressed with Madame Crotet, the wife of the chef, and clearly a reigning force behind Hostellerie de Levernois. At one point we observed Madame dressed most elegantly, in a diaphanous, gauzy top, carving meat as graciously and effortlessly as though she was waving a baton. As is customary in most restaurants in France, big and small, Madame's chief responsibilities lie in making sure that all goes smoothly in the dining room while her husband (and, in this case, also their sons) does the same in the kitchen.

Everyone had an important role here, especially since they were playing to a full house of highly discriminating diners. Serving the cheese course was in itself a sort of processional. Little tables were first set up in front of our table. Then immense silver platters, laden with a huge assortment of cheeses, were ceremoniously carried over by four people (two per platter) and placed on top of the tables. There was an extra large platter for all the cows' milk cheeses and another for the goats' milk cheeses. "I could make a dinner out of the cheese course alone," I said to Pete.

"I can't believe they bring all this out after the huge meal we just had," he answered.

"I know. But it's all so good, we must have a good sampling. Just wash it down with more wine," I joked.

The pre-dessert sorbet, made from Marc de Bourgogne (a spirit made from Burgundy grapes), was not only extraordinary but also cleansed our palates perfectly in preparation for the real dessert. I nearly swooned over the baked peach crowned with pistachio ice cream.

"I am beyond sated," I said to Pete as we padded off to our room.

"That was outrageous," Pete replied.

"A meal we'll alway remember," I added.

"And how."

How I loved that he enjoyed these feasts. As long as they didn't interfere with cycling, his enthusiasm for French gastronomy rivaled mine. It was so much fun to share all this with him. In many ways, being with him in France—and sharing in his excitement and discoveries—was like experiencing my beloved land for the first time.

Needless to say, we woke up the next morning not feeling terribly refreshed. We calculated that we had cycled about thirty-six miles and then drunk close to two bottles of wine. Thankfully, it was the good stuff. I was surprised that my legs weren't heavier, and decided that Pete was right, I have more in me than I am willing to test. Still, we started pounding water from the get-go.

We checked out of our glorious retreat, sad that we had barely had a chance to rest in such elegant surroundings. The members of the hotel and restaurant staff bid us a gracious *au revoir* but, sadly, no foie gras sandwich was produced. (That was a relief, actually.) Next stop: Beaune, where I wanted to spend some time checking out the boutiques and walking around this little town, one of my best loved of France. Pete wanted a haircut, too, so I talked about splitting up to accomplish our tasks.

We hit Beaune during the two-hour lunchtime closing, but Pete finally found a *salon de coiffure* that had remained open. (Yes, even they typically close for lunch.) I desperately wanted to let him go on his own—I felt like sitting out on a café terrace to write a few postcards, and it seemed to me that it would be good to have some time apart before moving on to our next region. Although Pete sometimes feels smothered by our togetherness, he was hesitant to break out on his own. His inability to speak French created barriers for him; so far during the trip he refrained from venturing even as far as a corner café without me.

"No, way," he protested. "You even come with me in Saratoga to put in your two cents."

Touché, I thought. "I only came with you because your stylist kept giving you that stupid bowl cut," I protested.

"Whatever," Pete answered, obviously annoyed.

"OK, I'll come in," I replied. "Maybe I'll be able to write a few postcards in the salon."

And as soon as we settled into the salon I realized that, as sweet and nice as the young lady was, hand gestures and facial expressions don't make for good communication, especially when it comes to a haircut.

"Would he like it just over the ears or behind?" she asked me in French. "Where does he make his part? And how about the sideburns?"

I felt a little stupid that I hadn't realized how many decisions needed to be made with a guy's haircut. It had made sense that I accompany him. When I recognized this, Pete appeared very self-satisfied. He was happy with our triangular communication, as it turned out, and pleased with the cut. He acknowledged and appreciated my help, he valued me being there with him.

What miscommunication, I thought. *Here I was trying to give him his space and it almost backfired on us. Helping him was more important than writing postcards. That's a perfect example of how easily things can go awry*, I thought to myself. There was no point going over it with Pete since he gets annoyed when I "over-analyze" our relationship. But if you don't review happenings such as these, they just repeat themselves. I guess I need to do more work on my end; I need to get more in touch with my needs and wants while checking in with him about his. Oh Lord, sometimes all this tip-toeing around feels exhausting.

We laughed about the whole experience, and I could tell we both felt happy about how we solved our little communication glitch. Our emotional needs had been met. And with his shorter hair, he was ready to face the beastly sun of Provence.

I caressed the fine hair on the back of his head and smiled at him.

"Hey," he cried.

"Hay is for horses," I hollered back.

He cracked a wily grin that stretched all the way across his slender face. He knew he was right and he was basking in his triumph.

Our salon experience helped me to appreciate our dynamic even more. And in understanding this and seeing how happy this made him, I loved him more than ever.

The Sun Doesn't Always Shine in Provence

Driving from Beaune to Provence was far more tiresome than expected. In all, it took nearly five hours since we encountered a lot of truck traffic along the way. As soon as we arrived in Provence, I was waiting for Pete to experience the "aaaahhhh" sensation that most people feel when they arrive in this glorious land. It wasn't happening, and, in fact, I wasn't getting it either. It was certainly the first time I had arrived in Provence that my senses were not seized by a panoply of fragrances and sounds. I couldn't catch one whiff of rosemary or thyme, and didn't hear the crick of a single cricket. The sky was dreary and the normally captivating landscape looked rather dull. We were experiencing a real rarity; the sun wasn't shining in Provence.

We arrived at our hotel, the Hostellerie du Prieuré in Bonnieux in the Lubéron, just barely in time for dinner. Pete was tired and suffering from an upset stomach—not so much, though, that it prevented him from drinking a few swallows of wine and nibbling on some cheese. He was definitely in the swing of things and had come to look forward to his wine and cheese nearly as much as I did.

"I miss Bourgogne," Pete blurted out. "I kind of wish I could do more riding there. There was some cool riding in Cluny."

"Just wait and see," I responded. "I know you'll love Provence, too."

The sound of cooing pigeons sheltered under the eaves outside our window and torrents of rain awakened us the next morning. Unable to resist being a wise guy, Pete said, "I thought it didn't rain here in Provence."

"I'm sure it will clear soon," I added, half convinced as I looked out at the leaden sky. I wanted things to go right on this trip. Even a wrinkle in the weather made me nervous. I wanted Pete to fall in love with France and in so doing, fall in love with me even more.

We breakfasted at Le Prieuré in a leisurely fashion. With all the rain, we felt in no hurry. A freshly dressed table in typical Provençal fabrics awaited us, a whimsical island in the bleakest of storms. Pete seemed resigned to the fact that we were forced to slow down and luxuriate à la Bessie.

"Oh look, toast," I cried out as a basket spilling over with golden croissants, *petits pains* and toast was placed on the table with our coffee and tea. "I'm thrilled! I haven't had a piece of toast since we left home two weeks ago." (Yes, one can become tired of buttery croissants.) The waitress carefully set down two little jam pots filled to the brim with thick, whole-fruit spreads to complete this ambrosial tableau.

Poor Pete. If only he could have felt the same contentment over this lovely *petit dejeuner*. I tried to gloss things over since I knew he was bummed about not jumping on the bike. I'm afraid, however, that my delight in the breakfast annoyed him even more. I decided to temper my enthusiasm and savored my tea and toast in silence.

Afterward I did my travel writer thing and visited more of the Hostellerie du Prieuré, a rather mysterious-looking old stone building built in the early eighteenth century. Formerly the Hôtel Dieu (a sort of hospice), the Marquis de Sade had been treated here for a period of time, a most convenient arrangement since his château was only six kilometers away in Lacoste. Pete and I were particularly taken by the old stone steps and tile floors, worn by time. It felt wonderfully Old World-ish to be staying in a place like this.

Before we ventured out for the day, Pete and I asked a few questions at the reception area. "What can you tell us about le Mont Ventoux?" I inquired.

"*Oh! Là! Là! C'est fantastique,*" replied the woman. She then began to describe in rather mystical terms the uniqueness of this famous mountain, the only one of its kind in Provence. "It is totally inaccessible in the winter, but you can go up it now—but be careful of *le mistral* (the infamous wind of the region). You must dress very warmly. It really is worth going up there. The terrain is very unique with a sort of vegetation that grows only in one other place in the world, on the Island of Spitzberg near Greenland. When it's very clear, you can see all the way to Marseille," she continued in perfect English.

"Ventoux is beginning to sound like quite an unusual place," I said to Pete as we walked away.

"It's mythic," he added with a nod.

"I'm glad you know more about a part of France than me," I teased as I intertwined my arm with his.

"Yeah, it's pretty unique," he added and then grabbed for my hand, which had curled around his forearm.

The rest of the day was spent just driving around and doing a few errands. We had picked up a brochure, "The Lubéron by Bike," at the hotel that outlined an exciting and challenging itinerary.

"Look, this route traverses the Lubéron region from east to west—from Cavaillon to Forcalquier—for just over one hundred kilometers," Pete said as he studied the brochure. "That's sixty-two miles."

"How hard is it?" Do you think I can do it?"

"It says that you can choose different parts of the ride according to your abilities. It says that road signs mark the suggested itinerary along the way."

Our hopes for actually doing this ride deteriorated rapidly as the heavy rain persisted and Pete became increasingly ill. When we stopped for lunch at the Restaurant du Logis, a cozy place near Isle-sur-la-Sorgue, the waiter said, "I can't remember the last time it rained in Provence." *How lucky we are to be here for such an uncommon happening*, I thought wryly.

Obviously we were meant to lay low, particularly since by now, Pete was spending a lot of time in the *toilettes* and at our bidet. We weren't sure whether or not he had some sort of a bug or whether his ongoing malaise was due to the excesses of the past two weeks.

"Maybe it's gastritis," I said.

"What's that?"

"I'm not sure exactly, but I came down with that toward the end of my research for *The Riches of France*. I was hit hard after I did the Southwest—too much foie gras, red wine and armagnac. Had the same symptoms as what you're having now. Couldn't even enjoy the *thalassotherapie* at the spa I was visiting."

"The what?"

"It's a sort of water/seaweed therapy. I was staying at La Baule in the Western Loire region of France. It was fabulous. But I was so sick I could only get up to go to the bathroom. I just had to stay in bed."

"Jeez, thanks for the update. Aren't we supposed to be going to the Southwest soon?"

I figured I'd better smooth out the situation instead of making it worse. "Anyway, I think we should find a pharmacy," I replied.

We ended up stopping at three different ones until we found just the right combination of medicines recommended by several pharmacists. (The French are so big on medications, it is widely viewed that a doctor is not considered very good unless the patient leaves a consultation with at least three prescriptions.)

The medications kicked in just in time for us to comfortably drive to our next destination, La Bégude de Saint-Pierre, outside Uzès, all the way to the far western end of Provence. Here we found ourselves caught in a total deluge, so it took some doing to settle our baggage and bikes into this hotel upon arrival.

"It actually rains as much in Provence as in Brittany," declared the young woman who greeted us. "Here, though, it comes all at once." I couldn't bear to look over and see the expression on Pete's face after that comment.

Light from a brilliant blue sky crept into our window the next morning, totally transforming the look of the region's craggy land-scapes. Pete and I were feeling good, anxious to head out and take a nice gentle ride. Our less-than-ten-mile excursion led us down bumpy back roads, however, completely devoid of any interesting views. It wasn't surprising to learn that this is an area known for its mountain-bike riding, something that became increasingly evident with each hillside scarred by trails that we passed. I had chosen this area largely because I had once visited this hotel and had always wanted to go back. Unfortunately, that wasn't turning out as anticipated, either; so, sadly, our spirits were not entirely lifted with the arrival of the sun.

We changed and drove into Uzès for lunch to take a quick look around. That, too, was disappointing since we didn't feel in any mood to deal with all the tourists. "I thought the villages in Burgundy were much more charming," Pete declared.

I found myself defending Provence. "Oh, you've seen it under bad conditions so far with all the rain and the subsequent traffic, and now people swarming about after the storm."

The only response from Pete was a slight, "Harrumph."

I was beginning to worry that he thought I was selling him a bill of goods. "How about we go visit the Pont du Gard, an ancient Roman aqueduct?" I suggested to Pete, hopeful of turning the tide on all this dissatisfaction. "That's one of the reasons I wanted to come here. Let's ride our bikes there since it's just a short distance from the hotel."

Pete seemed agreeable to this, so we quickly drove back to La Bégude, changed again, and sped away. I had never been there before and didn't realize that there was more to a visit here than just pedaling up to the aqueduct. It was the heat of the day by now, and as much as I thought I was organizing our little cultural jaunt nicely, I couldn't help noticing that Pete was beginning to fume. He became ornery, which I imagined was because he needed a good ride. Still, I was astonished that he was not enjoying being in such a magnificent place. I sensed a communication breakdown setting in.

By the time we made it to the aqueduct, we were barely speaking to each other. "I told you, I don't like to visit anything in sticky bike shorts," he said, finally revealing the nature of his irritation.

"Why didn't you tell me?"

"I told you that back in Burgundy," he countered. We continued to protest to each other for a few more minutes until we finally realized the futility of it all. That magical moment at the Pont du Gard would have to occur another time.

That evening we hunkered down in our hotel room, very happy not to dine out and content to munch on the sandwiches and salads we had picked up in Uzès. I had an article to write about our adventures for a website on France. Needless to say, it took me a while to drum up the enthusiasm. I toiled away until midnight while Pete caught up on some sleep. The silver lining to our cloud of unpleasant experiences over the past couple of days was that I had miraculously found a way to make my laptop work. Thank God for small favors.

Our itinerary required us to cross all the way back to the other side of Provence to our next destination in the Vaucluse, not far from the Lubéron. I knew that this was not ideal when I made the plans, but I didn't think it would turn out to be such a hassle. There wasn't much I could do about it, though, since it was October 1, the height of the tourist season in this part of France. This meant many fully booked hotels. Plus it was Sunday, a big day for French tourists as well. Crowds and traffic jams were an issue throughout.

I had another romantic vision of having lunch in a sunny café in Avignon on our way from La Bégude (near Uzès) to the Vaucluse. We pulled into this famed Provençal town famished and then turned around and around its maze of streets—most of which seemed to be going one way in the wrong direction—for a seemingly endless amount of time before we finally gave up and decided to move on. I imagined that Isle-sur-la-Sorgue, a town best known for its lively antique markets on the weekends, would also be extremely crowded, but I knew of no other town in the area where we would be able to grab a bite to eat mid-afternoon.

Hunger had truly set in by the time we hit Sorgue, but we tried not to think about it as we drove round and round for a parking spot. The situation here was as bad as in Avignon, not to mention that by now we were beginning to be concerned about leaving our car, loaded with all of our luggage, in such a touristy place. The bikes on the roof stuck out like two colorful parking lot beacons for all to see. Our fear of theft was very real, since my belongings were once stolen right out of the trunk of my rental car in Saint-Paul de Vence, not far away on the Côte d'Azur.

We spotted a teeny space into which Pete somehow squeezed the car, so we decided to stop just long enough to pick up something to eat. The center of town was swarming with tourists, as expected. Pete and I loitered for just enough time to order a couple of wood-fired pizzas from one of the traveling pizza oven trucks and sat down to eat them alongside the river Sorgue with cool cans of Orangina. We were flooded with one brief moment of calm at the water's edge staring into the river which was clear and high from all the rain.

Next it was time to battle the crowds once more, in search of a restroom. The public toilets near the park entrance were revolting. Having seen that, I opted to slip into a café instead where the conditions—as it turned out—were almost as bad. Unfortunately, I began to feel that a lot of the magic of these Provençal towns had faded, and then told myself that it's best to pick and choose the right time to visit them or be prepared to suffer the consequences. Generally speaking, early in the morning is a good bet.

At this point I was even less convinced that we would enjoy Gordes, our next *lieu de repos*. It had been many years since I had been there, and even then, it was bulging with tourists. My fears were somewhat alleviated when we pulled into the Hostellerie le Phébus, a veritable sanctuary in the hillside village of Joucas, just outside Gordes. Finally, we both breathed a big "aaaahhhh." It seemed as though we had come home to Provence, the land I first fell in love with twenty years ago.

Handsome stone terraces surround much of this establishment, positioning the guests for magnificent views of the nearby hillsides and fertile valleys below. All is about quiet seclusion at this stunning, four-star Provençal hotel, and almost as soon as we arrived, Pete and I labeled it "the perfect honeymoon retreat." Six of the suites have their own private mini swimming pool and terrace and fortunately ours was one of them. We had no time to luxuriate in this grand setting, though—at least not yet. Upon looking at the rugged terrain, we determined that the cycling must be good, so it was high time we checked it out. I changed into my bike clothes faster than a Tour de France rider could eat from his feedbag.

It was recommended that we visit some of the neighboring hilltop villages, or *villages perchés*, little enclaves of activity perched high on hills, characteristic of much of the southernmost parts of France. I was enthused but apprehensive, not sure whether or not I would be able to handle such hefty climbs. Pete could tell that the cycling looked good, so he was all business.

"C'mon, let's move it," Pete shouted as we pedaled off in the direction of Roussillon. I felt enamored by this delightful route that disclosed many of the charms of Provence—olive groves, cypress trees and seemingly untamed vineyards. Still, aware of Pete's urgency to get in a good workout, I pedaled as fast as I could.

"It's nice that there aren't any cars, isn't it?" I shouted. Pete didn't respond. *I'm really not clueless*, I thought to myself. *I'm just not you!*

Just as we were beginning to bite into the healthiest part of *la montée*, Pete moved forward into his own breakaway, yelling, "I'll meet you at the top!"

I had to dig down deep to keep up the momentum I had established from the base of the hill. That fraction of élan eventually slowed, then slowed some more, then more, until I once again found myself in that state of excessive physical exertion somewhere between pain and pleasure. My tongue was almost to my knees by the time I arrived at the top, but nevertheless, I felt extremely proud of my accomplishment.

Pete was nowhere to be seen, so I decided that he must have been waiting for me in the heart of the village, the focal point of Roussillon. I cooled off somewhat weaving in and out of the old cobbled streets of this charming town, making sure not to stray too far from the beaten path so as not to miss Pete in case he was coming to look for me.

Finally I arrived at the core of the village, one of the most spectacular sites I had ever seen, rich in red rock for which Roussillon was likely named. The main attraction seemed to be an overlook where the full splendor of the valley could be seen along with adjacent cliffs the color of the richest terra cotta imaginable. As I gazed up at these sort of high, hanging bluffs, I wondered for a half second whether Pete might have gone up there and then decided, *no way, it's not like him to venture so out-of-bounds*. So I sat patiently and waited for him to appear, thinking that perhaps he had done a little extra jaunt up and down the hill to double his fun. I had picked the perfect place to wait, too, for at this hour of the day, the sun already hung low enough in the sky to cast a radiant glow.

Soon I was being asked by people, all of whom were couples, to take their photo. I suppose they thought that I had nothing better to do. I didn't mind at all at first, but as time passed, it became rather irksome, probably not the picture-taking as much as being loverless on this lovers' leap. As much as I resisted it, I began to be annoyed. More than half an hour had passed, and still no Pete. I knew we didn't have much time left to cycle, either, since dusk would soon approach, and we had, after all, only begun our ride. I waited another fifteen minutes and then thought, *to hell with him!*

I bombed down the hill like the wicked witch of the west. Pedaling, pedaling, pedaling. I was seething. I was totally convinced that Pete had somehow tried to ditch me, consciously or subconsciously. There was no explanation whatsoever about his disappearance and it seemed impossible that he would not be able to find me in such an obvious spot. I was also sure that he was not hurt. It just seemed like the cycling was too good, and I was too much of a ball and chain. So it was time to part ways.

How could he do this to me? I practically hollered out on my bike. *Well, I'm not going to take it.* I began to make plans in my head for us to really go our own way, for us to end our travels altogether, for him to go home and for me to carry on on my own. A slew of outcomes and schemes flew through my head—totally obscuring any sort of cohesive thoughts. Issues concerning the flights home, my book project, the rental car (more precisely, how I couldn't drive it since it's a standard and I don't know how to use a stick) boggled my mind. I was like a crazed woman and he was all to blame.

Slowly, softly and ever more steadily I became absorbed in the peaceful Provençal countryside. Backcountry roads led me to little hilltop villages beautifully locked in time, privileged places where people appeared to live at their own rhythm, not one imposed upon them by the demands of work, home, life or travel. People were taking the time to sit quietly on a café terrace to exchange a few words with their neighbors, whether they were engaged in meaningful conversation or not. Suddenly I felt much more serene.

As I pedaled to the next village and then another, I felt empowered by my ability to navigate the untrammeled roads of Provence on my own. *Maybe we did need a separation, maybe we both needed to spread our wings some more—each day—in order not to lose ourselves so completely in our coupledom. And what prompted such a violent reaction? Was it fear? Perhaps I'm still not entirely in touch with old feelings of abandonment. How can such a rational person become so frightfully irrational?*

I rolled into Le Phébus just as night was falling, my odometer registering twenty-four miles. Pete anxiously awaited me at the door, full of love and worry. Sadly, I could not allow myself to totally warm up to him—I still felt angry. After all the "where were yous" and "how could yous" were dispensed, we finally found out what had happened.

"I was up at the top of the bluffs—the place where everyone goes," Pete explained. "I can't believe you missed it—it was the most spectacular place."

"You were up there?" I asked, shocked. "I was sure you wouldn't go there. It almost seemed too touristy for you. And how could you not have seen me from up there, anyway?" I added, in a lame effort to get in the last zinger.

"C'mon, Bessie, we both ended up fine didn't we?"

I sighed and then said, "How about we try out that big bathtub? I don't think we've ever taken a bath together before. I'll even add bubbles."

I could tell Pete appreciated me backing down as he beamed back at me. Despite our upset, he looked transformed. He had gotten in his ride and he was stoked. "That sounds like fun," he added with a wry smile.

Fences were further mended in the elegant dining room of Le Phébus, where we swooned over the outstanding meal of Chef Xavier Mathieu. Provence had managed to seduce both of us by the end of the day, and throughout the evening we were enticed into a total state of satisfaction by Chef Mathieu's haute Provençal cuisine. We had found our little corner of paradise and wanted to stay. We drifted off to sleep that night tightly wrapped in each other's arms. I couldn't help but think about how the day—like so many other days—had felt like we had experienced a week's worth of events in a single day.

After having been rewarded with a stretch of sunny weather, we woke up the next morning to a very uncertain day. Once again, it seemed strange to see cloudy skies spitting rain in Provence, but we soon learned that the weather can be fairly unpredictable in the fall. Just as we padded out onto our terrace to take a dip in our own private swimming pool, we were blasted with gusts of wind that neither of us had ever experienced before. Pete and I bent down to stick our hands in the water and said, "No way!"practically in unison. Both air and water were *glacials* (icy). The cause of this big switch in weather was *le mistral*, the famous wind of Provence known to blow incessantly for days or even weeks on end. Mistral means "master wind" in the Provençal language, a most appropriate and reverent term for this cold, dry, violent wind that whips down the Rhône valley from the north.

Once again, it looked as though weather was going to foil our cycling plans for the day. Pete was determined, though, not to let it deter him from his cycling program, so off he went to tackle the challenging hills of this unique area. During his absence, I organized and repacked my personal belongings and research information, a neverending task that I knew would become even more laborious as the trip progressed. Pete returned an hour and a half later effervescent and breathless from a great ride. He had climbed about forty kilometers (twenty-five miles) over precipitous terrain that sent him careening all the way down to the Abbaye de Sennanque, a twelfth-century Cistercian abbey, before returning to our hotel. Both Pete and I were over-the-top about the cycling in the area, and, as a result, sad that we had only planned to spend one night at Le Phébus.

It was time to shove off once again, but, as in Burgundy and Alsace, we departed vowing to come back soon. Now the question hovered about whether or not we were going to Mont Ventoux. From the get-go, Pete was hopeful about attempting that climb, but now that the mistral had kicked up even more than earlier in the day, that was looking like an impossibility. "We'll see," said Pete.

"Well, it would be neat to drive up there anyway, just to have a feel for this epic ascent," I said. I could tell he was weighing heavily the idea of doing such a ride. I didn't want him to feel that he had to do the climb just because we were there.

After a brief stop in Gordes on the way out to buy fresh tomato and mozzarella sandwiches for the drive, we meandered beyond the Abbaye de Senanque on a twisting road that once was part of a stage of the Tour de France. As we wended our way through gorgeous gorges chiseled out of towering, greyish-beige rocks, we both commented that this rather Southwestern landscape did not look very French.

The glorious scenery took on grander proportions in Venasque, where we captured our first look at the famous Mont Ventoux. It was truly awe-inspiring. Pete's reaction was one of excitement—mine, nervousness. The majesty of the mountain is surely enhanced by the fact that it emerges from rather flat land—it stands mightily on its own with no other mountains to rival it. Mostly shrouded, its huge peak hooked all the clouds in the area; the rest of the skies were blue. Straining a bit to see, we observed an area at the top, almost like a huge patch, that looked either like snow or the barren zone for which this monolith is renowned. (I found out sometime later that this strange baldness is due to deforestation that took place here centuries ago. Apparently many of the trees from the summit of Ventoux ended up as ships' masts.)

We kept our focus on it much of the way into Carpentras until in the center of town we saw a sign for Mont Ventoux Sud or Mont Ventoux Nord.

"There are two approaches to the mountain, either by the south or the north," Pete explained.

"Which one is it?" I queried, not wanting to slough off on my job as chief navigator.

"Let's just keep going in this direction."

"I think it would be a good idea to stop and ask at the tourist office right there," I ventured.

"Nah, let's not bother."

So I decided not to push the issue. At one point, we saw a team car from Crédit Agricole, fully loaded with bikes, veering off in the direction we had chosen.

"That's a good sign," I said. Pete didn't utter a word. Clearly, he was on a mission.

When we arrived in Malaucène, the town closest to Ventoux's north face, Pete started to suspect he was in the wrong place. "I don't recognize this town as having appeared on the coverage I've watched," he said.

"Oh wait, there's the tourist office," I cried out. "Let's stop there for directions. Oh no, it says closed for lunch. Bummer."

"That's typical of the French, it seems," Pete grumbled.

"How about we ask those old gents across the way? They're playing pétanque. It's similar to bocce ball—the older men play that all day long in the south of France."

I stepped out of the car and politely interrupted their game. "Do you know which way the Tour goes?" I asked *en français*. Proud as podium winners, each one of them perked up to answer me. I then trotted back to the car and announced to Pete, "The Tour always starts in the south and ends at the top, since the north slope is far too dangerous to climb or to descend."

"I feel stupid not listening to Bessie 'cause Bessie knows best," Pete chirped, almost on cue. I knew enough not to say "I told you so."

In all, we drove thirty-six kilometers (about twenty-two miles) out of our way. These were not straightaways either, so by the time we approached the base of the south side of Ventoux, my head and stomach felt as though they just experienced a roller coaster ride.

"I think I'll do the climb," Pete said.

"Are you *sure*?" I implored. I could still feel the mistral's gusty force rocking the car at times, plus the day was on the wane. I knew, though, that I should not Mother Hen Pete. "Well I guess you won't have many more chances to climb this mountain again in your life." By now, a good number of cyclists charged by us (all on their way down), an inspiring parade of superior ability that only served to pump up Pete even more. "I'm sure it will be memorable," I added, with a note of encouragement.

Now it became time to deploy Plan Mt. Ventoux. Way before we even picked up our rental car in Paris, we had laid this plan out, and even then the outcome seemed dubious. But we both thought it would be worth a try. I was to drive the "team car" up the mountain behind Pete in case he found himself in distress or even in a state of collapse. Pete was convinced I could do this, figuring that he would give me a little refresher course on shifting five-speeds (I had tried to learn before without much success) and off we would go. His total conviction that I could actually learn to drive the car in ten minutes or less made me believe that I could do it, too. This was important, after all—there was no backing down; it was potentially a do-or-die situation.

I sat down behind the driver's seat with all the confidence in the world, a feeling of self-assurance that was greatly reinforced by Pete's surprisingly magnificent patience with me. I probably cruised along about a half mile, I carefully attempted to shift into first gear, then second. Just as it seemed as though I was going to carry out this nearly impossible feat, I had to slow down and stop due to construction on the road. Reminding myself to take deep breaths and not to wig out, I carefully attempted to put the gear into first, once the construction worker waved his flag for me to go. Stall. I tried again. Staaall. Now I was feeling like I had an audience—the construction worker was watching me along with the front end loader operator, and, of course, Pete.

With soothing words of encouragement, Pete cooed, "Just slip it into first." Staaaaaallll. By now a car had pulled up behind us, which the construction worker patiently waved by. Staaaaaaaaaaaaalllllll. "Don't hesitate—just put it into first," Pete said, careful not to roil me.

"I'm trying."

I made several more attempts at shifting then bellowed, "This is just a slight incline here—how's it going to be on top of the mountain?"

Pete remained silent while I made more attempts to advance the car. *Damn, why can't I be one of those chicks that keeps up with the dudes?* I asked myself. *I really do want to drive this five-speed rental car up that f-ing mountain. I want to stay with my guy.*

"Don't worry about it," Pete said as he stepped out of the passenger side of the car and took over the controls. He drove a little farther up the road until he found a good spot where the car could be safely parked. There was no time to discuss my ineptitude with basic car mechanics, my inability to grasp that feathering feeling, or my inadequacy in locating that certain G-spot on cars, the point at which you let out the clutch just enough as you put your foot down on the accelerator. It was time for Pete to ride, otherwise he'd surely be descending Mont Ventoux in the dark. He changed into his bike clothes, quickly checked his rig to make sure all was looking good, and powered away at the sixteen-kilometer (ten-mile) marker. It was 4:20 p.m. He said that if he didn't return in two and a half hours, it would be time to call in the troops.

He barely said "See ya," but I had the good sense not to feel slighted. I knew his focus now was on his ride.

Having recovered from my nerve-wracking essay at driving and having decided not to be a worry wart about Pete, I settled into the car for a nice, relaxing stretch to myself. With lots of notes, maps, a few books and a bag of grapes, I had all that I needed to content myself. Time sped by, and then inevitable concern crept in about Pete. With every ounce of disquiet, I double-wrapped Pete in a pink light of safety. By now I was chilled; the wind howled and the sun was in as much as it was out. I could only imagine how brisk it was on top of the mountain. From the moment I settled into the car, a consistent stream of vehicles passed by, most of which were descending, a putrid smell of burning brakes trailing behind them. A couple of cyclists bolted by in the beginning although I hadn't seen any barreling down in quite some time. There weren't any that started the climb after Pete took off either.

About 6:30 p.m., a very fit-looking, young woman whizzed by on the descent, a reassuring sign that there was still life on top of the mountain. Dusk had settled into this forested spot by 6:45 p.m. and worry was beginning to take hold of me. It had been almost two and a half hours and still no sign of Pete. A couple of minutes later—just as I was figuring out a plan about how to find help—Pete zoomed into view. Shivering, yet totally ecstatic, Pete attempted—in the sort of frozen-faced manner you employ when skiing—to describe to me the thrills of his Mt.Ventoux conquest. Clearly it was the most punishing climb he had ever ridden.

"My head felt like I was going into la-la land," he said as he attempted to explain the incredible range of feelings—both physical and emotional—that he felt both on the way up Ventoux and down.

It wasn't a time for talking, though, since Pete was visibly on the fringe of hypothermia. His body trembled and I could tell that the light jacket he had donned on top of the mountain served as little protection for the freezing-cold downhill plunge. He quickly changed into his warm clothes. We sat in the car and cranked the heat to the highest of high. He was knackered, so we rounded up a can of coke, a half a bag of nougat from Montélimar and a piece of baguette to provide the instant sugar fix he so desperately needed. We waited about fifteen minutes, during which time Pete provided snippets of his climbing exploits. But, clearly, you had to see it to gain a sense of the intensity of this endeavor.

So we decided to drive up the mountain in order for me to experience it, too. The excitement of the Tour grabbed me right away when I saw so many cyclists' names and words of encouragement painted on the pavement by fans. *"Allez Ja Ja,"* "PANTANI," and "I like them apples, Lance" passed beneath us, conjuring up visions of famous cycling champions passing along the same route. As we entered into the thick of the forest where craggy, windblown trees provoked eerie, almost foreboding feelings within me, Pete began to give me the blow-by-blow commentary of his ride.

"Right here, I shifted it into the lowest gear—39/26—and I never got out of that gear all the way up. I was crawling up this—I don't know how those guys do it, particularly after all the miles and climbs they log before arriving here." Then a ways up the road, Pete admitted, "Here I was thinking about giving up. Then I said, no, let me go to the tree line."

After a relentless series of twists and turns (with few switchbacks) up through the thickly-wooded hinterland, the terrain finally cleared—just before seven kilometers—and we were allowed our first glimpse of the awesome lunar-like landscape so characteristic of Ventoux. The vast barrenness of the land spread out before us with all the strangeness of a desert prairie. "Just after Chalet Raynard, there was a wicked tailwind so I managed to ride up this quite easily," Pete continued.

"The landscape is spectacular," I said as I took in these hugely expansive rock surfaces sprinkled with tufts of mountain brush. "This is definitely a must-see for any visitor to Provence."

Pete nodded as he scanned the mountainscape of the mighty Ventoux. "It really is something to see–TV just doesn't capture it."

"My ears keep popping," I said as we ascended. Remnants of a setting sun cast a golden glow throughout, and with virtually no cars around, we felt as though we had landed on another planet. Cottony clouds hung over our heads like a heavenly ceiling.

"I've never seen anything like this before," I said in an almost whisper.

"It's freaky, isn't it? Everyone says so."

We were at the two kilometer marker and all signs of vegetation had vanished. All rock, only rock. "The bike was getting blown around quite a lot by now," Pete continued.

"I can only imagine," I said and moaned as I heard the creaking of our bikes on the roof as they were pummeled by the ferocious winds of Ventoux, mistral or not. Just as we entered the fog, we solemnly passed by the memorial to Tom Simpson, the greatest British cyclist ever, who perished up here during his attempt to conquer mighty Ventoux in 1967. "Thank God, I didn't test my fate at driving this," I added as we veered up the final turn. "I would have had a fit seeing you ride up here even if I was in an automatic."

"There's a ten percent gradient pretty much from start to finish," Pete couldn't help but add.

It was 7:25 p.m., dusk, and 0 degrees celsius (32 degrees Fahrenheit) by the time we reached the top of this 1738-meter (6,265 feet) mountain. That's freezing, and with the wind whipping so hard and fast, the wind chill factor must have plunged the temperatures to near-Arctic levels. "It's like Mount Everest up here," I declared in a rather panicky voice. "I want to step outside to take a picture, but I'm not going to—I'm afraid I'm going to be blown away." There was still enough light, however, to take in this high-elevation view, one of the most plunging I had ever seen, providing wildly impressive vistas all the way down into the valley. Pete stepped out for less than a minute and held the car door the whole time.

A sliver of pale-orange sky guided us most of the way down the north side. Here the road became considerably rougher and more narrow, a veritable suicidal tract for anyone who dared travel it in anything but a motorized vehicle or by foot. The terrain was different, too; here pine trees pierced the sky, creating a much more alpine look than the more Provençal landscapes of the south side. "Have you warmed up?" I asked Pete as the interior temperature of the car soared to sauna-esque heights.

"Yeah, but I'm still shaking," he replied.

"You need some fuel after that effort," I said.

"I know. I feel completely depleted."

An almost endless drive, accompanied by a seemingly eternal search for food, led us back to a pizza truck at Isle-sur-la-Sorgue. Parked in a different place, it wasn't the same truck we had grabbed food from the other day. Thankfully the pizzas were much better. Or perhaps they just tasted better since we were both so starved (for me, from all the emotion) and also there wasn't a soul around to disturb the nighttime quiet of this little town. Bellies full, from there we drove rather sleepily to Abbaye de Sainte-Croix, a blessed retreat, a four-star hotel outside Salon-de-Provence, where we knew we could nestle into a restful stay. Pete zonked out practically in mid sentence while I tossed and turned for hours as I listened to the constant whirring of the mistral. They say that it can be relentless and that it has made some people crazy.

A phone call yanked us out of our slumber the next morning at 9:30 a.m., otherwise I think we might have slept until noon. After a leisurely breakfast in the room, we decided that we would designate the day as a day of rest and catch up on a few of the necessary evils of travel, laundry in particular. It came as a huge relief to learn that I could leave our more specialized laundry—namely anything that needed a touch of ironing—with the hotel's laundry service. By now we had an exceedingly large quantity of bike clothes, socks, unmentionables and a few semi-ragged casual items that we didn't have the gumption to wash by hand. So off we went to Salon-de-Provence, where I was hopeful of unloading our washing of secondary importance to the local pressing for a normally price-efficient wash and fold. No go. None of the local cleaners could do the job in twenty-four hours or less, so we had no choice but to trudge off to the local *laverie* (laundry).

As mechanical as Pete is, and as fluent as I am in French, we could not figure out the highly sophisticated, token-operated, state-of-the-art machines that were housed in this lone *laverie* in this quiet little Provençal town. Talk about a recipe for disaster! Laundering together back home often creates friction between us. (He has his way; I have mine.) But, in France, in a sweltering laundromat with equipment that would challenge even brain surgeons, we were asking for trouble. Fortunately, I was able to ask (actually, beg) for assistance from the resident ironing mistress who was holed up in the back room. Then off we went to have a look around town after finally launching a few machines.

Our stomachs were beginning to growl. But we didn't dare venture for lunch, since it was made implicitly clear to us that we would have to empty the machines—washing and drying—as soon as the cycles were completed. As much as we didn't want to cower to the ironing warden, we figured we'd better comply. So after a good amount of hanging out, mixed up with a quick trip to the neighboring pharmacy and newsstand for more necessary supplies, we were on deck promptly when the buzzers rang.

Now we really wanted some food, particularly since Pete was still in need of restoring his reserves from his Mont Ventoux climb. Seeking out a pleasant lunch spot—perhaps shaded by a plane tree—turned out to be another fiasco. By now it was 2:30 p.m. and the restaurants had stopped serving. There wasn't even a halfway appealing café that would serve us a sandwich and a Coke at that hour. In the end, Salon fell way short of our expectations—we couldn't wait to seek refuge in our hotel.

Still starved, we picked up some quiches and sodas at the Monoprix (the grocery store—even the bakeries were still closed for lunch) and gobbled them up in the car on the way back to the Abbaye de Sainte-Croix. What a contrast here—we were finally able to soak up the serenity of this Provençal oasis by the light of day. Rest beckoned, for our jaunt in Salon was almost as taxing—albeit in a far less rewarding manner—as our adventures at and after Ventoux. Formerly a monk's cell, our room definitely exuded a certain calm, a divine tranquility found in religious dwellings and the finest hotels.

It was too beautiful outside, though, not to take in the splendor of this old abbey's surroundings. Plus the mistral had departed that night, leaving a clearness and crispness to the air that only massive gusts of wind can produce. First Pete and I sat on the terrace outside our room facing the large cypress trees—barely exchanging a word—for half an hour. It was nice just simply sitting together in such a peaceful place. A little too cool to go swimming, we still padded up to the pool area where we laid out on chaise lounges—fully clothed—for another sweet stretch of time. Not wanting to bring out our bikes, we then walked around the grounds where we visited grottos and the vestiges of a little village that had existed here centuries ago. (Parts of the Abbaye date back to the twelfth century.) Rest had finally seeped into our lives and its effects were blissful.

Before dinner we relaxed on the hotel's grand terrace with some Ricard (an anis-flavored apéritif typical of the region) and *tartines de tapenade* (little toasts served with rich olive spread). From there we could fully appreciate the expansive views of the valley below, the cypress trees standing like proud soldiers defiant against the wind, the centuries-old stone walls that marked the land where these peoples' forebears once farmed. Way off in the distance, we could see clear to Marseille and the Mediterranean beyond it.

Just as the chill in the air became too much for what little warmth my Souleiado shawl provided, we moved inside for dinner. Relaxed dining in all its casual elegance could be the motto of this one-star Michelin restaurant, and as I looked around the room, I noticed that shirtsleeves—not sports jackets—were de rigueur. Pete and I both dove straight into the full panoply of typical Provençal dishes and flavors here. Aromatic quantities of rosemary, thyme, dill, garlic, tomatoes and olive oil mark the cuisine of the Abbaye, resulting in a palette of Provençal flavors both fresh and uncomplicated. All, a perfect ending to the day.

At breakfast the next day, Pete talked more about his adventures at Ventoux. (I think he was still numb the day before.) "It's too bad I wasn't in better condition to have tackled such a climb," he said. "Last summer was the first season in many years that I hadn't raced. I haven't been training at all."

"You go on a lot of rides," I said.

"Nothing like before. I used to ride all the time before we started to go out."

I wasn't sure how to respond to that. It was hard for me to validate his feelings, since I still viewed cycling as a big part of his life. I was happy he had that passion, however, it still took time away from "us" back home. Yet I could understand where he was coming from. It's true—by his standards—he was not in very good shape. He had a bit of what the French call *une brioche* (a bun, known as a beer belly in America). I still found him fit and super handsome, though.

"Just think how great it is to have done the climb, even if you didn't do it at top speed," I insisted. "Plus it gave you an incredible workout."

"Yeah, I had been feeling too much under your thumb," Pete said offhandedly.

Ah-ha! I almost exclaimed and then decided it was better not to bring up my having-been-ditched-in-Roussillon outcries from the other day. Surprisingly, Pete's remark didn't make me feel angry or annoyed. I felt like I understood him. I felt like I was taking in his comment more like a guy than a girl. This was one of those beautiful moments when I felt fully in touch with Pete's needs and didn't think that satisfying them took anything away from my own.

The owner of the hotel, Madame Catherine Bossard, debriefed us on the excellent cycling in the area. We learned that there were two itineraries—each about twenty-five kilometers (about sixteen miles)–that sounded nice. She obviously knew what she was talking about since the hotel regularly receives groups of cyclists; plus they arrange bike rentals. It all sounded good, so we decided to drop our film off at the one-hour photo in Salon, pick it up by the end of the morning, and then whiz off for a quick ride. With a bit of coaxing, Pete agreed to drop off the film in Salon while I caught up on some office work. This was his first real expedition out on his own—aside from being on a bike—so I was hoping it would go well.

He returned grumbling about a language barrier with the guy in the photo shop and that our photos wouldn't be ready until after their lunchtime closing. That nixed our plans for the bike ride since we had hoped to do just a short stretch of one of the two rides on the way out of town. It also created another problem: where to have lunch in Salon.

Arguably the most alluring place for lunch was the Abbaye, but being the die-hard traveler that I am, I was determined to give Salon another try. It failed miserably—once again—after we ended up spending a painfully long amount of time at a restaurant terrace (the best-looking one we encountered, the one that had turned us away the day before), waiting for one lonesome waiter to serve an entire patio overflowing with people. Most remarkably of all, the waiter was totally unruffled as he ran crazily from one table to the next. He smiled the whole time, taking the whole lot of disgruntled clients in stride.

Pete and I chalked all this up to the experiences you have while traveling. As with life, events don't always turn out the way you want. This was very much how it went for us in Provence. Still, we were happy with our stay here and grateful that the good and the great balanced out the more tedious times.

Navigating Languedoc-Roussillon

During my research for *The Riches of France*, I came to know Languedoc-Roussillon well and was looking forward to traveling back there at another time. I had discovered then that Languedoc-Roussillon possesses many of the endearing qualities of its neighboring Provence—with far fewer tourists. It was also wonderful to work with my tourism contact from the region in planning my trip on that book, so I was thrilled to learn that she was more than willing to help me out once again. After having touted the region a good deal to Pete, he was anxious to discover it, too, and was eager to find out what all my quacking was about.

   This time around, though, my tourism contact didn't appear quite on top of her game. But, still, I was confident it would all work out. She had faxed me the name and address of the first two hotels on the itinerary just before leaving Provence, and explained that she would provide the rest of the program in a few days, all very last minute. The address of the first hotel was Hôtel du Midi, 48000 Barjac. No street address was furnished nor were directions about how to find the town. I suppose I could have asked for the precise coordinates but instead I told my contact I'd just use my map.

   Lo and behold, I located the little speck of a town of Barjac on my Michelin map. Pete and I calculated that the trip would be about one and a half hours—mostly by *l'autoroute*—from Salon to Barjac, the town I had managed to find on the map. The last part of the drive here—the section near Pont Saint-Esprit and Les Gorges de l'Ardèche, was lovely, and Pete and I already started to imagine ourselves riding around this countryside, soaking up more of France's sensational southern sun.

As we pulled into the sleepy little town of Barjac, we circled two and a half times around the village center and still did not find the Hôtel du Midi. It was late afternoon by now, Pete was understandably tired of driving, and we didn't feel like looking any more. We needed water anyway, so I hopped out and stepped into a little grocery store in search of *l'eau fraîche* and some direction.

"You're not going to believe this," I announced to Pete a few minutes later as I settled met Pete outside the car. "We're in the wrong Barjac."

"What are you talking about?"

"We're in the wrong department in the wrong region," I explained. "This is Barjac in the Gard department in Provence. We need to be in Barjac in the Lozère department in the region of Languedoc-Roussillon," I said, stifling my laughter about such a ridiculous mistake. "It's all in France nonetheless." *Thank you, God.*

Just as Pete appeared to be working himself up into a bit of a lather, I showed him the map so that he could see for himself. "I was not sleeping on the job—that error could have been made by the most skilled of navigators. Plus the grocer said that people confuse those two towns all the time." Indeed, the little town of Barjac that I had circled teetered on the tiny crosshatched line that delineated the border between Provence and Languedoc-Roussillon.

Pete studied the map that was now outstretched on the hood of the car. "This blows."

"You see, there's only one Barjac on this map and that's the one in Languedoc," I exclaimed as I poked the map.

I decided to call my contact at the regional tourist office. She, fortunately, had not yet left for the day. She squawked in a how-could-you-make-such-a-mistake sort of way, but, instead of falling into a downward spiral of accusations and allegations, I encouraged her to tell me exactly what to do to assure my arrival at Barjac in Lozère sometime that evening. Per her request, I phoned the Hôtel du Midi and asked for directions. I'm not sure whether it provided much solace or not, but once the madame on the other end of the line finished her long series of *"oh-là-là, oh-là-là, oh-là-là,"* she finally added that the mistaken identity problem about the two Barjacs happens all the time.

I stopped wondering why no one gave me a heads-up about this and forged on with my direction taking. As the bird flies, there were only about seventy kilometers (about forty-three miles) between the two towns, or one and a quarter of my pinky finger across the Michelin map. The line was but a serpentine scraggle across what appeared to be mountains, all of which was confirmed by the woman on the phone. "You'll be lucky if you make it in two hours."

Once back at the car, I broke the news to Pete, who, thankfully, took it like a good sport. (Fortunately neither of us were so incredibly seduced by Barjac in Provence that we were sad to leave.) As it turned out, nearly every inch of the way from Barjac to Barjac was truly spectacular. This is the sort of drive, however, you want to take on in the early part of the day, before you've accumulated a load of fatigue—both mental and physical—the kind that so often comes with the travails of travel. As we eased our way into Languedoc and eventually Lozère, we climbed and climbed and then climbed and climbed some more. By now, Pete was beyond the point of pondering how great it would be to ride this sort of terrain on his bike; he just wanted to maintain a firm grip on the road beneath him. As much as the climbing was impressive, the twists and turns were even more so.

"You're doing great, sweetie," I said encouragingly. "I'm so grateful you're doing all the driving. You're really doing a fantastic job. Plus you know how I like being chauffeured around." I could tell these kudos pumped him up, so I restated my appreciation for his efforts numerous times throughout the drive.

The landscape had changed dramatically from the sun-scorched terrain of Provence. The mountains contributed a sort of lushness to the countryside here, fertile ground that is not exactly alpine, but more reminiscent of the slopes of peaks you find in the Adirondacks or the Appalachians. The sun had disappeared many kilometers ago, and, in fact, a fine mist clung to the air, meteorological conditions that seemed particularly well-suited to this most unusual part of France, somewhere between West Virginia and the north of Wales. Completely enchanted, we crept through a number of little hamlets, at times attempting to peer beyond the stone walls that surrounded the centuries-old stone houses.

"What do these people live off of here?" I asked Pete, both of us slightly bewildered about this surprising sort of never-never land in this exceedingly remote part of France.

"Agriculture. Or maybe dairy?" Pete guessed.

"I don't know," I responded. "There's hardly room for a field and I haven't seen any cows either. It does look like people have been hunkered down here for ages though."

"It's amazing," Pete replied.

"Oh, take a look at that château," I exclaimed as I caught a glimpse of a small Renaissance wonder tucked into the fold of a mini valley as we veered around a corner.

"I better keep my eye on the road," Pete answered.

Finally, just after Mende (a bold-lettered-sized town on the map of France) we emerged from this sinuous trail and out popped a sign for Barjac. In truth, we missed it the first time, and only after winding around a bit did we locate Barjac in Lozère, a teeny trace of a place, barely a village, and certainly no more than a hamlet. "No wonder this wasn't on my map!" I couldn't resist declaring in my best three-quarters volume. In all, the drive from Barjac to Barjac ended up taking us two and a half hours.

Darkness had long ago fallen and by now we were extremely road weary, so it didn't seem to matter much—at least not to me— that the Hôtel du Midi lacked the luster and charm of our previous places of lodging. Combination *bar-tabac, hôtel-restaurant,* I could literally see Pete's nose twitching as we settled into our sixties-styled *chambre.* "Oh, c'mon," I said to Pete. "It's only for one night, plus I think it's kind of kitschy, a new experience for us."

"We don't need this kind of experience," Pete mumbled as he flopped down on a squishy mattress and adjusted the orangey lamp on his faux, mountain-rustic nightstand.

"It will be an adventure," I said in a cajoling manner.

"I can't believe we traveled so far out of our way to come to such a place."

"You're sounding like more of a critic—and a snob—than me. I think it's great to have varied experiences—we don't only have to stay in super nice places."

As I suspected, I knew we would be able to uncover some of the hidden charms of the Hôtel du Midi. The patron, both owner and boss of this humble two-star establishment, kindly offered us a beer as soon as we came downstairs for dinner. With hardly a soul around except for a small group of diners in the next room and the occasional person who dropped in to buy smokes, we garnered monsieur's undivided attention at the bar for what appeared to be as long as we wanted. Or, perhaps I should say that he claimed us as his audience. Right away, I inquired about this unusual part of France that we had just ventured across. "Oh, that's very typical of Lozère," monsieur responded as he hand dried glasses behind the bar. "Only 70,000 people live in the whole department. That's the smallest number of people per square meter in all of France."

And just as I started to inquire more about the people of this region, monsieur, a strong, well-built athletic type, supposedly passionate about cycling, took over the questioning himself. "So Americans are beginning to take to cycling. Is this because Lance Armstrong won the Tour de France these past two years?"

With the help of a good amount of translating from me, Pete explained to monsieur, "No, it's probably been since Greg LeMond's victories."

I could tell they both had a lot to exchange, and I had my questions, too, so all of a sudden our conversation had blossomed into staccato snippets of questions and answers, each of which was repeated by me in the language of choice. Soon madame joined in and I quickly discerned that they were both busting to tell us something. "Lance stayed with us three times," monsieur finally offered up, with all the discretion of a town gossip. Next monsieur and madame were providing me with the extraneous details of when, why and how Lance and his teammates took over this hotel. Pete listened to my translations totally unfazed and obviously not at all impressed that our own tour de France led us to one of Lance's regular rest stops.

With all the excitement of a teenage groupie, I listened earnestly to every detail of the champion's stay. He and his teammates had stayed twice for the Midi Libre race, the other time for the Tour de France, each time reserving the entire hotel for themselves. Monsieur and madame recounted that the mechanics arrive first with the luggage and gear and settle everyone in before the cyclists show up after the day's race. The team brings their own chef, who takes full charge of the kitchen, cooking up bushels of pasta throughout their less than twenty-four-hour stay. (The brand used at the time was Barilla, most likely one of their sponsors.) Mundane details about the guys possibly drinking a glass of beer after the day's race or their friendly demeanor with fans waiting outside also captured my attention, a funny sort of curiosity that I had never felt before for anyone, famous or not. Pete poked me, nudging me out of my investigative mode, and, with that, we moved on to a late dinner in the adjacent room.

As we squared ourselves away into our less-than-luxurious accommodations that night, I couldn't help but rib Pete about the Hôtel du Midi being good enough for Lance. "They stay in all kinds of places," he replied knowingly. "Sometimes they don't have a choice."

Pete and I were jostled out of our sleep by the near ear-piercing sound of a *villageois* scraping a thin layer of ice from his windshield that had accumulated overnight. I peered outside and discovered that within less than twenty-four hours we had gone from summer to winter. Dressing for such an occasion involved a lot of layering in addition to warm socks and gloves. When I went downstairs for breakfast, I stepped outside to breathe in an invigorating blast of fresh, mountain air. It felt—and almost looked like—an early autumn morning in northern Vermont.

After a breakfast meeting with a representative from the local tourist department, Pete and I were finally back on our bikes after an extended break. A most informative patron—who had observed us from another table—had kindly left us a map of Lozère with his recommendations for a good ride. He had circled an area a short dis-

106

tance away that we were to drive to from the hotel (about twenty minutes) and then cycle a twenty-something-mile loop from there. We were told that the area was unique but we didn't find out to what extent until we pulled up and parked at Château de la Baume, the historic landmark that was to be our starting and stopping point.

We set off on our ride and instantly became enraptured by the beauty and the strangeness of the countryside. It didn't look or feel at all like France. Instead it seemed as though we had blinked our eyes and landed in Ireland. The raw, dewy, overcast day further contributed to the delightful impression of having discovered a brave new land, one quite unlike any other in all of France. Rolling hills the color of moss carried us gently along, establishing a pleasant rhythm that maximized our hill-and-dale experience to the fullest. And everywhere you looked, there were rocks either in the form of low-lying stone walls that cut precisely through the countryside, or in the shape of a squat little house, or even just as a pile of rubble, a haphazard assemblage of God's litter.

And around almost every bend, there were cows, and then more cows. Cattle, actually—since we had learned that the Aubrac, this part of Lozère, is best known for its beef. In fact, the *race d'Aubrac*, or Aubrac beef, is considered one of the finest in all of France. Colored a vast range of shades of brown—from chestnut to burlap to dun—similar to the local stone houses, these peaceful animals appeared as permanent fixtures of this countryside, much like the manger animals of the nativity scene. It truly felt like God's country.

Suddenly Pete seemed in the mood for instructing, and once again, it came at a time when I was much more focused on the beautiful scenery than on my bike-riding skills. "Now, when you pedal, have your feet make nice, smooth, round circles. Be consistent. Don't just push down hard on the downstroke. There's a rhythm to cycling."

"You mean like this?" I yelled as I pedaled a long series of perfectly concentric circles.

"That's good," Pete replied. "Be sure to focus on that when you're going uphill, too."

"I knew you'd say that. That's much more of a challenge."

I watched his even pedaling and contemplated the power in his legs and the strength of his long, smooth back hunched over his bike. *What a turn-on.*

"Now let me explain drafting to you," Pete announced, breaking me from my thoughts. And before I knew it I was learning how a cyclist can use up as much as thirty percent less energy when being sucked along by the rider in front of him (or her). I had gained a sense of this before from some of the bike races Pete and I watched on TV, and, having done so, came to understand how bike racing is a team sport, how the cyclists all work together. "You want to follow six to ten inches behind my back tire," Pete continued. "Don't look at the wheel—it will mesmerize you—focus on the rider and the road."

I said "OK" as I made a rather half-hearted attempt to become caught up in Pete's wind, to be pulled along by his efforts.

As much as it was a mini fantasy of mine to zoom along in a pack of cyclists—my own little peloton—with the speed of gale-force winds, I could not overcome my fear. It seemed to go contrary to everything I ever learned on a bike or in a car. "Don't follow too closely," my parents still cautiously advise, so how could I possibly be comfortable doing such a complete 180 out here on a remote route de France? Obviously that takes years of practice and great confidence in one's bike-riding skills—either that or a wildly exuberant, breakneck attitude. I couldn't move beyond the idea that somehow I was going to rear-end Pete or he would suddenly throw on the brakes or some other fool thing and we'd both end up together in one big tangled mess.

"I'll try that again some day when I'm in the mood. Now I just want to relax and be serene," I cowardly called out to Pete. I couldn't bear to look at what I knew to be a very disappointed face. Instead I just sallied forth a short distance head-down, feeling somewhat guilty that he didn't have a buddy with whom he could properly ride. I raised my eyes just in time to see Pete catching up to an old tractor hauling some unsightly piece of junk up the hill. Pete must have been as happy as a cyclist sailing through a race on the tail of a competitor because, despite the smelly exhaust, he had positioned himself within inches of the vehicle's back end and allowed it to pull him right up the hill! I thought that summed up the differences between him and me pretty well. And despite these differences, I viewed his little trailor-drafting as a turn-on, too. Opposites do indeed attract.

Soon we came upon Nesbinals, the tiny village where it was recommended we stop for lunch. We needed to take a break anyway, since my toes were frozen and my reserves were low. Stepping into the hotel-restaurant, La Route d'Argent—pretty much the only eatery of its kind in town—we managed to order lunch just seconds before the chef closed the kitchen. "We can cook you a steak," the waiter declared. And after a bit of coaxing, he agreed to an order of *frites* (French fries), too, with a salad.

"*Allez,*" I added, "bring us *un quart de rouge,* also," concluding that a quarter of a pitcher of red wine would not only help to warm us up but would taste great with the meat, too. Meat, the famous *race d'Aubrac*—I tried not to think about all those sweet-faced animals when I ordered.

Out came an immense piece of beef served on a huge platter with an equally abundant order of fries. We had asked for it to be cooked *à point* (medium rare). But when I cut into it, I realized I should have asked for *bien cuit,* or well done. It was doing the proverbial mooing on the plate, so I had no choice but to ask the waiter to have the chef toss it on the grill a few minutes more. He kindly obliged, which, in my eyes, redeemed many a French server. "I was once told in a Paris bistrot that I couldn't order a steak unless I was to eat it rare," I told Pete shortly thereafter, as we reveled over one of the most delicious meat-and-potato meals we'd ever tasted.

"That sounds typically French."

"Well, I think it's their pride in their cuisine—they don't want to serve you something unless it's good. And to them, meat isn't good if it's cooked too much."

"So what did you do?" Pete asked.

"Oh, I think I just ordered a chicken or something."

Pete and I chuckled about this as we dove into a super savory lunch. Our *steak/frites* were enhanced by a big fresh salad of greens, tomatoes, carrots, red cabbage, hard-boiled egg and the most flavorful vinaigrette—all for a mere pittance.

Shortly before we left, two cyclists (I believe Germans) pulled up and stopped to enjoy *une pression*, a draft beer. There were no other encounters with cyclists (and few with cars either) throughout the whole ride in this wonderfully rural and desolate place.

"It's a big change from Provence," Pete commented.

"Indeed it is. And the countryside is quite different, too."

As Pete predicted, our legs felt like lead beams as we pedaled off after lunch. "It will become easier once our muscles re-enter a more athletic mode," Pete said encouragingly. "We need to get the blood flowing through our veins."

For this part of the loop, we were blessed with the benefits of a good tailwind, a nice switch from the endurance-challenging headwind we battled on the way out. At first, the rain threatened, and as it began to spit, I prayed that the heavens would not open up and pelt us with a full-fledged downpour. Miraculously, the weather cooperated, and at one point I stopped to gape at a glorious column of light streaming down in the distance. It looked as though the skies had parted and a big spotlight shone on the pastures below. Dark, ominous clouds hovered off to the other side of us, however, so Pete and I decided not to linger around to see what was going to happen. We were told before we'd ventured off this morning that the weather is always unpredictable in this section of France. Aubrac actually sits on a plateau at an altitude of approximately 1,200 meters (3,936 feet).

The weather, cold and thick with humidity, had triggered an ongoing series of sniffles on my behalf. Apparently Pete had become annoyed with my constant search for Kleenex, whether or not I actually stopped or just slowed down on my bike.

"Just do a snot rocket!" he hollered.

"A what?" I responded, rather insulted by his vulgarity.

"That's what all cyclists do," he replied defensively. "You just blow it out of one nostril while you pinch the other closed, and continue on." I'd heard about how deftly cyclists are able to relieve themselves—with a quick yank of the shorts and a little tug-tug on their manhood—during big races when not a fraction of a minute can be lost on anything as frivolous as peeing. But never had I heard of a you-know-what rocket. Maybe it's the word that left me screeching in horror. "Well, then, just wipe your nose on your glove," Pete yawped.

"Oh, that's disgusting," I said.

"No, they're made for that," he insisted. And with that morsel of information, he stopped to show me that there were two bands of terry cloth on each of my gloves.

"Well, isn't that something," I exclaimed, admitting, once again, that there was much more to all this cycling than I realized.

By now we had reached a fork in the road, so we decided that Pete would take the more challenging route back to the château and I would go the shortcut. Unlike in Burgundy, however, our separation represented no emotional distancing from each other. Today we had found a way to respect each other's rhythm without creating a cacophony of discord. I found myself cycling on a lovely little road—just Bella and me—in the middle of this unexpected quadrant of *la France profonde*, or deep France. It was empowering and wonderfully rejuvenating to be amid all this nature of the most extraordinary quality. And to make this one-with-the-universe sentiment even better, I felt totally liberated by wiping my nose on my gloves. *I wonder what's in store for me next?*

Once Pete and I met up at Château de la Baume, we loaded up our gear, fastened the bikes onto the roof rack, exchanged quick hugs and kisses, and prepared to set sail for our next destination in Languedoc. I whipped out the map in my most expertly navigational mode and proceeded to plot the drive. It was at this point that I noticed how incredibly close we were at Nasbinals to Laguiole, the town famous for its handsome hand-crafted knives. I remembered how beautiful the countryside is around Laguiole and thought that it was a pity we didn't have time to spend a few days in this area since the cycling was so good.

We plodded on, however, picking up the A75 just outside of Marvejols, pretty much the spot at which we noticed a dramatic change in the countryside and weather. With the unusual microclimate of the Aubrac to our backs, we drove right into sunny skies and warmer temperatures in a matter of minutes. The terrain was noticeably less verdant, but I couldn't help thinking how nice it is for the people of the region to have two such highly contrasted regions cheek by jowl. The plan was to drive about 120 kilometers (seventy-four miles) to an area some thirty kilometers (nineteen miles) west of Montpellier. Our travels took us longer than expected—approximately two hours—since a good portion of the roadway was a *nationale*, a highly-trafficked route that much of the time snaked around rugged hillsides punctuating more of the backcountry of France. Our journey ended in Gignac at a pay phone from which we called Robert, a representative from the local chapter of the FFCT (Fédération Française du Cyclo-Tourisme). He was to debrief us on cycling in this new area.

Robert swiftly escorted us back to his home, laid out a table full of various drinks, peanuts, and chips for the apéritif, and proceeded to highlight on an outstretched map the best places for cycling. Per my plans with the representative from the regional tourist board, the point of interest was to be Lac du Salagou and Robert's job was to clue us in on the best routes and their varying degrees of difficulty. We learned that the area is best known for its *vélo à tout terrain* (V.T.T.), or mountain bike riding, and, in fact, there was to be a big competition around this lake throughout the upcoming days. Fortunately, there appeared to be more than enough to amuse Pete and me on our road bikes. Once we formulated a plan and exchanged a few pleasantries with Robert and his equally friendly wife, we were finally on our way.

It all sounded pretty exciting, and Pete and I chatted about the plans for the next day during the short drive to our hotel. Our spirits plummeted, however, when we pulled into this totally charmless establishment that didn't at all live up to our expectations. Even with its three-star ranking, the Hostellerie Saint-Benoit lacked any real ambiance, or more importantly, a trace of coziness, something of primal importance to me in my home-away-from-home. To make matters worse, I was suddenly consumed by a sort of allergy attack (triggered possibly by the recent change in temperature or more likely by the spray of rank eau de toilette I tested in the *autoroute* restroom), which left my eyes and nose running like a mountain stream. Surprisingly, though, dinner was quite good here and if it weren't for the ultra-bright lighting and the Musak rendition of songs such as the theme to Titanic, the evening wouldn't have been half bad.

A very loud and annoying rooster crowed us out of oblivion the next morning (quite a contrast from the church bells of Cluny and Mulhouse and much of a surprise since we had hardly landed in farm country). We ambled out to breakfast utterly exhausted. Happily, though, all looked much better by the light of day (except for the woman who shuffled out in her old robe and slippers with ratty hair). An enclosed deck surrounded the poolside and here we munched on our croissants and buttered baguettes seated at rustic-looking tables and propped up on sturdy wooden chairs. The sun shone brilliantly and the air smelled sweet and crisp; somehow the entire scene exuded that certain allure we'd been craving.

I went back to my room, made a few calls, and then approached the management at the desk to see if I could possibly log onto their computer to check my emails. (My laptop, of course, would not work here.) I was quickly rebuffed but instead of putting up a fight, I just turned around and scuffed back to my room. I'm sure it must have been the dejected-dog look I assumed that spurred the hotel manager to ring me up a few minutes later and offer to drive me to a place where I could check my emails without inconveniencing the hotel. (It's best not to protest in France and better to have the French feel sorry for you.) What a delightful turn of events; off we went to her friend's office, where I was able to check in with doings on the other side of the Atlantic. As I made a mental note of this hotel's A for effort, I also realized that it's very conveniently located next to the Salagou Lake and the abbey of Saint-Guilhem, a gem of a cultural landmark and village. Perhaps with the right expectations, it could be quite the find, after all. (Hopefully their special niceties aren't just reserved for *journalistes de voyage*.)

Finally, by noon, Pete and I were off to Salagou, a manmade lake that—according to all reports—would beguile us with its charms. By now the bright sun had warmed up the day, and if it weren't for all the wind, we would have been back to near summertime conditions. Just beyond the small town of Clermont l'Hérault, we picked up the D156, one of the roads that partially encircles the lake. Here on the western side, we located a couple of huge parking lots next door to a restaurant-café, the perfect place to park our car for a few hours.

If yesterday we were in Ireland, today we were in the great American West, red rock country, the likes of which you see in parts of Colorado and Utah. It might be a stretch to dub this unique share of the country the Moab of France, but not a huge exaggeration. The lake is alluring, but the most intriguing part of Salagou is the rich red soil and rocks bolstering the surrounding area. It felt amazing to discover this sort of spectacular Spartan scenery in France. Just as noteworthy, too, is that along the more than twenty-kilometer (twelve-mile) loop of *départementales* that hem most of the lake—and a bit beyond—rich, fertile land also dances into view with all the freshness of a bouquet of garden flowers in the dead of winter. Vineyards, fields and clusters of little stone houses provide visual respite to the more inordinate scenery for which Salagou has become most known.

At one point Pete and I passed through a particularly lunarlike zone punctuated with the most poetic sort of graffiti we had ever seen. Charlie & Sabrina, Pierre *aime* Marie, and Catherine 1995 were just a few of the writings from the sea of scribbles that marked the land, all lyrical compositions formed from rocks and pebbles of varying shapes and sizes.

"I'd like to stop and do one for you," Pete announced on an astonishingly romantic whim. I paused for a moment and considered Pete's spontaneous expression of affection for me. He's not what I would call a romantic kind of guy. But he would occasionally surprise me with truly heartfelt gestures, sweet overtures that would almost make up for the times he'd forgotten to buy me flowers or candy or had neglected to woo me when I was counting on his attention the most. Pete was romantic when I least expected it, and this was one of those times.

"We better stick to our plan or else we'll come up short in the lunch department. Remember we were going to stop in that café in Salasc?"

"Yeah, we better not arrive late for lunch. It's not like in the U.S. where you can eat most any time."

I often think about what sort of stone testament to me Pete would have created, but actually that doesn't matter much. What's most important is that he thought about doing it for me in the first place.

As it turned out, the kitchen had been pretty much cleared out by the time we showed up shortly after 2 p.m. Only half a baguette remained, so we had the café make a sandwich for two out of it, with their remaining rations of smoked ham and Brie. A few swills of Orangina later, Pete tore off, vowing to meet me at Octon—in the center of the village—a short while later. He was adding a good climb to his ride, an approximately fifteen-kilometer (nine-mile) detour that apparently promised sweeping panoramic views and a heart-pumping workout. Once again, I enjoyed riding along at my own pace, truly absorbing this breathtaking scenery, and not having to listen to the commands "Pedal, Pedal, Pedal harder!" every quarter mile.

I thought about our relationship. *There's no doubt we get along better when we give each other space, especially when Pete gets to do his thing and I do mine. There's no sense trying to do everything together, particularly since we're as different as the seasons.*

We were both happy to have met up at Octon without a hitch—so much so that Pete even agreed to linger a while longer to take in the peacefulness of this village *place* and to snap a few pictures. There was a flurry of activity in and around the local wine co-ops and much animation amid the vines. We were hitting the height of the harvest here as well. Unfortunately, the ride back to the car ended up being far more exhausting (at least for me) than expected, since we had to ride up and around the dam at the far end of the lake. This challenge hit me particularly hard and in a fitful moment of weakness, I dismounted Bella and walked us both up the hill. And, as they say, once you get off, you never get back on—until the descent, at least. Thankfully, Pete made no comment.

Despite heavy legs and an accumulation of fatigue, I knew we couldn't drive directly back to the hotel. I wanted to investigate another hotel that I had heard about, Ostalariá Cardabela, in the little town of Saint-Saturnin de Lucian. While Pete waited in the car, I ventured in and cordially asked for the Cook's tour of the premises. My heart wept. *This is just the kind of place I want to find myself in when traveling,* I thought. *Part Old World castle, part cozy contemporary digs, all I want to do is flop myself down on their big wrought iron bed and call it a night.*

My now almost infamous tourism contact had also informed me that the owners of Ostalariá Cardabela also ran a restaurant, Le Mimosa, in the nearby village of Saint-Guiraud. Not to be defeated, we drove off in that direction, crossing through rambling vineyards, practically in tears over the beauty and quaintness of the scenery and villages, and most especially over our regret that we were not residing here instead of next door to the overly excited rooster. Just slightly northeast of Salagou, we had hit upon another one of the vast areas of Languedoc that so closely resembles Provence, but without all the crowds. I knocked on the door of Le Mimosa in Saint-Guiraud, but sadly, it was too early for anyone to answer to an unannounced guest.

Pete and I scurried around our now-even-less-enticing place of lodging attempting to clean up from the ride as we lamented that travels don't always work out the way you hope. "I'm glad you enjoy the same kinds of places that resonate with me," I said.

"Yeah, I'm beginning to like this travel writer's life—except for the times when something turns out to be a wild goose chase," he said with his wide grin.

"That's all part of the job," I replied as we jostled for space in our tiny bathroom. "I guess we won't bother to shoe-horn ourselves into that shower then," I joked.

"No, I don't think you'll find your romance there," he teased.

"You never know," I said as I whipped the towel off of him.

"Hey," he cried.

"Hay is for horses," I replied, placing a big, juicy kiss on his lips.

We received a phone call from Mr. Pugh, a British gentleman and the owner of the two outstanding establishments we discovered earlier, just as we were about to leave our little cookie-cutter room for dinner in the hotel restaurant. He was apprised of my visit by his hotel manager and graciously offered all of his apologies for us not having had the opportunity to experience his properties firsthand as he had attempted to arrange with the tourism department. He then invited Peter and me to check into the Ostalariá for the night and to dine at Le Mimosa. At first it sounded as though our discerning traveler dreams had been answered, but after consulting with Pete, we decided that we were just too tired to change hotels at eight o'clock at night. Dinner did sound tempting, though.

"All set," I announced to Pete once I got off the phone.

"That's my Bessie, Queen of France."

"And don't forget *la journaliste américaine* part either," I kidded.

Little did we know that dining here would turn out to be one of the best culinary experiences of our trip. The chef was not only a woman—Mrs. Pugh—but also a New Zealander. Perhaps this explains the glorious paring down of the courses, the divine freshness of each ingredient (mostly organic), the simple combinations of flavors that gave birth to creations as imaginative as cake made with Muscat and olive oil, served with ginger honey ice cream. With each course, Mr. Pugh poured us a local wine, every one more astonishing than the one before. It's true that Languedoc is known to be the biggest producer of table wine in France, however, the winemakers in the region are also developing more and more wines that would rival your finest Burgundy or Bordeaux. The entire evening was a success, and Pete and I totally relaxed not only over such a fine meal but also as a result of dining in such comfortable surroundings. Call it nouveau chic or sophisticated eclectic, one thing is for sure: there is absolutely no pretension at Le Mimosa by the décor, the staff, the clientele (about fifty percent local artist types), or, of course, by the food. I guess this was just one of the good, unexpected discoveries of our travels.

There was no time for dilly-dallying the next morning because, once again, we had a road trip ahead of us. Our program commanded that we be in Limoux in the Aude department by 11 a.m. We were told the drive would take two hours, so *this* morning at least, we were glad to hear the rooster crow. Upon our arrival at the tourist office in Limoux, we were warmly greeted by Christophe, a local representative, who fortunately spared any excess of formalities. Soon the clock on the old bell tower in town struck twelve, the sacred hour in France, when all civilized folk rush to the table.

By now we were particularly hungry for a good lunch since we found French sandwiches to be too bread-y. Christophe led us through a smoke-filled *café/tabac* replete with PMU (France's lottery and also a major sponsor of the Tour de France) displays and many heavy gamblers. I followed him up a set of stairs toward the back, and just as I was about to answer Pete's inquisitive looks with a shrug of my own, we stepped into a totally smoke-free dining room set up with small tables draped in crisp linens. Almost *toute de suite* we were served a Blanquette de Limoux, the oldest sparkling wine in France said to have served as inspiration for Dom Perignon, the most praise-worthy monk who created champagne centuries ago.

I could tell from the way this was beginning that we were in for a feast, and in this part of the country bordering the Southwest, I knew that didn't mean a light and simple repast. Over *confit de canard, cassoulet de canard*, and a couple of pork-product dishes, we discussed the wine and food of the region, the native peoples' love for rugby, the proliferation of mountain bike riding here in recent years, and the Cathar people. The latter subject interested me considerably, mostly since I knew nothing about these folks but had occasionally heard mention of them in France.

Over the strains of Shania Twain, Christophe began to explain. "Catharism existed in this region between the twelfth and fourteenth centuries. The people who practiced the tenets of this religious movement led very simple lives, virtually void of rites and icons. They only believed in the teachings of the New Testament. This so-called sect did not sit well with the King or the Pope," he continued. "So the Crusades set about eliminating the Cathars, and, of course,

Catharism. I suggest part of your program this afternoon involve visiting an old Cathar castle. You'll see it's one that has been reconstructed from ruins."

Armed with much literature on the Pays de Cathare (Cathar Country), also known as Pays d'Aude (Aude Country), named for the Aude river that runs through this department, Pete and I felt excited about discovering a whole other section of France—yet again! (Note that in France, the *départements* are either named for a river, or, as in the case of the Lozère, mountains.) It was close to 3 p.m. when we emerged from our hearty lunch, and more like 3:30 p.m. by the time we actually started to tour after having dropped our bags at our hotel in town. At that point (and after such indulgence) we weren't at all sure we'd do the program on two wheels or four. So we set off with the bikes on the roof of the car and our gear in tow saying, "We'll see." We were to stay on the D118, direction Alet-les-Bains, a road that appeared well traveled.

"This is far too traffic-y for me," I exclaimed. "We've already visited an old abbey, a pottery workshop and the Cathar château and I still feel like we've just stepped away from a village feast. How did the organizers possibly expect us to do all this on a bike after having sat down to that medieval mid-day banquet?"

"I know. I don't know how much more of this I can take. I better get in some tough rides in the Pyrenees."

I urged Pete to press onward in the comfort of our luxury sedan since I still wanted to travel another good distance on the D54 and D70 toward Bouisse to check out a bed-and-breakfast. I was tipped off by the tourist office in Limoux that there was a place I might want to visit—little did I know, though, that it was at the end of the earth. Soon Pete and I found ourselves climbing, climbing, then climbing—quite a different sensation in a car than on a bike. With each turn we ascended, I could tell that Pete was wishing he was on his bike.

Finally, we arrived at a place that did appear to be at the end of the earth and also the top of the world. Truly a slice of bucolic paradise, I later learned that this delightfully remote B & B is actually situated in Corbières, the rugged foothills of the Pyrenees Mountains, which also span a good segment of this region. With no signs of life in view save for sheep and goats grazing on the fertile pastures beyond, this site is just the place for feeling one with nature. Also an apparent haven for cyclists, many push-it-to-the-limit types stay here just to have good reason to embark upon an especially Herculean climb when they return home at the end of the day.

Monsieur and Madame Delattre showed us around their little sanctuary that they created here nearly twenty years ago. (Their B & B, Les Goudis, actually opened about eight years ago.) Once again, I yearned to move right in, for the charm, warmth, and genuine rustic quality of this unique place pleased me immensely. To further enhance this scene, a huge fire blazed in the hearth of the kitchen where many of the guests had gathered to share their tales of the day from their discoveries in this magnificent countryside. All settled in nicely, no one had to leave for dinner, since madame serves up country fare nightly.

So with all-too-familiar feelings of a letdown, Pete and I silently drove back to our hotel, hoping we would somehow find some redeeming qualities in our Hôtel Moderne & Pigeon Limoux. It was 7:30 p.m. when we pulled up—a good four-hour tour entirely carried out by car. "We would have had to have had rockets on our back tires to have covered all that territory on our bikes," I exclaimed to Pete. "As it was, we did all the visits at lightning speed."

He didn't comment, but I knew what he was thinking. I'm sure he would have liked to stay at that B & B high in the hills and taken a huge ride with the guys in the morning. I squeezed his thigh and said, "We'll have fun tonight." But somehow, I didn't think that helped much.

We could tell that our hotel must have been quite a grand establishment in its heyday. Unfortunately, that was a long time ago. Still, we made good use of our marble bathroom and freshened ourselves up for what we hoped would be a pleasant dinner downstairs. Sadly, the restaurant here seemed to be more consumed with pomp and circumstance than fine dining. My poached turbot in cream sauce was served to me not only cold, but rubbery to boot. I voiced my discontent in my most diplomatic voice, which in this establishment rebounded like a fishwife attempting to open a charm school. *"Moi, j'y suis pour rien. Qu'est-ce que vous voulez que je fasse?"* exclaimed the server in the ultimate expression of his "it's-not-my-problem" poor attitude. He actually said, "It's not my fault. What do you want me to do about it?"

Next thing I knew the chef and the maitre d' became fully engrossed in this *scandale*, capturing the attention of every other diner in the room. Mortified, Pete shrank into his chair while I stood my ground, knowing that any decent restaurant in France would willfully accept the complaints of their clients. (Granted, there is not much to complain about in France, since even the simplest meal is generally quite good. But if something is wrong, I'm a big proponent of speaking up.) A hot salmon was placed before me instead and Pete and I finished the rest of our meal feeling like scolded schoolchildren.

The next morning we woke up at 10 a.m. after having slept ten hours. I was revived, and set about making some real changes with the remaining two days of our program in Languedoc-Roussillon. I decided that I would arrange our place of lodging for the next two nights. After a few phone calls, I was able to locate a hotel that sounded attractive in Collioure, a quaint seaside resort, not far from our previously arranged engagements. Pete and I were relieved that we would not have to be so locked into an itinerary that was not working well for us. With these freshly laid plans in our back pockets, we proceeded to check out of the hotel where we were cast off with a less-than cordial *au revoir*. (I guess hard feelings remained from the night before.)

None of this mattered, though, because we were working as a team now. If there was one positive outcome from having to contend with traveling great distances to less than thrilling accommodations, it was that Pete and I banded together in our dissatisfaction and were in total agreement about how to resolve the situation. Thank goodness, at least *we* were on the same page.

Fortunately, we were able to savor one more delicious facet of Aude Country before straying too far. It was Sunday, October 8, a lovely fall day, and clearly the perfect time to go to market. I had heard that the *marché* at Espéranza was especially colorful since many of the mountain folk—mostly French hippie types—congregate here *en masse* to sell their products (lots of goat cheese, not surprisingly) or just to socialize. Indeed I hadn't seen so much long hair, dreadlocks, African jewelry and Birkenstocks since I watched footage of Woodstock '69. Pete and I felt extremely clean cut—he in a Polo shirt and fresh jeans; me in khakis, a denim top, and a Souleiado scarf. We didn't care, though, since it just felt great to be part of such an animated scene. Here, too, we ordered a couple of pizzas from the roving pizza truck and sat in a café and gobbled them up among the locals. *La vie est belle, quoi.*

From Espéranza—or more precisely Quillan—the scenery became even more dramatic. First we passed through magnificent gorges, then we arrived in the Pyrénées Orientales department where, once again, that most agreeable Provençal/Mediterranean feeling seized our senses. The combination of vineyards, cypress trees and parched rugged terrain boldly announced that we had entered a land where the sun typically shines throughout the better part of each season.

By the end of our two-hour drive, we approached the coast and gathered up the expansive view of the azure waters of the Mediterranean. For Pete, it was his first time at this bright blue sea, the moment we had been waiting for, the moment we had built into our itinerary since the earliest planning stages of the trip. We spotted our hotel, Les Trois Mas, easily and were delighted to see that we'd be staying at a place right on the waterfront. Our room, too, was graced with spectacular views of the sea and of a wide swath of the centuries-old fishing village of Collioure beyond. As much as we wanted to rush right out and explore, we took a few minutes to unpack and to admire the extraordinarily Old World scene from our window. It was time to relax, release and let go.

A short while later we were out mingling with the throngs of Sunday afternoon strollers—mostly French—that had practically overrun this little town. It didn't bother us, though, since we were in a touristy frame of mind and knew that we had no imperatives to meet. After a bit of shopping at Sardane, one of my favorite addresses for Catalonia-inspired clothing, we whiled away some time at Les Templiers, a landmark hotel-restaurant-café of France. The service here was awful, but, this, too, didn't matter, since after all the long stressful drives and challenges navigating the region on many fronts, we were content to just go with the flow.

People watching was entertaining here, too, a pastime that took on a whole new meaning for me with Pete as my companion in France. "Triple *oui* is like a word, isn't it?" Pete suddenly inquired.

"What do you mean?"

"Well, I rarely hear people—including you—just say *oui*. It's usually *oui, oui, oui* in rapid succession."

"Oh, *oui, oui, oui*," I answered with a chuckle.

"I also noticed that French people lace their shoes differently," Pete continued. Once again, I replied with an inquisitive look. "They lace them horizontally," he explained.

I found his observations marvelous. Clearly, as a male, and as someone who did not speak French and was traveling in France for the first time, his findings were quite different from mine.

Inevitably the conversation led to talk of flies, since in one of the establishments we had recently frequented, there was a fly in the milk pitcher, which I consequently poured into my coffee—*horrible!* We both concluded that the French don't consider this sort of happening to be nearly as offensive as Americans would. "In Burgundy," Pete added, "There was a fly buzzing over my digestif and the waiter just waved his hand through the air explaining that there were many flies because of the wine harvest."

"Well, despite the flies, it *is* nice to look out windows without screens," I said.

"*Oui, oui, oui*," Pete answered, puckering his lips like a Frenchman. "It is much nicer without zee screens," he added, lips still puckered as he gave me a kiss.

We both laughed hysterically over this, remembering the moment vividly, already reminiscing about our travels.

Before moving on, I urged Pete to take a look inside the bar area to admire the many paintings that were once offered as payment to the original proprietor by artists such as Matisse, Picasso and Derain. We also looked in at the restaurant and hotel area and concluded that we'd like to try both at a later date.

Then, like many of the other tourists, we walked out to the far reaches of the breakwater and looked out upon the horizon as far as the eye could see. We finally experienced the arm-in-arm, romantic, touristy moment we'd missed at Roussillon in Provence. We walked alongside the Mediterraen as two lovers on a quiet holiday.

"This is an emotional postcard moment," I said. Pete just smiled and gave me a hug.

After stopping for some souvenir picture taking, we wended our way back to our hotel along the ancient ramparts, the same stone pathways that had been navigated by man for ages.

It was fantastic not to feel rushed, not to experience the constraints of being a travel writer, not to be on a schedule. It was nice just to be.

This newfound vacation mode prompted me to take a leisurely bath, especially since the Mediterranean-tiled bathroom in our room was well equipped for that very thing. Use of the jacuzzi bathtub was definitely encouraged. Next to the bath, laid out on a fresh white hand towel, were packets of special *balnéotherapie* bath aromatics with instructions on how to use them (fifteen- to twenty-minute bath, then fifteen- to twenty- minute rest on the bed was what stood out the most to me).

"I smell Italian food," Pete hollered from the bedroom.

"It's just the bath therapy," I yelled back, which was indeed a delicious blend of rosemary, thyme, and essential oils.

We dined inside at the hotel's one-star Michelin restaurant amid an explosion of primary colors. (There was too much of a breeze in the air to brave the terrace.) The meal was good and artistically presented. For me, the highlight was the entrée, where I was served a silvery flower-like fan of fresh anchovies seasoned with dill, olive oil and Banyuls (the local sweet wine), presented on a bed of finely chopped peppers, mushrooms and *oignon confit*. I wouldn't consider having anchovies—not even a few on a pizza—any place but Collioure. Here, though, they are the sweetest and most flavorful you can imagine—not surprising, since the town has been known for them since the Middle Ages. Today these tiny delicacies are still fished from the Mediterranean from June until September on nights when there is no moon, current or wind; they are cleverly coaxed toward the boats by the light of a single lamp on calm waters. As soon as the catch is brought in, the anchovies are freshly salted and preserved in a briny mixture for at least three months.

Even after the array of countryside we had experienced up until now, that night we almost felt as though we were in a different country all together. Lulled to sleep with the sound of the gusty sea breeze blowing through the pines outside our window and by the crashing of the waves on the beach, we both felt like contented captains of our own ship. Our union provided a perfect ending to what turned out to be a lovely day. The lovemaking was extra special here, too. It was divine to feel so one with each other, so one with the world.

We remained scot-free the next day until early afternoon, when I met briefly with the director of the tourist office from nearby Argelès-sur-Mer, the town where we were supposed to have spent our last night in the region. This didn't intimidate me because by now I had already stated my case with my main tourist contact over the phone and felt confident that I was handling matters appropriately. It was a little awkward at first for Monsieur le Directeur to greet me. But once he realized that I was an affable person with reasonable grievances, he began to ease up on his rigid demeanor.

Pete showed up just in time for the fun. Minutes later we were suited up for our ride with the Vélo Club des Albères from Argelès-sur-Mer, a tour arranged by the tourist office. A fifteen-minute drive inland from Collioure took us to the established meeting point at St-Genis-des-Fontaines, where we joined up with four of the members of this bike club. Ranging in age from fifty-three to sixty-eight, each was a prime example of how incredibly fit you can be when you're older. From the moment of the introductions, I could tell this was a relaxed crowd, charming people—three men, one woman—who conveyed all the warmth of the Midi (the south of France). There would be no monsieur this, madame that; instead we were to be a group of cyclists out to have fun.

Before casting off we visited the abbey at St.-Genis- des-Fontaines, a baby jewel of Romanesque architecture, dating back to the eleventh and twelfth centuries. We were informed that there would be more visits along the way during this *cyclo-tourisme* outing, and with that news, I said a little prayer at the altar that Pete would be able to endure such touring without becoming too irritable in his sticky cycling shorts.

No sooner did we pull out onto the road than I realized that there was an art to group riding, even if you weren't part of a peloton. The language seemed to be international because Pete caught on right away despite his inability to say more than a handful of French words all at once. For me, though, it was quite new. This was, in fact, my first group ride—ever—so I knew I needed to stay on my toes, and most importantly, pick up the pace.

Everyone had a purpose at one point or another, or so it seemed. Jean-Marc was the *capitaine de route*, the guide and pacesetter, who led us all out on a well-defined, pre-determined course. Michel, a former pro cyclist, exercised particular vigilance in his role as *serre fil* (line tightener). He was our own sort of broom wagon on this little tour, a kind soul quick to pull in any stragglers. (The broom wagon is the final vehicle of the Tour de France race; it serves to sweep up the last of the riders.) I hung back with him, of course.

Along the way everyone exerted much caution in pointing out various obstacles on the route such as potholes, broken glass, sewer lids, parked cars or just a bump in the road. There was more finger-snapping followed by pointing down to potential hazards than I cared to register. Apparently, though, this is all part of group-ride etiquette because Pete had no problem joining in on the gesticulating.

Next thing I knew I heard Pete yelling "*Voiture derrière*" in French, just like the rest of the team, to indicate that a car was coming up from behind. At one point I was almost blown off the road by a lady who bombed by in an *auto-école* (driving school) car—a rarity since French drivers are normally respectful of cyclists. But fortunately I was tipped off by someone else's *"voiture derrière."*

Pete was in his glory, and if I could have read his mind at that point, I'm sure he was saying to himself: *This is great, now that I have Bessie in training camp.* Indeed, I pushed myself more than perhaps I would have alone with him. I was caught up in the momentum of the group, not to mention the fact that I didn't want to keep five other people waiting. At one point, we were pushing it so hard that we had just about emptied our water bottles in quenching our thirst. Just as I started to think about stopping someplace to buy water, we pulled up to a cemetery. I had assumed that it was another one of the special visits planned along the way, but, no, this was a spontaneous one to replenish our reserves. Then it was explained to me that you always find fresh water in cemeteries throughout France and that it's common practice among cyclists to refill their *bidons* there.

Our grand tour led us to Brouilla, Ortaffa, Villeneuve-de-la-Raho (where we took pictures alongside the lake), Pollestres, Nyls, Ponteilla, Trouillas, Monastir-del-Camp, Villemolaque, St-Jean Lasseille, Banyuls-dels-Aspres, then back to Brouilla and St-Genis des-Fontaines. In all we traveled twenty-six miles at an average speed of 12.7 miles per hour (slightly higher than my usual speed). We had a glorious time together and truly enjoyed the conviviality and camaraderie of our little group. Peter even seemed to appreciate the visits, the most lengthy one to a handsome Romanesque church and cloisters at Monastir del Camp where we reveled in a tasting of local Roussillon wines including Côtes du Roussillon and the sweet nectars of Muscat and Vieux Rivesaltes. Fortunately, we only had about fourteen kilometers (nine miles) to pedal after that, because needless to say, we felt a little otherworldly once back on our bikes. More pictures were snapped on the steps of the beautiful little fifteenth-century church Banyuls-dels-Aspres in the quaint town of the same name. In the end, both Pete and I were thrilled to have discovered such a marvelous region with such wonderful people.

The pace remained quick back at our hotel with only a fraction of time to shower and change before the planned dinner that evening. My hair was still damp when our tourist director acquaintance whisked us away to The Cottage in Argelès-sur-Mer. Our whole little group was awaiting us (how did they get ready so fast?), including Jean-Marie, Michel, Antoine and Josée. It was nice to see everyone in a different context, all spruced up and looking forward to sharing a fine meal.

In the beginning, the tone was very official and formal (perhaps due to the presence of Monsieur le Directeur). First there was a speech by Michel, then Jean-Marc. But, as the wine flowed, and one delicious course after another was consumed, everyone began to loosen up. Monsieur le Directeur—Jean-Marc—began to *tutoye* me (use the less formal version of you), and the rest of our cycling buddies soon settled into a really good time. We talked about how the language of cycling is international and how thankful we all were to have shared such an experience. Scrumptious desserts (yes, two) of *crème catalane* and a strawberry/meringue/ice cream mélange added an extra dollop of sugar to the mellifluous words that followed.

I could practically hear a drum roll (or perhaps, the musical theme to the Tour de France) in my head, when it evidently became the moment to more formally honor Peter and me. We were both presented with medals of cyclists hanging from red-and-yellow striped ribbons, the colors of Catalonia, the emblem of the region. Each was engraved with the name of the cycling club and the date of our excursion together. What at first appeared a tad corny grew into a most appreciated display of affection, for it was all extremely sincere and heartfelt. Peter and I were deeply touched.

What a happy ending to our sometimes-unnerving adventures in Languedoc-Roussillon.

Living Large in the Southwest

It was Tuesday, October 10. As much as we felt blessed with what we had experienced so far, we were also sad that our trip was winding down. The Southwest was to be the last region of France that we were to explore *à vélo*—at least for this trip—and on many levels it seemed as though we had just begun to stretch our legs. This was to be the mother of all regions for Pete, since the first half of our stay here was to encompass much of the Pyrenees, and Pete had his sights on taking a chunk out of one or more of these mountains' mythic climbs.

After a lengthy drive from Collioure, we finally landed in a highway rest stop just outside of Pau, the designated place where we were to meet François, our contact from the Béarn (pronounced Bay-arn) department of France, one of the many *départements* of this region. Accompanying François was a very jovial Frenchman by the name of Jean-Renée (J.R. to his friends), who we were told knew his way around France's most impressive cols (mountain tops). With all the aplomb of an official tour guide, the tall and handsome François expedited this parking lot rendezvous, instructing us to follow him to a more appropriate place to converse. Immediately Pete and I felt as though we were in expert hands and that it was unlikely we would have to do a lot of time wasting and unnecessary travel in this province the way we did in Languedoc.

We blew through Pau like a team car on the day of a big race. "The Tour always goes through this town," Pete said. "It's the gateway to the Pyrenees."

Soon afterward, we found ourselves pulling up to L'Horizon, a modest country hotel in the Jurançon, a picturesque section of this department that we were to explore for the rest of the day. It was just past lunchtime, so it was out of the question (thankfully) to sit down to do an extended lunch. We were, however, installed at a table where a magnificent feast of an autumnal dessert was laid before us—truly a meal in itself. If I were to judge the cuisine of this unassuming restaurant by the quality of its sweets, then a meal here is topnotch. On a plate the size of a platter, each of us was served an elegant *crumble de saison*, the French equivalent of our homespun dessert, made from seasonal fruits and nuts and topped off with chestnut ice cream and a *coulis de figue* (fig sauce). Of course, the beverage of choice accompanying this sweet confection was a perfectly chilled Jurançon, the white wine of the region that is either dry or (most often) sweet. We were served a *moelleux*, a sweet one, an exquisite *vin doux* with about half the alcoholic content of your more heady Muscats. Our plan was still to do some cycling before the end of the day.

It didn't take long to figure out that J.R. was not one to remain idle and that cycling was definitely on his mind. We learned that since his retirement about six years ago, he had cycled more than 10,000 kilometers (6,200 miles) over more than eighty-five cols throughout France's most spectacular mountain ranges, including the Pyrenees, the Alps, the Jura, the Vosges and the Massif Central. As the head of the Club Cyclo-Tourisme for these mountain ranges, he organizes many rides that would make even the most ardent cyclists feel faint. Today, though, we were to cruise around the Jurançon on terrain that supposedly even I could handle.

But before I was to be allowed out with the guys, I was to spend some more time with François learning about the delicious Jurançon wines. (I suppose they were possibly hoping that after more tasting, I'd be so unfit to ride that they'd only have to accompany me just long enough to humor me.) Behind their respective parked cars, Pete and J.R. changed into their Lycra. They were quite the pair, the two of them—Pete as tall as J.R. was short, with neither of them having much means to communicate with each other except their common language of cycling.

François and I set out in his little Renault, traversing cornfields just on the verge of harvest and passing by gardens with tomatoes still ripe on the vine. I noticed beautiful, still-blooming hydrangeas of the sort you see on Nantucket or Martha's Vineyard, a sight that I had only seen in certain parts of Brittany before. There were palm trees, too—clearly the local climate was quite particular. With daytime temperatures easily reaching seventy-five degrees and sunshine a more frequent occurrence than rain, this delightful weather is due to the fact that the Jurançon sits at the foot of the Pyrenees. As with every other wine-growing area of France that we visited thus far, here, too, we were lucky enough to have arrived during the harvest, this time right at the beginning. The grapes for the *moelleux* would have to wait another two weeks, allowing the fruit to become extra ripe and rich in sugar content before being tenderly plucked from the vines.

As we chugged up this hilly terrain, I was happy I was not riding it on my bike. There was absolutely no one around on these sometimes single-lane country roads, and I couldn't help but think that any enthusiastic cyclist in search of a challenge would be thrilled to land on this turf. It looked a little too much for me, though.

The vines were unique to the area, too. All extremely well-pruned, here they were coaxed to grow up high, a good five feet off the ground so as to avoid the frosts of November and early December. (Many grapes are actually left on the vines that long, drying into concentrated, shrunken nuggets of flavor, perfect for the production of the sweetest *vin doux* of the region.) François and I ended our wine tour at La Commanderie de Jurançon, a showcase boutique where visitors can taste wines from more than twenty-five domaines. I was careful not to *déguste* too much, though, and drank plenty of water, since I still had my heart set on experiencing some of the super cycling in this area.

Soon Pete and J.R. zipped into view, both grinning like little kids. Obviously, communication posed no problem for them, and instead, they stood before François and me praising each other's bike riding skills in their respective languages.

"Nous avons fait que dix kilomètres," J.R. began. They only did ten kilometers (about six miles).

"Yeah, but it was a nice climb." Pete added. "Probably with a ten percent gradient, then a little spit of fifteen percent. It went up through the steepest sections of the area."

"Les Côteaux du Jurançon," J.R. added.

I smiled at Pete because I was happy he was having fun. I also felt proud—and somewhat mystified—about how he seemed to understand J.R.'s French. "Do you want to hit some more ambitious climbs?" I asked. They both looked at me as if to say, *what do you think?* Suddenly I sensed François' presence even more.

Then Pete and J.R. said, each in his own language and practically in unison, "That's OK. Why don't we all take one together?"

They patiently waited for me to conclude my visit and change into my own bike garb and then off we went.

I was lucky that the ride started with *une belle descente,* and as I found myself freewheeling down the undulating hills of this bucolic countryside, I, too, felt like a kid that had just experienced the real joys of cycling for the first time. About two miles into the ride, though, we encountered our first significant climb. I felt proud of myself for automatically raising my fanny out of the saddle and for beginning to power-pedal, all the time determinedly counterbalancing my weight over the handlebars.

"Non, non, non, ce n'est pas comme ça qu'il faut faire la danseuse, Mariebett," or no, no, no, that's not how you do the dancer, Maribeth, J.R. instructed. (The "th" always poses a challenge for the French.) Instantly deflated, *OK,* I thought, *now I have two instructors with me, so I guess there's no room for any indifferent behavior.*

La danseuse that J.R. was referring to is that exquisite motion a cyclist makes while standing up on his or her pedals, truly dancing in perfect synchronization so that bike and body work together, arms and legs cooperate without expending the slightest amount of useless energy. Imagine Lance Armstrong on one of his alpine climbs.

Sadly I have never been much of a dancer on or off the dance floor and my coordination is about as keen as a marathon runner

132

attempting to simultaneously run and do the fox trot without missing a beat.

"C'mon Bessie, be more even with your pedaling," Pete chimed in. "Remember what I told you before. Smooth."

This time I was eager to learn a few pointers, so I tried to assume a nice, even rhythm.

"You always have to keep something in reserve," J.R. continued in French, just as Pete seemed to say the same thing in English. I was beginning to think that they had collaborated, that they had discussed my bike riding inadequacies and that they were jumping at the chance to bring them up.

"Like don't go into your granny gear (the easiest gear) when you're only halfway up the climb," Pete added.

"Always keep something under your wheel," J.R. continued.

Jeez, so glad to be out with my two instructors, I thought. *Maybe I should have sampled more wine with François during our tour. That Jurançon was delicious.*

Instead I decided to give up my stubborn ways and began to really apply myself. I was under expert instruction after all; J.R. was a *moniteur*, so how could I refuse his lessons? Soon I felt myself really progressing, really gaining confidence. I was riding faster than I had before.

"See," Pete said, "It helped that you pushed yourself yesterday with the group ride. Today you're even stronger."

"What does *à bloc* mean?" I asked Jean-Renée. And he explained that it meant that you were going full speed or that you had reached your maximum. *Hmmmm*, I guess I was going *à bloc*—at least by my standards. "What about *faire une valise à quelqu'un*?" I ventured. I learned that was an expression used to say that you had really left someone behind, as in leaving them as baggage. By the end of the ride, I couldn't help but think that it was sweet that Pete and J.R. hadn't made a valise out of me.

At the conclusion of it all, I felt proud of myself and of Pete. His knowledge of cycling and polite ways were clearly charming the French. I couldn't imagine doing such a trip with anyone but him. His sweetness and superior cycling ability were conquering me on each step of our adventure. As much as we were opposites in many ways, we did complement each other well. There's no doubt that in most instances, he had what I was lacking and vice versa. In considering our unique balancing act, our own *danseuse*, I felt more content with our relationship than ever before.

After a country-style dinner in a little restaurant tucked away in the woods (most of the dining and lodging establishments are hidden away like this in the Jurançon), we checked into the Maison Rances, a bed-and-breakfast where we were to spend the next two nights. We both woke up during the night to the sound of rain, a melodious din that normally would have pleased us and gently lulled us back to sleep. But with the cycling plans we had afoot for the next day, we rolled over and grumbled.

At breakfast the next morning, Simon Browne, a large and gregarious South African who had recently moved to this remote area to start a new life with his family as the lord of this seventeenth-century manor house, loudly proclaimed at breakfast, "No Col d'Aubisque today. It hasn't rained like this since last May, even though this can be a rainy part of the country. Today there's rain throughout all of France," he continued. I wasn't sure whether or not this last bit of information brought any consolation to Pete or not. I could tell, though, that he was desperately hanging onto a little shred of a possibility that the weather would be clear enough up in the mountains.

"Yesterday was the best day of riding yet that I've had in France, and I was hoping for another good one today," Pete said gloomily, as we slipped off to our room.

"I know, I'm sorry. I know how much you were looking forward to tackling the Aubisque."

François picked us up as planned and the three of us headed out to the mountains with Pete's bike standing defiantly on the roof, boldly slicing through mother nature's teeming rain. (Bella rested comfortably back in the Browne's barn, as it was never part of my plan for me to attempt the Pyrenees.) We stopped at the entrance of La Vallée d'Ossau in a café where Jean-Renée greeted us. True to form, the fireball of some sixty years made the effort to drive a half hour here from Pau to see first-hand the conditions of *la metéo*. As we all conferred around our cafés—with me already chilled to the bone—the dreaded verdict was given; there would be no riding up to the Col d'Aubisque today. With many shakes of the head and numerous *non, non, non* pronounced, J.R. confirmed our fears, and convinced us that as a veteran cyclist of the Pyrenees, the weather would be *"plus que horrible"* up above.

After sharing a few more stories and laughs with our new friend, we regretfully bid Jean-Renée goodbye with vows to cycle again together at some point in the not-too-distant future. So it was to be a day filled with tourism rather than cycling.

"I guess I just have to accept the fact that we're going to follow your program today rather than mine," Pete said. I bit my lip and gave him a big hug. Although somehow I sensed that my love and affection wasn't going to provide much solace.

First stop was to the Vulture Museum at the base of La Falaise aux Vautours. I questioned this curious sort of attraction, prompting François to say, "The vultures of the Pyrenees are revered almost as much as the sacred cows of India."

"Who would have imagined?" I responded.

"Well, that might be a bit of an exaggeration," François replied. "But they do play a vital role in preserving the natural habitat of this mountainous region. The mountain folk send their animals out to graze in the high mountain pastures once the snow melts. The grasses, flowers, herbs and even roots such as licorice at this high altitude are much more aromatic. The cows, goats and sheep love it, and they yield milk far more flavorful than an ordinary animal grazing at sea level can produce.

"That makes sense," I said. "I've always found *fromage des Pyrénées* to be particularly tasty."

"Yes, it is," François replied, however, I could tell he was eager to talk about the vultures. "Obviously accidents can occur; a sheep might fall into a ravine or an old cow might expire at the top of one of France's highest peaks," he continued. "When this sort of consequence of nature transpires, the vultures are the heroes, picking the carcasses clean so as not to leave behind a single gram of rotten meat to spread disease."

"That's interesting," Pete said. "I'll never look at vultures the same way again."

I winked at Pete to show appreciation for his interest. The museum was fascinating, and from April to October, four cameras monitor the activity of the vultures perched on the two cliffs above this center. (Some 300 vultures populate the area during the fair weather season.) Since it was almost mid October, the action was turned off until next year, a situation that disappointed François greatly.

"Oh, that's OK," I said to François, relieved that I would not be seeing these creatures up close and personal. I looked over to see Pete's reaction and saw him shooing away an excessive amount of flies that were circling the dark and small exhibition space. I joined in, too, since they soon moved my way.

François noticed our flailing arms and said, "There are a lot of flies this time of year because of the wine harvest."

Pete poked me, rolled his eyes and whispered, "That must be the standard phrase for the French." I squeaked as I attempted to suppress my laughter. Fortunately François was already moving toward another exhibit. Pete and I lingered in our shared joke for a moment, choking on our chuckles. I think we were both happy that a funk hadn't set in about his ride being called off and it just felt good to laugh.

Just down the road from the vulture museum, we visited the cheese cellars of the Fromagerie Pardou, a must-see for anyone who has an appreciation for *fromage*. Housed in an old train tunnel, up to 20,000 wheels of cheese carefully age here on shelves some twenty-one feet high. Before the aging process begins (it generally lasts about two months), it all starts with wheels of cheese brought in by the local shepherds. After a sixty-hour, saltwater bath, each cheese is laid out to age on moisture-absorbing pine shelves; and depending on the type of cheese, rubbed with a dry cloth, salted, and turned every couple of days until a golden orange crust finally forms. I noticed that each wheel was marked with a different symbol or letter, a sort of branding that was put on there by the shepherd in order to insure the proper identification of his cheese. Upon completion of the aging process, most of these shepherds/producers reclaim their cheeses, and others are sold at the Fromagerie Pardou cheese store across the way.

We lunched in the informal restaurant adjoining the cheese store. "I can't wait to try this cheese," I said.

"The most delicious Pyrenees cheese comes from the Béarn department of France, not the Basque region," François proudly declared. "The Basque people don't let their animals graze nearly as high. Plus the peaks aren't as significant there anyway."

"How do you know when you buy *un fromage des Pyrénées* where it comes from if you are not in either the Béarn or Basque regions?" I queried.

"You have to have a very trusty and knowledgeable cheese merchant and ask them," François responded.

"I can hardly wait to ask a *fromager* about the exact provenance of their particular *fromage des Pyrénées*. Won't they be impressed!"

The change in weather brought out our mountain-man appetites, and as the rain continued to fall outside, we opted for the *garbure*, a hearty soup consisting of ham, duck leg, sausage and cabbage. We finished off this Béarnaise specialty with a couple of cheeses, of course, from *le tunnel*.

"These cheeses are delicious, François," I said.

"They really are good," Pete added.

"The very best ones may be consumed in the months from November to March since those contain the summer milk," François added, still in his perfect English.

"If only we could stay through November," I joked. "Then we could have even better cheese and another stab at the Aubisque."

"It would probably be snowing by then," François said.

On our ride up to the Col d'Aubisque, we did indeed pass many animals, the divine producers of delicious milk but also the nemesis of many a Tour de France rider. Most have bells—if they haven't lost them—sonorous instruments that not only served to alert us to their presence but also to enhance the Sound-of-Music experience of this alpine landscape.

"The Tour riders know that they risk encountering an animal at breakneck speed," Pete said from the passenger seat.

"How do you know that?" I asked.

"I know some things about France."

"The shepherds are not always able to keep them away during the Pyrenees stages of the race," François added. "Especially on the other side of this tunnel."

"Yeah, there have been some bad crashes because of that," Pete said.

"Whoa, aren't you the tour guide," I teased.

Between intermittent patches of fog interspersed with torrential rain, the jagged snow-capped peaks of the Pyrenees loomed. "That's the difference between the Alps and the Pyrenees," François offered, as if reading my mind. "Here the range emerges very quickly. For the Alps, this is the case from the Italian side." We twisted around turns in a seemingly unending succession of undulations. Many of the roads only allowed for the passage of one car. Some weren't more than paved cow paths. There were no guardrails. Pete and I commented that roads like this don't exist in the U.S.

"You just can't tell what's around the corner," I said more as a warning than a comment. "Plus with this weather, the visibility is hugely decreased. You can't even see just ahead—not even on the more straightaway sections."

"Take it easy. Take it easy. It's fine, Bessie. François has everything under control."

About one kilometer from the top, virtually every bit of the road was covered with names of famous cyclists, primarily those of the Spanish riders. Armstrong was there, too, though, and upon passing his name, I couldn't help but imagine Lance sailing up this behemoth of a mountain *en danseuse* with no visible distress. Clearly the hardiest animals remained at the highest elevations, for here we passed thick-legged, workhorses breathing the frosty air, sturdy beasts that seemed to prefer to brave the elements instead of heading down the mountain. It was a nippy two degrees Celsius at the top, just barely above freezing. Add to that monsoon-like winds and pelting rain, all of which provided me with good reason not to leave the comfort of the heated interior of the car. Pete braved it just long enough to have his picture taken next to the summit marker at 1,709 meters (5,605 feet), an eternal remembrance that he made it to the top of the Aubisque regardless of the fact that he was in a car rather than on a bike.

We stopped at one point on the descent so that Pete and François could take a look at where the Swiss rider, Charlie Koblet, flew off the mountain and fell sixty meters (about 200 feet) during the 1958 Tour. It was foggy then, too. Miraculously, he survived. Cycling accidents make up a considerable part of these mountains' history.

"Can you believe that J.R. thought I could do the descent of this?" I exclaimed. "Then he thought I could attempt part of the climb of the Col de Soulor."

"That's a baby of a mountain in comparison," Pete teased.

"Yeah, that's just what I'm reading here," I responded as I studied the map. "Oh yeah, here it is—Soulor's a mere 1,474 meters (4,835 feet). Can you imagine? Thanks for the vote of confidence, J.R., but no thanks!"

François remained silent with his eyes set on the road. Jean-Renée was right, though. At least about the rain. "It looks as though it's going to rain tomorrow since all the cows are lying down," he kept saying the day before. It was hard to believe, since there wasn't a cloud in sight.

By the time we were making our descent, Pete fortunately let go of the fact that he was not going to attempt one of the great cols of the Pyrenees—at least not today, with all this rain. At mid-mountain, we all finally began to relax and enjoy the scenery. We marveled at this rustic area, the unspoiled scenery totally void of any significant commercial development—all so different from many parts of the Alps. We passed green pastures dotted with sheep and a variety of little houses crafted of stone hauled from the nearby rivers, all of which were topped off with roofs made of mountain slate. And virtually every man we passed sported a beret, the quintessential French hat that is actually made in Béarn, not in the Basque country.

To further reinforce the Béarn's veritable claim to fame on the so-called *béret Basque*, we stopped at the Musée du Béret in the town of Nay. This also happened to be the site of one of two remaining beret manufacturers in France. Originally knitted from local sheep's wool, church statues of figures wearing berets give evidence that they have been around at least since the thirteenth century. With the typical damp, often drizzly weather of the Pyrenees, it's no wonder they are the headgear of choice for old and young alike. The most authentic one still today is the black wool with the silk (more like acetate) lining, encircled with a leather band. It's waterproof, of course.

"So how come the *béarnais* people have been shortchanged in the recognition department for this iconic French product?" I asked François.

"The Basque people have worn the beret for many years as well," he explained. "But it caught on as a fashion accessory once the sophisticated people—mostly British— began to vacation in Biarritz during the nineteenth century. That's in Basque country. They saw many fisherman and other workers wearing berets, so they adopted them, too."

"Yes, I remember now from my research for *The Riches of France*. The artsy crowd and then the cognoscenti liked the jaunty look they provided."

"Jaunty?" François asked.

"Kind of lively," I answered.

"Chipper," Pete added.

"Well, aren't you the wordsmith!" I smiled.

"Well, from then on, the beret was associated with the Basques and the poor *béarnais* were only recognized for their Béarnaise sauce," François continued.

"Oh, so that's where bearnaise comes from," Pete exclaimed as I shot him a glance to hush up. François, forever the proud Frenchman, likely preferred to think that most people associate this delicious sauce with his region.

After a quick tour around Nay, we were off to visit Tissages de Coarraze, a famous *basco-béarnais* linen manufacturer. Here, too, the *béarnais* have remained wrongfully unrecognized since what is commonly referred to as Basque linens are also made in Béarn. By now, Pete and I were growing a bit weary, perhaps by all this deciphering and injustice, but more likely as a result of too much time spent in the car navigating dizzying terrain.

"Maybe we should head back now," I said.

"We just have one more stop to make at Biraben, a high-end gourmet food store," François piped up. "I know you will love it." Pete nodded at me from the back seat as if to say *thanks*.

Since this is the Southwest, it made sense that the Béarn garner its own notoriety (no matter how small) as a fine producer of foie gras, *confit de canard* and the remaining panoply of delicious heart-attack inducing products associated with this immense quadrant of France. For me, it was teatime, but for the folks shopping at this near supermarket-sized food emporium, samplings of foie gras and Jurançon were de rigueur. Oh well, I couldn't refuse, plus I hoped that it might settle my stomach a bit from the tedious ride.

"What are some of the other differences between the *basque* and the *béarnais*?" I asked François between munches and sips in the cocktail hour-like atmosphere of this high-stepping shoparama.

"Well, the people from Béarn are known to be shepherds and wine growers, those from the Basque region are largely shepherds and fisherman."

"That makes sense to me. And do the basque make foie gras, too?"

"*Pas vraiment*," or not really, François replied with an edge of chauvinism addressing the subtle sort of rivalry that exists between these neighboring departments of France.

François did his job well. I was sold on the Béarn and vowed to return again, particularly since, along with Paris and Bordeaux, the city of Pau—the gateway to the Pyrenees—is almost always included on the Tour. Loaded down with a ton of information, plus our own *bérets béarnais*, we thanked François for such a whirlwind tour and settled into a quiet evening *chez les Browne*. We only had time to steal a short rest in the solitude of our rooms where there was, thankfully, no TV (another of Pete's passions) and no phone. Soon it was time to gather downstairs around the fireplace for the apéritif.

Over chilled glasses of Jurançon we chatted with our hosts, Simon, and his elegant wife, Isabelle, and their gathering of guests that included a couple from Wales who love to frequent B & Bs, a couple of avid golfers and a sculptor from South Africa. Conversations included many travelers' tales on subjects as far and wide as cheese smuggling, shopping for booze in nearby Andorra, the size of the towels at the Ritz, Spanish bullfighting, British hooligans at soccer matches and rugby, to name just a few. Simon, a big strapping man who happened to be a former rugby player, had much to say on the latter and all of the above since his presence was as thundering as his wife's was demure.

It was all quite entertaining although I could tell that, as two rather private persons, Pete and I could not make a steady diet of this sort of socializing with people whom we had never met. As usual, all kinds of questions were directed my way, and once again, I learned that it was every other person's fantasy to become a travel writer. I didn't bother elaborating on the downside of the job. Instead I tried to turn the tables a bit and ask my fellow diners and hosts the questions.

"Do you cycle, Simon?" I ventured.

"Oh, yes," Simon responded and launched into his own diatribe about the sport and his tip for wearing cycling shorts. "I double them up. Of course they make me look like one of those wrestlers, but they certainly serve the purpose."

"I'll have to try that sometime, since I don't find sitting on a bike saddle to be very comfortable," I said. "Not sure if it would be worth the added puff though."

A classic Southwestern meal was served with much grace, and at one point, the only thing interrupting our dining experience was a fly buzzing around the room. Thwack. Simon took care of it in one fell swoop with the help of his enormous South African fly swatter.

Very much the gentleman, Simon said, "If you don't mind, I'm just going to get rid of this fellow."

Then one of the guests added, "You know when flies take off, they jump backwards."

Pete tapped my foot under the table and I tapped him back. It was hard to quell our laughter. At least no one blamed these little buggers on the wine harvest.

We were talked out or else perhaps the dinner would have seemed more novel. There wasn't an idle moment with François, and with all of the note taking and information processing, my brain was fried.

"I can't wait to be on our own tomorrow," I whispered as we were falling asleep.

"Me, too."

Pete had toyed with the idea of taking another shot at the mountains the next day but the weather was still dubious. Plus we had another program to follow and were expected at Saint-Jean-Pied-du-Port in the Basque country later in the afternoon. François had outlined a nice fifty-kilometer (thirty-one-mile) loop for us to do that day beginning and ending in the town of Salies-de-Béarn which passed through Orthez, Orion, Laàs and Sauveterre along the way. It would have been a perfect ride for me, but once again, the weather was not cooperating. Pete and I decided to take it in by car and arrived in Salies-de-Béarn in time to explore its labyrinth of old streets. Chocolatier Lavignasse won hands down as our favorite shop.

"I'm so glad you like chocolate," I said as I savored an espresso-imbued ganache that melted in my mouth.

"They're so good here—how could you not?"

"And they look beautiful, too. Look at how glossy they are—that's the sign of an exceptional chocolate."

"Maybe we should just pass on lunch," Pete suggested.

"Good idea. It's an unthinkable one in a country that never misses a meal, but it makes sense for us today. Plus I doubt I'll be hungry after all this sampling."

Instead, we ambled over to the baths for which this town is famous. Although most of the French check themselves in here for a cure of a minimum of eighteen days, we discovered that it was also possible to catch a quick soak and a massage more or less on the run. With the renowned waters here as salty as those of the Dead Sea and boasting an even higher mineral content, Pete and I were intrigued. But as we looked out onto the main bathing area at the center's array of *curistes* bobbing up and down like over-sized rubbery bath toys in this heavily salinated solution, we couldn't help but feel that this is the sort of communal experience for which you really have to be in the mood.

"What do you think?" I asked Pete.

"About what?"

"About going in. What'd you think–I was going to ask you about our relationship!"

He laughed and said, "No, I don't think it's for us."

"At least not today," I replied.

On we went past rows and rows of cornfields with stalks standing proudly (some ten feet tall) leading up to the fairytale-like village of Laàs. It was to be the corn festival here over the next couple of days, a festive, folkloric event that celebrates this little community's prized product: *le maïs*. How this part of France became known as the corn belt was unclear to me, but I could only attribute it to the weather for just as we approached Laàs, the skies miraculously turned brilliant blue and the sun shone brightly on the golden fields below.

Apparently no trip to this village is complete without stopping at Auberge de la Fontaine, a pretty corn-yellow and husk-green colored restaurant where chef Alain Darroze works his magic, often in the form of corn-based dishes. Beret-clad, and most welcoming in a very down-to-earth manner, this former chef to the late President Mitterand insisted that we try at least one of his *spécialités*. Lunch service had ended by now, but it wasn't too late to whip up *un milhassou*, a corn-based sort of flan, served warm with chocolate ice cream, chocolate sauce, and almond *tuile* cookies.

"Boy, this is good," I said to Pete as I lapped up every last trace of sauce.

"I can't believe you had all that after all the chocolate we ate."

"*Oui, je suis gourmande.* Plus you had some, too. Next time I'll have something more sensible—the chef's famous tomato salads made with six different types of tomatoes from his garden sound wonderful."

"Well, enjoy your sugar high," Pete teased.

"I'm sure you're sailing some, too, *mon cher.*"

Pete and I zoomed off to the Basque country guzzling liters of water and chattering about all that we had experienced in such a short amount of time. As the drive inched away from the Béarn and closed in on the *pays basque*, the rooftops slowly turned from dark slate to distinctive red tile. Soon virtually every façade was crisp and white, punctuated by doors, shutters, railings and exposed timbers painted in characteristic blood red.

"It's incredible how much the architecture changes in France," Pete said.

"Isn't it? You can say the same for the landscapes, the food, the light—everything. You drive an hour and a half and you see a whole different scene."

"I like the look here."

"Me, too. It's especially nice because you don't see any random dwellings that don't fit in. I don't see any Tudors thrown up here. People save them for Normandy," I added.

"That's because there's so much tradition in France," Pete replied. "If people threw up a different type of house here, they'd be thrown out of the village."

"I suppose you're right."

We were just about crashing from a lack of solid sustenance when we arrived at Les Pyrénées, an elegant Relais & Châteaux establishment in the charming town of Saint-Jean-Pied-de-Port. We had already heard great things about *la table* here, so we planned to experience it on the second night of our stay. After just a nanosecond of settling into our room, we passed diners commencing what looked like a magnificent feast. Crystal tinkled and silverware chimed as Pete and I discreetly ducked past the oh-so polished dining room on our way out the front door.

The rain continued to fall here, but having never visited this historic town, I was determined not to let it curtail my ability to glimpse at a couple of its centuries-old back streets. We were in search of a restaurant, some quiet place where we could delight in a modest meal and then turn in early. So I thought it best to check out a few different places in order to avoid falling into a tourist trap in this well trammeled destination.

"What are you doing?" Pete hissed. "Why are you looking around so much? Let's just go directly to the restaurant."

"Which restaurant?" I snapped. "How can you expect me to land upon the right one without having any indication as to where to go?" Clearly he had become spoiled with so many plans previously laid out for him. "What about the adventure of travel?" I insisted. By now, he must have been hypoglycemic or something because he was just acting like an ornery bear.

His outburst had upset me and I was angry that he had ruined the nice time we were having together. I felt that he didn't appreciate my efforts toward scouting out the right place for us. And it annoyed me that he seemed to have forgotten, too, that it was part of my work to size up a town upon arrival. I was pretty good about not lashing out at him, since I didn't want to further escalate our arguing. Instead I ended up leading him into the best bargain restaurant in town where we solemnly dined on a surprisingly good *poulet à la basquaise* and a local red wine.

By the end of the meal, I couldn't resist bringing up his bad behavior. "See, it all worked out," I said as we paid the bill. He knew I was referring to the upset we had earlier. I should have let it go. *Remember, if you don't want a tug of war, let go of the rope.* But somehow I hoped he'd give me an apology—or some kind of acknowledgement for having been impatient and unreasonable.

"Don't get me going," he growled as we walked out of the restaurant.

Despite the heart-shaped bathtub and the crisp floral Porthault linens at our fine hotel, our moods didn't improve much the next day. It was still rainy outside, a situation that seemed to augment our dampened spirits by the hour. *Is this why he had become such a crank? I thought everything was going well.* Pete logged some major TV time, while I attempted to bang out a few pages on my computer. Finally, it was time for lunch and we were once again confronted with the question of where to go in this touristy town. I made a tentative attempt to peruse a menu or two before Pete became upset with me again. "Let's just go here and not make a big deal out of it," he barked.

Not surprisingly, I ended up eating the worst *piperade* of my life in the most smoke-filled café you could imagine. Tears began to roll as I embarked upon a discussion of our relationship and our frequent inability to understand each other.

"Oh, c'mon, let's not go there," Pete clipped, completely invalidating my feelings.

We headed back to our room to suit up for a ride along the Vallée des Aldudes, rain or not. As though God's grace was cast upon our shoulders, the sun began to shine as we pulled into Saint-Etienne-de-Baïgorry, just a short scenic drive from our base of operations. With our civility toward each other improved, we ventured about exploring this authentic little town, taking in the sounds and sights of a region that doesn't quite seem French, or Spanish, but rather an odd assemblage of the two. In a dusty, old hardware store of the post-war genre, we discreetly observed an elderly man conversing with a young fellow in Basque, a language unlike any other existing tongue and which is spoken with spitfire rapidity with nary a single word comprehensible to my ear.

Now that the sun continued to shine both figuratively and literally, Pete and I settled into a nice bike ride alongside the river in the Aldudes Valley. The rain had drawn out all the dampness of autumn; a rich, earthy smell permeated the air and big, spiky, brown chestnut shells the size of tennis balls littered the roadway creating a mini obstacle course along our path. Huge expanses of dried, brown ferns enveloped the hillsides, a pleasing fall scene that prompted me to think of how lush these slopes must appear during the summer season. The dead silence of the valley was interrupted only occasionally either by the passing of a car or the ringing of bells around the necks of the sheep grazing high above. Our little climb on the way out was rewarded with a largely freewheeling descent on the return.

"How about we stop to take a picture on the bridge?" I asked. Pete responded by dismounting from his bike but he didn't seem too happy about the idea.

"Yes, right there close to that Basque house. The one with all those hams hanging on the porch." Pete positioned himself where I indicated with a snarl on his face. "Great, I think I can even get that mystical castle in the distance."

"Will you take one of me now?" *Damn, I hate this walking on eggshells bit. This guy has no patience.* "I suppose we can't hang around to see if someone might be able to take a picture of us?" I ventured.

"No, let's get on with the ride."

Well, would a little picture taking prevent us from doing that? Still, I hopped on my bike as fast as possible in order to avoid any more conflicts.

After loading our bikes up at Saint-Etienne-de-Baïgorry, I thought we would stop in at the recommended gourmet food shops on the trip back. Pete agreed to stop at Laurent Petricorena, the famous Basque restaurant and food shop, but insisted upon waiting in the car.

By the time I exited with my nearly one dozen bottles of special hot sauce (not a very practical, easily transportable purchase), he was once again fuming mad. "What took you so long?" he shouted.

"I took some notes and bought some souvenirs," I replied as calmly as possible. *I've had enough of his impatience. I thought he was partly on this trip to support my endeavors.*

"It shouldn't take you that long!" he hollered with his face all screwed up and his eyes darting wildly.

"What are you—my keeper? You're nuts—I can't believe you're acting this way. You're going to therapy as soon as we return home!"

I bellowed. *Clearly the wrong time to bring up such a request. Plus, you didn't phrase that like a request, Maribeth.*

"That won't be necessary 'cause it's over between us!" Pete countered.

"Yeah, well I wanted to end it back in Provence—when you ditched me in Roussillon. Maybe you should just go home."

"You know darn well I didn't ditch you in Roussillon. Are you still beating that dead horse? You're unbelievable," Pete said as he finally put the key in the ignition. "Maybe I should go home," he mumbled as we drove off.

We rode home in silence. My head was a swirl with all kinds of crazy thoughts. *What was his problem anyway? Is this just about miscommunication or is it something greater? Did he mean it when he said he wanted to break up with me? How could we leap from bliss to such a cauldron of nastiness? We'd had three ugly episodes within the past twenty-four hours. What was he thinking? Should we break up? And then where would we be? Where would I be? My hopes for having a child with a wonderful man would certainly be dashed.*

Then finally a lightbulb turned on and I realized that Pete was feeling too much under my thumb. *Maybe he's feeling controlled by me. Yeah, that's it—he's hung up on the control thing, the power struggle. I know I sometimes press his buttons. Well, he certainly presses mine. Blowing up over hot sauce—how ridiculous is that? He must not be in touch with these feelings or else he would find a healthier way to express them.*

We had been traveling together for more than three weeks by now and were not having enough time apart. If I wasn't setting up the itinerary—intentionally or not—someone else was doing the job. *He needs to establish his own time frame—I get that. I guess I should just be more aware of it. He needs to climb a mountain. He needs to challenge himself. Yes, that's it. Enough of the froufrou boutique hopping and sightseeing. Pete needs to strike out and do some real guy stuff on his own.*

Miraculously we were finally able to work out the vagaries of love back at the hotel in the glorious heart-shaped bathtub. Our chemistry—our physical attraction toward each other—seemed to pull us back from the brink every time. Thank goodness we had that going for us. As we creamed and caressed each other, we promised to change our ways.

We dressed in our finest clothes and sauntered downstairs for dinner as though all was right with the world and us. Surprisingly people were dressed rather casually for such a high-stepping restaurant, a general *laissez aller* that we noticed throughout all our travels. And here, it seemed as though we were the only Americans. We felt simply dashing anyway and more importantly, were sure that our presentation paid proper homage to the restaurant's distinguished chef, Firmin Arrambide.

Known to be the finest restaurant in the Basque country, our meal at Les Pyrénées showcased numerous sensational products of the land. Stuffed red peppers *à la morue* (cod); grouper in a lemon, butter, garlic and parsley sauce; and filet of duck served with roasted fig, apple purée, ginger fig purée and prunes stuffed with foie gras tantalized our tastebuds with an increasingly progressive intensity of flavors. A different Irouleguy—the appellation of local wine that includes the smallest number of vineyards (and tiniest production) in all of France—accompanied each dish. We particularly delighted in a white from Domaine Brana, a fresh, slightly lemony-tasting wine that enhanced the fish dishes exquisitely. Service here was very professional and happily more relaxed and friendly than usual for such a highbrow establishment.

Our conversations at dinner touched on a variety of subjects from whether or not we should eat the fig skins (we decided we could since Pete insisted that everything that is put on a plate is supposed to be edible) to cycling.

"Have we been to a flat region yet?" I attempted to recall.

"Alsace was pretty flat," Pete responded and segued into a whole sermon about my bike riding practices. "You need to raise your level," he continued. *As if I was not in touch with that tidbit of information.* "You should have been doing that this past summer. But I guess you couldn't since you were on deadline for your book. A fifteen-mile ride five times a week would be enough for you. Consistency is what's most important."

"You're right. I just wish I had more time to ride," I said.

"You've got to make the time."

Dessert arrived, a total of five *gourmandises* that—along with the little tray of pre-dessert cookies, candies and baby pastries—could have more than satiated a whole roomful of sugar addicts. Mini portions of orange soufflé, crêpes suzettes, raspberry-filled lemon *macarons*, chocolate tears and raspberry sherbet in a pastry cup were carefully placed before us, producing an over-the-top tableau created from the master pastry chef's vivid imagination. "This is gorgeous," I said to Pete. We sampled a little of each, vowing to put ourselves on a strict brown rice and veggies regime once we returned home. (As it was turning out, we were obviously gaining more pounds than losing them during what had become our gastronomic tour de France.)

As is often the custom, Chef Arrambide stopped by to say hello just as the coffee was served. A most genial man, he filled us in on the history of the restaurant and many of the lesser-known highlights of the region. It was a family affair since 1939, when his grandfather and grandmother started the business, and Chef Arrambide expressed his contentment that the tradition follows not only with him and his wife but also with his son in the kitchen and his daughter at the reception. Talk changed to the marvelous countryside just outside of Saint-Jean-Pied-de-Port, as Chef Arrambide waxed enthusiastic about the forests, lakes and chalets of Iraty.

"That area sounds pretty magical," I said to Pete back at the room. "Plus it's supposedly only thirty minutes east of town," I added as we both studied our handy Michelin map.

"Yeah, but the region looks pretty mountainous," Pete said as he pointed to the topographical characteristics of the map.

"It might be a bit of a stretch, but Iraty *almost* looks as though it's on the way to our next destination—what do you think?"

We greeted the next day with real vigor, excited about seeing a more remote part of the Basque country and our plans to travel to a whole different area by the end of the day. Plus, somehow, the dark cloud of dissension had been lifted from us.

"I think I could make one more attempt at the Col d'Aubisque early afternoon," Pete said. "That would be my last crack at it."

"By the looks of this map, it looks possible," I cheerily replied. It was Saturday, October 14, and the days were ticking by, so we thought we'd better make the best of the remainder of our travels.

As much as the day started out bright, we spied a huge mass of storm clouds clinging to the mountains upon our ascent to Iraty. Soon we were plowing through rain and fog even more treacherous than what we had encountered a few days previous on the way to the Aubisque. The vertiginous ascent was mostly marked with a gradient of 11.5 percent. It seemed as though we were off to the hinterlands. We were clueless about what was down (or rather up) the road. When Chef Arrambide talked about Iraty, we had no idea he was referring to such mountains. There was hardly a car on the road— thankfully—since much of the time there was only room for one car to pass. The hairpin turns were wicked, and after almost an hour driving, we kept wondering when we were to come across civilization again. Fortunately, there were many signs as we wended our way along the *Route du Fromage*. The signage indicated that cyclists were frequent travelers here, too, but, of course, on this day totally unfit for man or beast, not one two-wheeled wayfarer was encountered.

Finally, we passed in front of the charming little chalets that Chef Arrambide had described. All in stucco with slate roofs, each boasted freshly-painted shutters in either rust red, forest green, burgundy or cornflower blue. The tippy-top of Iraty painted a charming scene even during such miserable weather. The summit encompassed a large plateau dotted with poetic ponds and little meandering trails.

Conveniently, hunger set in on top of Iraty or else we may never have stopped at the area's lone restaurant where we delighted in one of the most pleasant eating experiences of our trip. As soon as we ducked into this little chalet, we knew that we were in for one of those rare, almost locals-only experiences. Hunters with hounds, hikers, Basque and Spanish families congregated here between the blazing fireplace and the rugby match that played on TV. All the tables were prettily set with the distinctively-striped Basque linens and a simple menu of *soupe paysanne, omelette au jambon, salade du jour, sandwich* and *gaufre* was displayed on the chalkboard against the wall. Pete and I were served a tureen of soup so big that we could barely finish it. Still, our affable waitress asked if we wanted more. Next we passed to a delicious tossed salad with an omelet chock full of Basque ham and *piperade*.

Pete and I were like two contented travelers that had had their first meal in days.

"Shall we top off this feast with *une gaufre?*" I asked Pete.

"What's that?" he quipped. "A little rodent?"

Our spirits were back. We passed on the *gaufre*—the waffle—and ordered up a couple of *cafés* to boost us for the remainder of the ride. All told, our bill rang in at way less than twenty dollars, large tip included.

"We'll be back again, Iraty," I said as we drove off. "And maybe next time, for a pedal or two."

It took about an hour to drive down the mountain; then more than another hour to navigate through all the rugged terrain that make up the foothills of the Pyrenees. Unrelenting rain accompanied us the whole way, forcing Pete to definitively abandon his hope of attempting a Pyrenees climb. As it was, we had totally miscalculated the amount of time it would take to travel to our next destination just outside of the town of Villeneuve-sur-Lot in the *département* of Lot-et-Garonne.

Evening was well underway by the time we pulled through the huge, wrought iron gate that marked the entrance of the Domaine de Clavié, the bed-and-breakfast where we were to spend the next few days. We cautiously rolled down the expansive gravel drive lined by a long alley of fruit trees. Two stunning Weimaraners, sleek grey specimens named Ixia and Igor, greeted us along with their hosts, Georges and Marc, as we pulled up to this massive and impressive home.

All the weariness from our day of traveling lifted as I entered this luxurious sanctuary of repose and fine living. Every inch of this beautiful home was handsomely decorated with lush fabrics and antiques. A host of collectibles of extraordinary quality shimmered within glass showcases and atop fine furnishings throughout. After checking into our stately suite, resplendent with heavy draperies and thick, cream-colored duvets, I flitted around our immense marble bath for a cursory freshening up.

Dressed with crisp Basque linens, fine china and sparkling crystal, the table—along with the room in which it is situated—looked as though it had been primed for a Merchant-Ivory production. An abundance of glowing candles highlighted this dramatic scene and Pete and I felt near giddy as we sat down with our hosts in such a privileged setting. Marc had prepared a lamb confit, a succulent piece of meat served with baby carrots and cloves of garlic that had cooked seven hours. Over much good food and wine, we talked about my work, our cycling and their lives. Georges revealed that parts of this *bastide*-like residence date back as far as the fourteenth century. (*Bastide* refers to a fortification—usually in the form of a village—built during the Middle Ages.)

Part of the recent history of the Domaine du Clavié, however, is centered around its plum orchards. First introduced here in the seventies, these fruit trees not only look stunning on the property but also generate income. The area surrounding Villeneuve-sur-Lot is after all plum—or rather prune—country. Prunes from this part of France, called *pruneaux d'Agen*, are considered among the best in the world.

By now it was time for us to retire to the red *salon* where we relished a delicious homemade plum eau de vie and listened to stories about traveling stills and fruit pickers. It was after midnight, and as I saw Pete give me a little wink, I looked for a break in the conversation to excuse ourselves. Thankfully Igor twitched and whimpered, indicating to our hosts that he was ready to have his collar removed and go to bed.

When Pete and I returned to our *grande chambre*, we noticed a small plate containing three plump prunes placed on each of our bedside tables, a thoughtful touch that allowed us to indulge in one of the region's best specialties. Truly seduced by their glossy appear-

154

ance and chewy texture, these were indeed the best prunes I had ever sampled, sweet confections that resembled a healthy candy more than a dried fruit.

The rain didn't let up the next day. "It's raining throughout all of France," Marc announced at breakfast. "Parts of Italy and Switzerland are experiencing devastating floods."

We were rained out again, so we decided to travel around by car to the *bastides* we had planned to visit on our bikes. Before heading off, we chatted with Georges some more. He was delighted to see that Peter had taken a keen interest in his cane and corkscrew collections. Each piece possessed a story telling of eloquent times when form was emphasized more than function. Georges became even more animated when describing his treasures, supplying Peter and me with a kaleidoscope of information concerning the lifestyles and social mores of the people of centuries past and their high regard for beautiful *objets*. Definitely an eccentric, Georges fascinated us both by his vast knowledge of antiques and by his choice of over-the-top pieces. I loved the fact that Pete, a guy with so much brawn, could be so interested in collectibles.

After a dreary drive around the fortified villages of the area, we landed at a pizzeria in Monflanquin. It was hard to appreciate the beauty of this quaint, historic town under such dark skies but with a little imagination we were able to conjure up images of an animated village square and sun-drenched façades embellished with an array of potted plants.

"Let's head back and watch the World Championships of Cycling on TV," Pete suggested after lunch.

"That sounds like our best bet," I responded. "And maybe we can even do some laundry." We had expressed our need to Marc earlier that day to find a laundromat and he kindly offered us the facilities of the Clavié since he didn't seem to think we would find one open on a Sunday.

Fortunately, when we returned, only the housekeeper was home, so we freely loaded up three washers without feeling like much of a bother. (The use of the laundry room is certainly not part of the package at this elegant *demeure*.)

Pete and I settled into the TV room to watch the cycling. We decided to relax and make ourselves at home the way Georges had suggested. Pete sunk into an immense armchair while I positioned myself crosswise on his lap—all five feet ten inches of me!

The commentary on the *Championnat du Monde du Cyclisme*, which happened to be taking place in France, amused us immensely since the French commentators seemed to be far more uproarious than their American or British counterparts to whom we had become accustomed. There was practically no need for translation either, since most of what we heard seemed to include a lot of *oh-là-là, attaque* and *allez, allez, allez* or some variation thereof. The word peleton was pronounced *pleton* more often than not, which distinctly reminded me of my early days learning French when I discovered that so many words were incomprehensible because of the French gobbling them up. It was good fun and through it all I learned more about bike racing as Pete absorbed more French.

We popped our clothes into the dryer and headed out for a little drive around Villeneuve-sur-Lot. This felt depressing but we couldn't tell whether it was due to the inclement weather or the town itself. I was in search of a hot cup of tea, but sadly the only place we could find that would accommodate us was a stinky café. We ended up braving the smoke and actually had a bite to eat, since we knew we were on our own for dinner and that the day was already on the wane.

It was time to hurry back to the Clavié to reclaim our laundry. I was embarrassed to find that Marc, a very meticulous Swiss, had finished off most of the job and left a laundry basket full of neatly folded clothing upstairs in our room. The remainder was still drying downstairs, so Pete and I sheepishly ducked into the laundry room to round up our belongings so as not to further intrude.

With the rainy day and our chores behind us, Pete and I cuddled up in our room for a cozy night. We felt like real teammates by now—there's no doubt that we were in it all together through rain or shine, good times and bad. Our spats and full-scale blowups were becoming less frequent, and even when they did happen the repercussions didn't seem as great or last as long. Even the laundry project didn't spur as much consternation as it had in the past. I felt like we were learning to live more harmoniously with each other. Our explosions in the Basque country had already become distant memories. We were allowing much more room for forgiveness, growth and understanding.

Before we left the next morning, we decided to brave the drizzle and mud (Marc actually provided boots) to walk through the orchards. Here we were stilled by the peacefulness and the sense of order created by the precise plantings of the trees. It was truly a wonderful place for contemplation, and we reflected on the many interesting people we had met during our travels and how great it is to discover so many different places.

Now it was time to travel to our last destination in the provinces. In many ways we were ready for our trip to come to an end, particularly since the constant shuffling of our belongings and countless over-indulgences were taking a toll. We had, however, felt somewhat cheated with the cycling, mostly due to the foul weather of the past week, so we weren't quite ready to pack up our bikes. Pete and I also knew that it being mid-October, road riding back in upstate New York was coming to an end. This was to be our last chance for a memorable ride in the French countryside and both of us hoped we had saved the best for last.

The prospects looked glum as we drove from Lot-et-Garonne, past Bergerac and Périgueux to Brantôme in the north of the Dordogne (also known as Périgord). "Look at how hard it's raining," Pete complained. "Our chances for riding today are nil."

"Well, there's always tomorrow. We have one last day to pedal around France." Pete looked straight ahead and gunned it to pass a small van that was already going faster than the speed limit. *Oh boy,* I thought.

"Look at this fairytale-like town," I exclaimed as we entered Brantôme, a picturesque enclave largely surrounded by water. "It's even more exquisite than how it looked on the Internet. I read that it's dubbed the Venice of the Périgord. Isn't this romantic?"

"It does look pretty nice," Pete replied as we approached the most heartwarming spot of all, an old abbey mill where this seventeenth-century structure was transformed into an engaging Relais & Châteaux hotel and restaurant of superior standing.

"That's it, that's the Moulin de l'Abbaye. That's where we're staying," I said. Our hearts jumped when we drove up, and suddenly the idea of not pedaling off didn't seem so bad. "Look at this place, Pete. I love those window boxes with cascading flowers. The Brothers Grimm couldn't have created a more bucolic place."

Covered in ivy, this French blue-shuttered building juts out into the meandering Dronne river, just across from a spectacular sixteenth-century stone bridge. "There's the old abbey I also read about. It was founded by Charlemagne during the fifteenth-century—can you believe it?"

"If it weren't for all those Mercedes and BMWs parked out front, you would think you *were* in a different time," Pete added.

Although the mill no longer functions as in years past, the sound of rushing water from the adjacent dams and waterwheel reverberates throughout the property and beyond. We were delighted to have been given a room just above all these waterworks.

"Come here!" I shouted to Pete. I stuck my head outside to take it all in. "Feel that whoosh of water—I love the mist."

Pete laughed and scooped me up in his arms. "Let me kiss the princess then."

"Well, aren't you something! Yes, please do," I coquettishly replied as I batted my eyelashes. "Aren't I lucky to have such a handsome prince charming."

We laughed about our silliness and threw ourselves on the bed and made deep love. Best of all: We didn't have to worry about making noise since the din of the rushing water drowned out all other sounds. Finally it seemed that Pete had let go of the idea of going for a ride.

It became even more of a storybook image at night when Hollywood-style lighting illuminated the old moss-covered bridge in a sensational fashion. (Sure, they didn't have electricity way back when, but I imagined the scene showcased by lanterns.)

Pete and I could take all this in from the table where we were seated in the Moulin's restaurant. It felt as though we were in a movie and to further enhance the experience we sipped Dom Perignon, poured from the bottle that awaited us at our table. The entire dining room sparkled; sunflower yellow and French blue reigned supreme in a décor highlighted by Provençal fabrics and Monet's Giverny-patterned china. Dinner was, of course, first-rate.

As we passed through the sitting area on our way up to our room, we couldn't help but notice a couple of New Yorkers—perhaps friends—leaning outside of the window overlooking the rushing water below.

"This is unbelievable!" the man exclaimed in a heavy New York accent.

"Unbelievable? I'm living it!" the woman responded since she apparently was lucky enough to have her room looking out onto the water like ours. "Last night I had to ask Leonard (her husband, I imagined) to close the windows. It made so much noise it was worse than central air conditioning!"

Pete and I escaped to our room howling with laughter. "It's funny how that lady's experience sounded far less poetic than ours." I said, poking him in the ribs.

"Well, I doubt Leonard's getting the action I'm getting."

"You never know," I answered, with a wink.

It was true. With the still of the night, the rapidly running water below did create quite a stir. And that does matter when you're trying to sleep. So I decided to sleep with one window closed, the other open.

"It seems like the rain is tapering off," Pete announced the next morning. "One of the Americans downstairs told me that the forecast for the afternoon is good."

"How about we tour Brantôme this morning and ride outside of town after lunch?" I suggested.

"Sounds like a plan."

It ended up being a perfect fall day. The air smelled crisp and fresh after all the rain and the sun beamed brightly as if it was joyously celebrating its return. Pete and I suited up one last time and headed east per the hotel manager's directions.

"It's great to be out on the bike again!" Pete shouted as we sped off.

"Yes, I feel electric!" We were elated to be riding after too many days off. But I also felt a mixture of happy/sad emotions. "This is going to be our last real ride in France for a while," I yelled to Pete. He smiled back, however, I wasn't sure he heard me.

The first part of the ride disappointed us with too much traffic and road construction. "Isn't there another way?" I protested.

"On rides, sometimes you have to go through some tough stuff to get where you're going."

"That sounds like life in general," I shouted back. So we forged on and I kept my eyes fixed on the road. Each time a big truck charged by me, I shuddered, white-knuckling my handlebars and murmuring more prayers of protection.

At one point I looked up to see Pete pedaling up the road in front of me, studying the map, without his hands on his handlebars. *Oh, no,* I thought, *I never should have asked him about another route.* And just as I was thinking that, a big truck rounded the corner in an attempt to pass another vehicle barreling down in the opposing lane. "SweetieEEEEEE!" I cried at the top of my lungs and just in the nick of time, Pete let go of the map, grabbed his handlebars and veered off to the far side of the shoulder.

"Oh, my God—I saw *your* life flash before my eyes."

"Don't worry—that was nothing. Don't be so nervous."

Fortunately, we didn't have far to go after that before we turned off onto a quiet road that led us to the beautiful medieval village of St-Jean-du-Col. "Look at this scene," I said as Pete road alongside of me. "Check out that that old turreted-château. Did you know they call this the land of 1,000 châteaux? Wow, look at that

Romanesque church alongside that cobbled street next to that old stone bridge," I marveled. "Let's take some pictures."

We stopped and Pete willingly posed for lots of them—many with these marvelous highlights in the background. He even took some of me. Obviously something had clicked in our relationship. I think we were both learning to slow down and appreciate the moment. We were in no rush to go anywhere and since this was to be our last day of cycling in France, we wanted to enjoy every bit of it.

From here, we ventured off onto a great road—a real country road that alternately crossed through cultivated fields, meadows, forests and then more of the same. This was the ride we were waiting for, and to fully express my joy, I gave several rings of my little bell. Pete turned around with one of his wide grins and in that moment, I know I loved him more than at any other time. He turned back around and continued to ride a good ten to twenty paces ahead of me. I couldn't help but think that I'd miss that view of him. Just the thought of the curve of his back, his tight butt and the power within his thighs made me swoon.

My thoughts drifted to yesterday's lovemaking—wow! *Has he thought about that today?* I wondered. *No sense in asking since he's not one to talk about those kinds of things. Still, I'm curious about what he thinks about on the bike. Probably nothing.*

I began to feel nostalgic about our times together on the trip and also grateful that we had discovered a certain simpatico that seemed to be working. The terrain cooperated, too, for the hills rolled enough to keep Pete happy and me reasonably challenged. In all, we cycled twenty-six miles, a perfectly respectable distance for the last ride of our own tour de France.

The evening was spent lounging in the heartwarming comfort of our room. It was like staying in a luxurious French country house. "Let's just breathe all this in one more time before leaving for Paris in the morning," I said.

"Sounds good to me. I don't think I could take more Dom and foie gras anyway."

We were awakened by the boisterous quack-quack of the ducks below, a welcome sound that sure beat the annoying buzz of our travel alarm clock. They put on quite the show at breakfast, and we were delighted to be able to view their comings and goings from the huge picture windows of the dining room. "Breakfast here is as quaint as the other night's dinner was theatrical," I said to Pete. "If we didn't have such a long drive ahead of us, I'd sit here all morning and sip tea."

"Time for the fairytale to end," Pete clucked. "I've got a big drive to do and I need my navigator."

"Well, at least I'll always be Queen of France in your eyes," I teased.

"C'mon, your carriage awaits you."

Room With a View in Versailles and Not-So-Romantic Paris

It poured rain from the moment we left Brantôme all the way back to Paris. Pete and I were grateful that we had lucked out with yesterday's weather and ride. Out of all the thousands of cars we passed along the *autoroute*, we didn't spot one other that was transporting bikes. Clearly any stragglers from the huge influx of summer visitors had already gone home. The big vacations were over, for the most part, and *le beau temps* probably wouldn't fully return until next April. "Boy, am I glad I didn't bring my Serotta," Pete declared as we commented about the weather. "It really would have taken a beating—I was much better off with my Reghin."

"Well, I was happy having Bella along. And now when we're back home, we'll have that shared memory together." Pete looked at me as though I was cracked, and I just winked at him and said, "It's a girl thing."

Dropping off the car at Renault upon our return posed no problem and fortunately we were able to retrieve the bike boxes without too much of a search. The last thing Pete felt like doing was disassembling the bikes, but thankfully he tackled the job without much complaining. Renault had been very accommodating and we even learned that one of the employees had stored our boxes in her office during our travels. I mustered up all the nerve of a travel writer cashing in on perks to ask if she'd keep them (this time with the bikes inside) for another five days. Pete planned to swing back and pick them up on the way to the airport after our time in Paris. I their baggage room—I'm sure they receive all kinds of crazy requests all the time.

An unpleasant experience with a Parisian taxi driver should have served as a forewarning to what was in store for us in Paris. (I thought it was a good idea to make Paris just a quick stopover, then go relax in Versailles for a few days, then back to the French capital for some touring.) Despite the perfect directions I gave him, the driver growled about having taken the wrong streets to our hotel, the Hôtel Mansart, on the corner of place Vendôme and rue des Capucines. When we finally arrived at the designated address, he seemed to expect Pete and I just to jump out so he could run off to his next fare lickety-split. Of course it was still raining. Pete and I scurried about as fast as we could to unload our four pieces of luggage, a couple of shopping bags loaded with souvenirs (namely hot sauce), and one extremely large and unwieldy box bulging with the research material I had collected during my travels. The disgruntled cabbie shouted some very rude (if not obscene) remarks to us just after he nearly wiped us out of our supply of euros for the the fare and the added surcharge for our baggage.

Pete and I ascended into our grand, high-ceilinged room and flopped on the bed. Suddenly it seemed as though all the loading and unloading of our car in the provinces wasn't so bad after all. At least we didn't have to deal with a surly cab driver and we always had more than adequate time to move our belongings. "Let's not have this ruin our time in Paris," I said. "Especially since it's so short."

This was the first time for Pete in the city of love and I wanted it to be special. It was up to me to keep us on an even keel since he was more of an outdoorsy kind of guy, the sort of person who sometimes becomes edgy in cosmopolitan areas. His uneasiness in cities was somewhat surprising since he lived the first five years of his life on Park Avenue in New York. There's no doubt, however, that he feels more comfortable surrounded by nature than by the hustle-bustle of a big city. I actually liked this about Pete, and that was a big part of what attracted me to him. But I could tell that this was going to put added pressure on me here in Paris and that it was up to me to make sure that all went smoothly.

"The size of the portions in Paris are much smaller than in the provinces," Pete said the next day as we lunched at Dalloyau, a stylish tea salon on the oh-so chic rue du Faubourg Saint-Honoré. "Dinner last night was pretty minimal, too," he added.

"I never noticed that, but I suppose you're right," I answered, savoring my delicious yet delicate *plat du jour*. "People here save hearty meals for the country. In Paris, everything is more refined." Pete rolled his eyes, so I said, "Why don't we order another dish to fill you up?"

"I don't want to be bothered," he said with a shrug. I could tell he was not satisfied, a situation that seemed to add to his growing disillusionment with Paris, something that unsettled me even though I understood his feelings.

We passed the rest of the afternoon strolling around the elegant streets and posh *places* surrounding our Right Bank hotel. It was nice but we couldn't help feeling like country bumpkins that had just rolled into the big city for the first time.

Being the expert Paris tour guide that I am, I lined up a *soirée* for us to captivate Pete with my beloved city's charms. Since it was already the third week in October, we were able to take one of the boat rides on the Seine (the Bateaux Mouches, of course) early in the evening and still have it be dark. This is indisputably the best time and best way to take in the majority of the city's attractions, as they are illuminated by both the monuments' spotlights and those of the boat. Pete and I ignored the damp chill in the air and sat on deck arm-in-arm and oohed and aahed over the sites. Pete was in awe of the grandeur of Paris and the dazzling views that this boat ride offered, and I was breathing a sigh of relief.

The tour ended just in time for us to run over to the Bar des Théâtres near the Pont d'Alma on the stately avenue Montaigne for a bite to eat. I had arranged for us to take in a show at the Crazy Horse, the sexiest cabaret in town, located next door. I'd hate to think that the best part of our entire trip in France for Pete was the couple of hours we spent at the Crazy Horse. That could very well be the case, though, since I don't think I ever saw him so fixated on anything other than perhaps the TV during a mountain stage of the Tour de France. As the curtain went up on this world-renowned show, he went completely bug-eyed.

"They're beautiful—aren't they?" Pete just nodded as he took in this lineup of ladies that marched, pranced and undulated across the Crazy's tiny stage. I was in awe as well, mesmerized by this bevy of beautiful women all scantily clad save for a few well-placed embellishments. Titillating, yet most tastefully done, is the best way to describe the performances at the Crazy Horse. Taking your mate to this show is a gift that only a secure woman can give her man.

We ended up walking a great distance back to our hotel that night because, in typical Parisian fashion, there wasn't a taxi to be found so far after midnight. This could have been the crescendo of our very full evening had we been more warmly dressed and had I been wearing more comfortable shoes. Our plans to celebrate our light and love back at our room in our own intimate manner fell by the wayside by the time we finally reached the front door of our hotel. We both fell into a pile on the bed and Pete zonked off to sleep instantly. We had opened the big, six-foot tall windows before we crashed, hoping that the fresh air would help us to sleep better. I tossed and turned intermittently throughout the night. Clearly I had imbibed too much and that, combined with the balmy fall night and the traffic noises below, was interfering with my night's sleep.

Neither of us was very fresh in the morning. "I feel bloated," Pete said, placing particular emphasis on the "o."

"Me, too. It must have been all the booze. My throat is scratchy, too."

"All this wining and dining is getting to be too much."

"I know—I doubt this is how the riders feel at the end of their Tour de France. I guess we crammed too much into our stay."

"Too much, except for cycling." Then Pete caught himself and said, "But you did a wonderful job pulling it together."

"Why, thank you," I said with all the grace of an appreciative host.

By the time our car and driver dropped us off at the Trianon Palace in Versailles, the princely hotel where we were to spend the next couple of nights, I had developed a full-blown cold. I could tell that this was not your average *rhume*: I had been hit with a nasty bug and it was attacking every cell in my body. It was time to succumb. Enough of being on the go, this was to be a weekend of rest; if I had to spend it in bed, then so be it.

"Well, at least we have plenty of room to spread out," I said as I sized up our suite. "It's as big as Marie Antoinette's bedroom at the palace."

Pete nodded in approval. "Look, it has two TVs."

"That's good, since I have a feeling we might be spending a fair amount of time here."

I had lined up a couple of treatments the next day at the hotel's spa weeks ago, thinking some pampering would be good after our travels. "I think I can go, especially since I'll just throw on a robe and not worry about how I look."

"You're fine, Queen of France," Pete said jokingly.

"Will you take the appointment for the facial, so that I can have the one for the massage?"

"Nooooo—what do I want a facial for?" he answered. "That's your deal. I could really use a massage after all that driving."

"But I can't go with this puffy, cold-infected face. I'm almost feeling like I shouldn't be going to the spa at all."

"OK, all right, I get it. I'll do the facial."

"It'll be a new experience for you," I reassured him. "I'm sure you'll like it."

"I've had lots of new experiences this trip."

I was hoping that the massage and soothing atmosphere at the spa would bring me back up to speed. But in truth, I felt more wiped out than ever. Pete loved his facial.

"Why don't you amble over to the château on your own? You don't have to do a full-fledged tour—you can just take a look around the grounds."

"Nah, I don't feel like it."

"C'mon, you feel more comfortable in France now. Just venture out and see Versailles." He was content to hole himself up in the suite with me despite all my sneezing and blowing. I'd like to think that it was because he wanted to be there for me but he wasn't much of a nursemaid. *It's too bad that even after more than a month of travels together in France, he still wasn't ready to cut the apron strings. Unless on a bike.* Plus the selection of TV channels in our suite was so extensive, I don't think one of those girls from the Crazy Horse could have pulled him away.

At one point I suggested we just sit and admire the glorious view from our window in our salon. The weather was once again drizzly and grey, but it was extraordinary to take in such an expansive vista across such a stretch of beautiful lawn. Green and fertile, the grass blanketed the grounds like the most impeccable fairway you could imagine. Upon this verdant plane stood numerous perfectly trimmed trees, many of which were hundreds of years old.

I flirted with the idea of cycling around Versailles Sunday morning as we had planned. They rent bikes there and I thought that would be a near-idyllic way to complete our own tour de France. But it was out of the question, since I barely had enough strength to deal with my luggage situation yet again. I was feeling better, though, and as we checked out of the hotel, I breathed a sigh of relief upon thinking that I had left the worst behind. Maybe now Pete and I could share a romantic time in Paris before he left for the States in a few days. (I was going to stay on a while longer.)

"I'm feeling kind of out of it," Pete mumbled as we were piling into the car to return to Paris. He looked ashen.

"I hope it's not your turn."

We both remained quiet on the ride back into Paris, feeling far from rested after our weekend in the country.

"You'll see—we'll have a nice time here," I said as we drove down a street lined with chestnut trees and marked by Paris's renowned, greyish-beige buildings in *pierre de taille*. "There's no itinerary—we can just do whatever we want. There are wonderful gardens here, too. We can stroll through Les Tuileries and Luxembourg. Wait 'til you see them. Let's just do lots of walking and spend long moments in the cafés. There are no meals planned. If you want to go to the Eiffel Tower, we can do that , too," I trailed off as we pulled up to our hotel.

We checked into the Hôtel d'Orsay, near the Musée d'Orsay. "Look at how large our room is here," I exclaimed. "It's much bigger than your average Left Bank hotel room."

Pete didn't express the same enthusiasm. "I'm getting a big headache, now, too," he moaned.

"We better head to a pharmacy," I said. "I'm in need of one, too, since I used up all my drugs over the weekend. All this stuff is costing a fortune." After inquiring at the desk as to the whereabouts of the nearest pharmacy, we learned that this being Sunday and this being France, only a few were open in the area. The closest one was at St-Germain-des-Prés, a good twenty-minute walk away, which normally would have been enjoyable had we both not been in such rough shape.

As we approached the designated *pharmacie*, we spotted a line all the way out the door and halfway around the block. I could believe it since I had lived eleven years in France, but Pete couldn't. "What's this, Russia?" he exclaimed, incredulous about the idea of having to wait so long to buy a supply of aspirin and vitamin C. "Let's just go to a supermarket," he added.

"It won't be any easier to find one of those open today, Pete. Besides, they don't always carry cold remedies."

"What do you mean they don't carry cold remedies? They must have aspirin and decongestants—that's just basic stuff."

"You'd think, but they don't. On the other side of the coin, my French friends think it's strange that drugstores in the U.S. sell cigarettes." Still, Pete seemed annoyed at this crazy French way of life.

"How about I do the waiting and you find a place to sit?" I offered. He shuffled over to a bench with his liter of Evian firmly clenched in hand. The wait appeared interminable, and all my feverishness of the past couple days returned with a vengeance. I stood on one foot, then another, as people around me sighed heavily and tried to cut ahead of me on numerous occasions. Pete remained within view, and if ever I looked over at him, I would observe him making wild gestures and mouthing, "Hurry up!" An hour later, weakened and exasperated, it was finally my turn, so I placed my requests with all the efficiency of an army drill sergeant, charged the whole bundle of French remedies, and then quickly trotted out.

"What took you so long?" Pete yelled.

"Did you see all those people ahead of me? That's what took me so long. What did you think—I was sitting down eating chocolates?"

"I can't believe in a country as sophisticated as France you have to deal with this shit. I can't believe you have to wait an hour for cold medication. It's not a third world country."

"I know, I know. Even though I lived here a long time, I still forget that these kinds of things happen. I think I've chosen to remember most of the positives about France, but there was a lot of stuff I had a hard time dealing with when I lived here. Remind me to tell you later about the post office and supermarket dealings—I had some real go-arounds. Come to think of it, I once ended up in a full-on fight with the dry cleaner. Actually, that happened with two different dry cleaners. I've never had such battles in the U.S."

After a few deep breaths about all the aggravation, we headed over to the rue de Buci street market. "Let's just get something simple that we can eat back in our room," I suggested. "That's not very French but what can you do in view of our circumstances?"

Once back in our room, Pete just picked at the *tabouleh* and *jambon de Paris* (Paris ham), two of my favorite French take-out foods. We settled in to another night filled with CNN and a seemingly endless amount of channel surfing.

Shortly after we dozed off to sleep, I was awakened by a loud commotion in the bathroom. "Are you all right, sweetie?" I asked. Pete moaned, and I could tell he was not OK at all. He barely had the strength to crawl back into bed, and when he did he was shaking intensely, almost convulsively.

"I'm sooooo-ooo cold," he stuttered. And with that, I wrapped him in all the bed coverings, tucking in every part of his body but his face. He shook wildly and his teeth chattered so much I thought they'd crack. Instinctively I laid upon him, practically pinning him down, covering him with every bit of warmth my body generated. We laid there together for what seemed an eternity until he finally calmed down and fell asleep.

I felt well on the road to recovery the next day, but unfortunately Pete was still hurting. The next couple of days were spent nursing him back to health. Clearly both of our immune systems had been attacked and we were not strong enough to ward off our maladies. We had overdone it, big time. Thankfully, now we didn't have a schedule to keep. It's true that the Musée d'Orsay just a few steps away beckoned, but neither of us could fathom any touring at this point. My only excursions were to buy food and more drugs. Keeping housekeeping at bay proved challenging, since we always had the room occupied. Being sick away from home is never much fun, but we were in a comfortable place with each other, both literally and figuratively, and handled it well. I believe there is a reason for everything, and it seems to me that this situation proved to be a test of our love for each other. It's easy to be loving during a romantic meal, but it means even more when you can be loving when someone's ailing.

Pete left for the airport that Wednesday morning, still tired and weak and also nervous about how he was going to travel in such a state. He managed to pick up the bike boxes at Renault with the Airport Express shuttle that had picked him up at the hotel. The hotel, however, notified me later to say that Pete's knapsack, which he left on the van's back seat, was going to be returned to me. Aside from that little hitch, we both carried on separately, basking in the love we felt for each other. We may not have accomplished the goals we set out to attain during our tour of France, but we definitely achieved others.

We had grown much closer during these last five weeks and had shared more experiences together than we had ever imagined. Pete had delighted me in many unexpected ways and each day I felt my love grow for him. It's true that we had some real battles, but all in all, we were actually good companions. I felt as though the trip had been a success—not exactly how I had envisioned it, but a triumph nonetheless.

And best of all, even though I had a lot of work to do, I began to miss him just as soon as he left my arms.

PART TWO

Prelude to the Tour

"What do you mean you can't go?" I said to Pete.

"I just can't—I have too much to sort out here. I can't afford to just take off and travel around France again, even if it's just for a couple of weeks."

"But you promised. This is something you've always wanted to do—how can you miss out on this?"

"I just wouldn't feel right going," Pete replied.

I paused and tried to gather my thoughts. *I could sort of understand Pete not feeling comfortable about taking another trip to France, particularly since he was still trying to figure out what to do with his life, yet it still came as a shock. Did it have something to do with me? Was our trip last time not so special after all? Was I a pain-in-the-butt travel companion/tour director?* I contemplated asking him these kinds of questions but instead we just sat in Congress Park in the heart of Saratoga on the cool grass, painfully trying to figure things out. I thought about my book project and wondered how this would affect that—likely not well, even though I still wasn't sure what shape it would take.

"That's like filming a movie with a leading man and having him back out of the project two-thirds into production. Why did you wait 'til now to tell me this? It's early June and the Tour begins in a month. I was going to line up our tickets tomorrow."

"Because I knew you'd be disappointed. I didn't want to disappoint you. I guess I've been putting it off. "

"Well, I *am* disappointed. I really thought we were going to the Tour together. Not only do I want you to go with me, but I can't help but wonder how this will affect my book." Pete just stared blankly at

"We're only talking about two weeks," I said, half pleading. "You know I want to write a book about our adventures, and you *and* the Tour de France are a big part of that."

"I'm sorry, I just wouldn't feel right going. I need to sort things out here."

I couldn't believe this turn of events. I couldn't help being annoyed with Pete. He had months to figure out what he wants to do with his life. I just wanted him with me in France—one more time—for only two weeks. And emotionally, I felt abandoned, almost the way I did on top of Roussillon in Provence. A big part of me did understand where Pete was coming from; I realized that he wasn't in a position—mentally and otherwise—to fully enjoy such a trip. But didn't he have a sense of how important this was to my work and me? Couldn't he just put his feelings aside for a couple of weeks? I was not asking him to go for a root canal. Attending the Tour de France was a lifetime dream of his.

We had talked so much about the Tour during our cycling adventure around France that we knew we would have to return to see it for real. Watching this great race on TV wouldn't suffice; Pete and I itched to become a part of it. Our shared passion had become the Tour and we both were hoping to attend it that following July. In many ways it felt as though we had only experienced half of the journey that we were meant to take together; the other half was to occur on the sidelines of this world-famous bike race. Plus we felt like it would be another step toward strengthening our relationship.

Our initial month-long odyssey in France did take us to a different level. But our lives were unsettled and we both had some issues to work out, individually and as a couple. We knew that until we addressed them—or at least learned to live with them better—we'd still keep butting heads with each other and our future would be uncertain.

Our close-quartered living situation in Saratoga didn't help us much—what a recipe for disaster. Our couples counselor—who we did see for a short while—called it a set-up. Within the confines of my tiny Victorian apartment, there was little room for Pete to do his guy thing, which typically included dropping and draping his clothing and gear throughout. As much as I tried to make him feel at home, he couldn't help feeling out of place in such fussy surroundings. He didn't have any of his own space and it was impossible to create some for him. So I suppose he tended to be even messier than usual, a vicious cycle that irked me even more. Even though we shared much closeness and were formulating our own version of partnering during this time, I think he sometimes felt like an intruder.

In the months following our big trip to France, Pete was even more unsettled with his life. He didn't know what he wanted to do or where he wanted to live, two minor details that prevented us from moving forward together. Yet he was pretty set on wanting to live out West. He made plans to test out Montana for a while, which I fully encouraged. The great American West held a lot of allure for me, too. But I was not yet ready to make such a move. I knew I could do it anytime, since as a freelance travel writer, I could work from anywhere.

So it made sense for Pete to scout out the possibilities first. Fortunately, we both felt confident enough about an eventual future together for such plans—along with an impending separation—to feel right. It was going to be another test for us. Pete and I had planned to spend a month in the Rockies and were hoping to leave early February, about three months after our first trip to France. Kitty, my much adored black-and-tan tabby—and also the most tangible reminder of my previous life in France—died suddenly from a brain tumor a couple weeks before we were to leave. Being one to read something into almost everything, I couldn't help but take this as a sign, perhaps one of change. (My personal mantra over the years had become "through pain comes transformation.")

Pete and I ended up spending a few weeks together in Bozeman, Montana. We were happy to find ourselves back in our travel companion mode after having been sandwiched in in Saratoga for the last few months. We had a fun time overall and became convinced more than ever that the West was where we wanted to be— we just didn't know where.

Then, as planned, I left Pete in Montana. I hugged him tightly goodbye, wishing him well on his new journey, quietly praying that we would come together at a later date at some mutually agreeable new frontier out West. So many uncertainties. I swore to myself that I would carry on with my own life while he attempted to seek opportunities and work things out on his own. This proved to be a challenge, for I did miss him greatly. Throughout this period, we both tried to trust that we'd be together again soon. We just didn't know where, when and how. But one thing remained certain, we both hoped to attend the Tour de France together that following July.

Pete returned to Saratoga for a visit May 1 and never left. We still hadn't formulated plans for living out West, but we knew it would work out. We just didn't want to rush into anything. I guess we viewed our relationship the same way, however, with that, I felt more pressure. The baby thing still weighed heavily on me and I had hit the eleventh hour of that clock.

At least we were moving in the right direction, or so it seemed. Throughout all this uncertainty, I could at least hold on to one constant, which was that Pete was going to accompany me to the Tour de France that summer. Now that he had cancelled out on that, I couldn't help but question our whole relationship. Clearly Pete had commitment issues.

I let a few days pass, thinking he was going to come around, and then finally had to reserve my flight and follow through with the rest of my plans. By then, I had adopted a to-hell-with-him attitude and was determined to have a great trip on my own. I wouldn't need him this time to drive a car or handle Bella as I would be traveling by train and renting a bike. His company would be sorely missed, but I was still miffed about being shunned. To me, his decision not to go was a rejection of sorts. I tried not to take this to heart since I suspected his decision was more about his stuff than mine. *Maybe he didn't feel worthy of such a trip. Maybe it was too much for him to take another once-in-a-lifetime trip for the second time in less than one year.* Unfortunately, he was the Tour de France expert and I knew that without him, chances were great that I'd miss out on many wide and varied aspects of this marvelous event. *Oh, well.*

By the time I was to depart for my travels, we had come to an understanding. There were no hard feelings; Pete sincerely wished me a good trip as I expressed my desire for him to have a productive stay at home. We kissed each other goodbye, once again stating that the time away would do us good.

I was to stay just short of a week in Paris before meeting up with the Tour at the beginning of the second week of *La Grande Boucle* (the big buckle or loop). I arrived in Paris on the first official day of the Tour, the day after the prologue. For the first time in my numerous trans-Atlantic crossings, my travels were impeded by a circuitous route through London from Boston, and my luggage didn't arrive. It was late afternoon by the time I arrived in my hotel—the delightful Hôtel Lutétia on the Left Bank. I was so weary that I just decided to don the plush bathrobe that was provided and crawl into bed. Coverage of the Tour on Eurosport kept me entertained throughout the evening, and I felt proud of the fact that I didn't experience one inordinate pang for Pete.

Most of the rest of the next morning was spent checking in with a variety of contacts—both professional and personal—in order to properly plan my week in Paris. I was cooking now. I had lived well over a decade in Paris—this was my turf. It didn't take long to notice the freedom that my independence provided; I also felt relieved that amid all this planning and appointment making, I didn't have to consider someone else's schedule.

There was one hitch, but I consoled myself in knowing that even if Pete had been here, he wouldn't have been much help. My luggage still had not arrived, a situation that was becoming increasingly aggravating since it was not only the first week of the Tour de France but also couture week in Paris. Prized invitations for the Hanae Mori Haute Couture show that afternoon had been delivered to the Lutétia for me and I was determined to make an appearance. I was preparing myself to go out and shop for a little something to wear when I learned that my bags had been found and would be delivered to the hotel by noon. I praised the Lord, since that sort of forced shopping often leads to spending too much on things you don't really need.

It was close to 1 p.m. when the concierge telephoned with the news that one of my bags had been delivered. I thanked him since he had already devoted a lot of time to tracking them down. I crossed my fingers that the right suitcase had arrived. I felt instantly disappointed when I spotted my sporty black duffle bag, knowing full well that it contained my assortment of cycling attire and that the chances of finding something presentable for an haute couture show within it were slim. Not to be defeated, I showed up less than an hour later at the show, sporting the same rumpled attire—save for a few additional baubles—that I had worn for more than twenty-four hours during my travels.

It worked, and through it all, I couldn't help but attribute this new sort of personal empowerment to the boost in self-esteem I received from cycling. Several years before, I know I would never have dared to attend such an event in such a less-than- polished manner, however, sports helped me to develop a seize-the-moment attitude that makes so much more seem possible.

The rest of my week in Paris remained full of contrasts. My major suitcase finally arrived, so I was able to bop to my appointments and special social engagements in proper Parisian style. The whole time, though, part of my mind remained preoccupied with the Tour. I found myself juggling my schedule to be able to race back to the hotel for special Tour coverage. My daily read of the *International Herald Tribune* captivated me with both Samuel Abt's articles on the Tour and Suzy Menkes's pieces on the couture shows. This was an interesting time for me, a short week where my passions collided. My interest in cycling and the Tour de France was doing circles around my familiar Parisian persona. "What happened to you *en Amérique?*" my French friends laughed and teased.

"I've grown a whole new me," I learned to reply.

Shortly after I arrived, the weather turned from blazing hot to bone-chilling cold. It's almost impossible to be prepared for this sort of Arctic blast that sometimes blows into Paris in the dead of summer—unless you happen to have been traveling in Scotland first and stocked up on woolens. I tried the old layering trick but soon found out that several T-shirts, a summertime sweater, and a shell were by no means adequate in dealing with the cold and rain that this particular week of July produced.

By July 14, I changed hotels and moved over to the Warwick, just off the Champs-Elysées, a prime location for trotting over to the Bastille Day parade. I attended the huge military *défilé*, honoring France's *fête nationale*, for the first time. (This, like attending the Tour de France, was considered rather low-class by my French husband and others that were part of our world at that time.) Thankfully, the front desk at the Warwick handed out large umbrellas to their guests in an attempt to prevent them from being totally rained out for this big event. I was thrilled with this spectacular show of French pomp and circumstance but by the time the last cavalcade passed, I was drenched.

The rest of the day was spent wrapped in the creamy luxury of my room at the Warwick, nursing a nasty cold that came on as swiftly as the change in weather. After a hot bath, I tucked myself into the soft sheets for an afternoon of television viewing. It was an exciting day for the Tour since France's darling, Alain Jalabert, claimed the stage victory. The French cheered him on ecstatically and the win seemed doubly important since it was Bastille Day, France's version of our Independence Day. By now, I yearned to be at the Tour. I'd had enough of the crowds and craziness of Paris, I just wanted to be out in the provinces again, perhaps do some cycling, and most of all, be a part of this stupendous sporting event. Thinking about all this and being under the weather made me miss Pete for the first time since I left home. As much as I tried to resist, I called him. (He had my itinerary with all my numbers, so he could have called me. But I couldn't help making the first move.)

"Did you see Ja Ja?" I asked.

"Yeah, that was great. It's always nice when a Frenchman wins the stage on Bastille Day. Doesn't always happen. So, how are you doing without me, sweetie?" Pete asked coyly.

"Oh, fine." I filled him in on all my activities and then said, "I do miss you, though."

"I miss you, too."

"So what have you been up to?"

"Oh, working at the shop," Pete responded, referring to his job at the bike shop, which he had resumed. "Getting in a lot of riding, too."

"Oh, that's nice."

"Yeah, some really good rides." We chatted more about our doings. The conversation was nice and I was sincerely happy that he was making the most of his freedom, spending more time out on the bike.

"Well, I should go. This is probably costing a fortune. Enjoy your time to yourself."

"I will—you, too. Love you."

"Love you, too." I couldn't help thinking about our travels together last time in France after I hung up. But then I realized that I'd better nudge myself out of such melancholy. There was no sense feeling forlorn with such an adventure ahead of me.

Alpine Adventures

Finally, the day came when I was to shove off to the provinces. My good health had been restored and the sun shone brightly once again in Paris. It was Sunday, July 15, and I was on my way to the Tour de France, the three-week-long bike race widely considered to be the world's most challenging sporting event. I stocked up on cycling magazines at the kiosk at the Gare de Lyon, the train station where I would board the high-speed train, or T.G.V. (*train à grande vitesse*), that was to whisk me off to Aix-les-Bains in the Alps. It felt great to finally be able to focus all my attention on the Tour. There was much to read up on, for I was still such a neophyte about the Tour (and cycling, I suppose). I needed to debrief myself.

With the help of my Guide du Tour from the magazine, *Cyclisme International*, I was able to trace the three-week, twenty-stage (plus the prologue) odyssey that would make up the 2001 Tour de France. The route changes every year but one thing remains the same: it covers more than 2,000 miles on its grand circuit around France, traversing precipitous terrain throughout, especially in the Alps and Pyrenees. Truly a unique international competition, the Tour generally slices through at least one neighboring country (this year Belgium), in addition to traveling through many different parts of France, big and small. Twenty-one specially selected teams from countries such as Italy, Spain, Germany, the Netherlands, the United States, and, of course, France receive invitations to attend the Tour based on their particular standing for that year. Each team counts nine members, or cyclists, from countries as far-reaching as Lithuania and Australia, along with their European and American counterparts.

I was beginning to really get that cycling is a team sport. Of course there are many stars such as Lance Armstrong, Jan Ullrich and Erik Zabel, but even these cyclists achieve their results with the help of their teammates, also referred to as foot soldiers, lieutenants, workers and *domestiques*. A bit of studying of my Guide helped me to decipher many of the Who's Who of the cycling world, the colors they were sporting, their country of origin and their birth dates. Fortunately, Pete had also provided me with the Official Guide from *Vélo News* that furnished additional information—and a somewhat different perspective—in English.

My knowledge of cycling and the Tour grew tenfold as we sailed through the beautiful French countryside on this sleek train, this magnificent specimen of French technology that cruises along at an average speed of 186 miles per hour. Here I was on the fastest conventional train on earth zooming off to attend the most dynamic bike race on the planet. *Yippee—boy, do I feel exhilarated!* I couldn't wait to arrive but I also knew that as with most traveling, getting there is often half the fun.

Amid all the vacationers around me, I wondered how many of them were off to see the Tour. It mobilizes millions of people throughout the country every year in July, for it is not just a sporting event, it's a happening. It costs the Tour de France organization twelve million dollars to stage this three-week extravaganza but for the public, it's free. Towns pay approximately $75,000 to host a stage, money which in most cases is well spent, since it typically results in an enormous boon to their local economy. I thought about all this hoopla and I still couldn't believe that Pete was not right here with me, sitting by my side. Traveling is most fun when you share it with someone special. *Oh, well—I tried.* Fortunately I was not harboring any hard feelings—however, I did feel a little lonely from time to time.

I looked outside and my mood turned blue when I discovered that the skies had become dark and it had started to rain. Foul weather was forecasted for much of France, but I figured I shouldn't pay any attention to it since the French meteorologists are quite often wrong. *Double ho-hum.*

I decided to change my attitude and revert back to thinking only positive thoughts. I was full of anticipation and enthusiasm about attending the Tour, so there was no point in being dismal about being without my sweetie. My best effort was put forth upon arrival in Aix-les-Bains to prevent the torrential rain outside from dampening my spirits any further. There appeared to be only two or three taxis at the station ferrying travelers to their hotels, so I took a deep breath and patiently waited my turn until the first taxi I had spotted came around a second time.

I was half soaked by the time I was picked up and delivered to the Adelphia, the totally unassuming establishment where I was to stay for the next two nights. Known for its baths and healing waters, the city of Aix-les-Bains enjoys quite a large following of spa-goers and vacationers alike. As I checked in at the front desk, several bathrobe-clad people padded by me, a sure sign there was pampering afoot at this hotel. Without even bothering to unpack my toiletry kit, I changed into my bathing suit and headed for the hotel spa. The next hour was divided up between the sauna, the steam room and the pool, where I lolled for a while in a sort of underwater chaise lounge that magnificently massaged my body. Every inch of my back was worked on by scintillating, therapeutic jets.

I rested on the bed for a while back up in my room as is recommended, fully appreciating this unexpected opportunity to totally de-stress. It was wonderful to find myself in such a relaxed mode and timely because there was not much to do until the next day when my real program in the Alps was to begin. The rain continued to pour outside, so much so that I could barely see the view of the lake and mountains outside my window. It was a good night to stay in, particularly since I still had a lot of Tour coverage to watch for entertainment. I felt so tucked in that I was wishing I had picked up something to eat in town, or at least that the hotel had room service.

I mustered all the energy necessary and dressed and primped (just a tad) for dinner. Only a handful of people occupied the large dining room downstairs, and that, combined with the dreary weather outside, made me feel as though I was at a North Sea resort in the middle of winter. The home cooking was heartwarming here, so I just decided to go with the flow and accept everything that came my way. Just as I looked up from my daily note taking, I spotted a little flurry of activity outside. A couple of cars pulled up emblazoned with the Tour de France logo and several very official-looking men piled out of each of them. Up until that moment, the only indication I had that the Tour was to arrive here was from the television up in my room. This bit of scuttling about (it was still pouring rain) also seemed to have piqued the interest of the smattering of diners in the room, and all of a sudden I heard a distinctive buzz.

"Are you going to have people from the Tour?" I asked my waiter in French. "I mean people actually involved with the Tour—not just spectators?"

"*Oui et même des équipes.*"

So officials *and* teams were expected—I had all I could do to conceal my curiosity. Instead, I decided to play coy and said, "So, we're going to have some good-looking guys here."

"Yes, but they are less impressive in real life than on TV. They aren't very tall." And so my waiter continued to provide details of well-known cyclists he had encountered here in the past.

That night I returned to my room with a little bounce in my step. I didn't know what to expect but I sensed that life was going to perk up at this sleepy spa hotel. I watched the day's cycling on Eurosport, then drifted off to sleep listening to the rain still pounding down outside.

Corinne, my contact from the tourist board of the Savoie department, had arranged for me to do some cycling in the Alps. I had stipulated that my level was intermediate at best, so the big mountain climbs typical of the Alps were definitely out of the question. "There is some 'soft' cycling in the area," Corinne said. "I've even arranged a special guide for you."

Pierre Lortet, an affable and good-looking man wearing a flannel shirt and shorts, met me at the hotel in the morning. "You could see your breath early this morning and there was snow on top of the mountains," he mentioned right off. "But the day should warm up and be sunny. You should be OK with what you have on," he said as he assessed my light biking attire. Pierre hooked me up with a yellow bike, and after a small seat adjustment, we were on our way.

I couldn't have asked for a better guide; Pierre was a city planner who specialized in bike paths. "I obtained most of my ideas from Boulder, Colorado," Pierre explained. "We're in the process of applying many of them in France, particularly in this area."

I expressed interest in Pierre's work as we stood there exchanging pleasantries. Then I asked, "What about the cycling? I hope Corinne told you that I'm just looking for a mellow ride."

"*Oui, oui, oui, pas de problème*," Pierre responded. My heart winced since his good looks, demeanor and now *oui, oui, oui* made me think of Pete. (I also couldn't help finding it interesting that my new cycling partner in France was named Pierre, or Peter.)

The first four kilometers of our bike ride alongside Le Bourget (the longest lake in France) were plagued with rather heavy traffic, but soon we found ourselves cruising along the bike path passing in front of cornfields, the university and tech center and neatly arranged commercial spaces. It would take an average cyclist about two hours to ride this entire *avenue verte*, or green way, but we opted to cycle on only the part that led us into the pretty town of Chambéry.

We rendezvoused with Corinne here and parked our bikes to tour around the cheery pastel-colored buildings of the town. "This is where Greg LeMond won his world championship in 1989," Corinne informed me. "That event and the '92 Olympics in Albertville spurred many improvements here." As I looked around at all those old stones, I couldn't help reflecting yet again on the incredible richness of France and the quiet beauty of its towns of all sizes.

After a savory lunch at La Maniguette, a newly opened restaurant with a Provençal flavor, we loaded our bikes onto Corinne's car and raced to meet the ferry that would take us across the lake back to Aix-les-Bains. In all, Pierre and I had cycled some twenty kilometers (about twelve miles) in the morning, and although it would have been a better workout to pedal back, we decided not to in order to save time. (The Tour was rolling into Aix later on in the afternoon, so

I wanted to be sure not to miss it.) Pierre and I kissed Corinne goodbye, thanking her for her hospitality, and jumped on the ferry in a flash.

The sun beamed in a practically cloudless sky and both Pierre and I enjoyed this pleasant crossing, which marked a welcome pause in our day's activities. Little did I know that life over at Aix was frenetic with all the festivity surrounding the Tour de France. When I left in the morning, all was almost deathly quiet and not even the Tour people from the night before were anywhere to be seen. It was part of my plan to attend the *départ*, or start, from Aix-les-Bains the next morning. But it wasn't until Pierre came to pick me up that he informed me that the Tour riders would also be arriving in Aix, so I could catch the Tour then as well. Boy, did I feel stupid not having realized that myself. Fortunately we were able to work it out so that I could take in the arrival, too, albeit on my own since Pierre had other engagements.

Tour mayhem hit us as soon as we stepped off the ferry. I approached the crowd just in time to see a brightly painted car with a giant grocery cart brimming with mock groceries zooming by. The famous multi-vehicle publicity caravan that passes before the cyclists, warming up the crowd and distributing all kinds of goodies—useful and otherwise—was already passing through. It appeared that this over-sized shopping caddie was the last of the bunch. Suddenly I realized that I had to step on it if I wanted to make it to the finish line in time. I thanked Pierre for all his help and relinquished my little yellow bike to him on the spot.

Then it was time to run. It was not hard to determine in which direction but forging my way through the crowds posed more of a challenge. Finally I found my way to the information booth, where, although I wasn't expected until tomorrow, I introduced myself and requested a special *laissez-passer*. The small crew from the tourist office of Aix was most agreeable, granting me a pass that allowed me access to the grandstand near the finish line. Just as I inched toward the special VIP section, I heard people yelling, "*Ils arrivent, ils sont à quatre kilomètres.*" My attempts to find a choice seat were in vain, since no sooner did people announce the cyclists' arrival at four kilometers, than they blew right in with all the speed of thoroughbred racehorses. I had missed my special VIP seat but still it was all very exciting and fun being caught up in the frenzy of the crowd.

To my surprise, the spectators thinned out quickly. (I later figured out that they were probably trying to catch up with the cyclists.) This allowed me to weave through to the tribune where I took in the day's ceremonies. I had viewed this daily ritual of the Tour numerous times on TV but to sit there across from this colossal inflatable stage with all the media, Tour officials, local dignitaries and pomp was really a hoot. When the theme song of the Tour began to play, I knew it was time for the ceremony to begin, even though some riders were still straggling in. The backdrop, attendants and flowers changed with each jersey that was presented. First came the winner of that day's stage, then the yellow jersey for the overall leader of the tour, then the green for the fastest sprinter so far, followed up with the red polka dot for the King of the Mountains, or strongest climber, and the white for the best young rider. I was proud of myself that even without Pete, I could follow all these presentations. And what I knew so far also told me that Lance would be up on the podium soon and that there was no reason to sweat it; the Tour had barely begun. (Up until that point, most of the riding was on comparatively flat terrain; tomorrow would be the first stage in the mountains and that's when the real action begins.)

A mass exodus ensued at the end of the ceremonies and I edged my way toward my hotel which turned out to be only a short walk away. It was hard to believe that it was the same place I had walked out of earlier that day because as I approached, I discovered that it was swarming with activity on the outside. My jaw dropped when I saw the huge, sparkling U.S. Postal team bus parked alongside my hotel. And as I approached, I realized that was where much of the crowd had gone. People were milling around, gawking at the bikes being hosed down after a long day of riding and peering into the gathering of Postal team cars that were there as well. I wasn't sure whether or not they were expecting one of the guys to step out of the bus at any moment, but I approached for a closer look. Then I put two and two together and in my characteristic un-shy manner approached one of the bike technicians. "Is the team staying at the Adelphia, too?"

Jackpot! I couldn't believe my luck—to think that I was right in the center of this hubbub. I walked through the throngs of fans that had already gathered in front of the hotel with all the confidence of an actress on her way to the Oscars. Inside, the hotel was in full swing, busy with check-ins of the Tour entourage and various other goings-on. I was relieved to see that I was recognized as a hotel guest and scurried into the elevator. My plan was to retreat into my room to regroup a bit and then decide what to do and where to go. Perhaps I could bump into some of the guys downstairs at the spa. Or maybe I could meet up with them at the bar for a beer. *Nah,* neither of those places seemed very likely for super pro cyclists in the middle of an extraordinary endeavor.

As I padded down the hall to my room, I noticed a scale, a cooler and a bowl of boiled potatoes outside of a door. *That's strange,* I thought, and with all the gall of a *National Enquirer* reporter, I stole a glance beyond the open door and spotted a massage table set up and ready to be put to use inside the room. The plot was thickening.

On my trip downstairs to the hotel gift shop (a good pretext for strolling around), I learned that indeed the whole U.S. Postal team was staying on my floor—including Lance. Thankfully, I found the discretion to avert my eyes as I passed two towel-clad cyclists in the hall back up on my floor, presumably changing places at the massage table. (The only thing I did see was very pronounced tan lines.) Once again, I retreated to my room to regroup and to freshen up for dinner. *What's going on here?* I asked myself as I vacillated about what to wear to dinner and how to style my hair. *I'm acting like some sort of a teenage groupie.* I hadn't experienced such sensations since I crossed good-looking senior boys in the halls during my freshman year in high school. The difference here, though, was that I was now a mature woman—nearly forty years old—and these guys were at least ten years my junior! In the midst of all this adrenaline rush, it occurred to me, too, that I was quite involved with a man, although he now happened to be on the other side of the Atlantic, who remained very close to my heart.

Oh, well, I suppose there's nothing wrong with a little flirt. It keeps you alive, after all. But still, I couldn't help wondering what all this giddiness was really about. I had been around famous people before—including when Larry Bird once ended up at my Boston apartment—but never had these encounters provoked such emotion. I just shrugged my shoulders and chalked it up to the Tour and my excitement about cycling overall.

Like so many others, I wanted to say hello to Lance, to congratulate him, and to tell him he's such a remarkable inspiration on so many fronts. I remembered that Pete told me he had a house in the south of France with his wife, so I thought maybe he'd enjoy receiving copies of my books, *The Riches of France* and *The Riches of Paris*. Books in hand, I chatted with Lance's bodyguard (who boldly stood watch outside his door) on my way to dinner. He was most amicable and encouraged me to wait a couple of minutes for Lance to leave his room to give him my best wishes in person.

Suddenly, I felt shy and awkward. Then I said to myself, *oh, what the heck.* Lance emerged and greeted me with all the grace and friendliness of a well-respected diplomat. He was truly charming, and much to my surprise, expressed genuine interest in my work, congratulated me on my books and thanked me for the gift. When I asked him if I could have my picture taken with him, he happily obliged, repositioning us so as not to capture the unsightly *sortie* (exit) sign in the background. We headed off to dinner together and picked up a few cyclists from the team AG2R on the way down in the elevator. Our chatting more or less ceased at that point, we said quick hellos to the other cyclists, and rode the rest of the way in silence.

In groupie mode, I shamelessly asked the maître d'hôtel to seat me at the table closest to the two large tables occupied by the U.S. Postal team. Tonight the dining room was packed, but much to my good fortune, there was a little table close to them that was discreetly tucked halfway behind a pillar. As usual, I had my trusty notepad with me, so I didn't look hopelessly alone and idle sitting there in such an animated room. I did steal glances from time to time over at my celebrated cyclists' tables, but, honestly, mine were not more frequent than those of the other diners. It was quite a sight to see all those handsome men from the U.S. Postal and other teams, all freshly showered and neatly dressed in their team warm-up suits congregating around their dinner table after a full day out on the bike. The adjacent table was made up of the team manager, Johan Bruyneel, the assistants, all the *soigneurs* (or caretakers whose responsibilities include tending to the needs of the cyclists, from laundry to massage) and the rest of the support staff that accompanies the team to a different location every day of the Tour.

I had read in my cycling mags that each cyclist burns an average of 8,000 to 9,000 calories a day, part of which is consumed in the form of sugary treats and drinks out on the road. This makes dinner more important than ever, not only for the calories consumed, but also for the pleasure of eating a meal together, and the camaraderie shared. The team's own private chef, Willy, a Swiss, served up the courses in huge quantity, each one looking more delicious than the other. Salad, pasta, chicken with roasted potatoes and vegetables, strawberry tarts and yogurts were all dispensed in copious amounts along with bread and wine. *Yes, wine!*

The guys seemed to be focused on more than their food, however, and the mood overall seemed serious. They were doing their homework. I could see that they were studying graphs of the next day's race, and I could tell from a distance that there were many pointy peaks, which, of course, meant that it was going to be a big day in the mountains. It was the eve of the Alpe d'Huez stage, that infamous grueling chunk of the Alps that truly separates the men from the boys, the elite cyclists from the slackers. (There aren't any true slackers in the Tour de France, but everyone has a bad day at some point.)

Two other handsome and fit-looking gents dined at a small table on the other side of me. Former professional cyclist Steve Bauer was one of them and by the end of the meal, I had moved over to join him and the other cyclist in a glass of wine.

"So what do you guys do?" I asked after I told them my reason for following the Tour.

"I operate Steve Bauer Bike Tours," Steve said.

"What kind of bike tours do you organize?" I asked as I sipped my wine.

"We specialize in high-end tours for people to cycle along the actual Tour de France route. They also attend the stages."

"Wow, that sounds fun *and* challenging. I'd guess that's the perfect vacation for high achievers. If ever I went on such a tour, I'd need to spend some time in the support van."

We had some laughs and finished off the evening in the bar where most of the Postal staff, including Johan Bruyneel, had congregated. (The cyclists had already retired to their rooms.) The atmosphere was clubby, and in between sips of coffee, we shared our impressions of the day. Steve filled me in on some of the ins and outs of cycling and I chatted with Johan about my love of Belgian—his native land—France, the French language, my work and my new passion for cycling and the Tour. "I initially spoke French with a Belgian accent," I told Johan, a Belgian that grew up in a cycling-mad country. "When I was sixteen, I did an exchange with a Belgian girl from a French-speaking family in Antwerp and that experience had a big effect on me. I love Belgium—the people are really nice. "

"So why did you lose it?"

"Lose what?"

"Your accent. Now you just have an American accent," he joked. The mood was considerably more jovial than earlier, and I thought to myself that was probably the first time all day that most of them had a chance to kick back.

It was time to say good night, which was fine with me since I couldn't wait to call Pete and fill him in on the day's adventures. "Guess who I'm hobnobbing with?" I asked, bubbling over with excitement. "OK, so don't bother guessing. I doubt you'd guess right anyway," I said excitedly. "I'm over here hanging out with the cycling world's crème de la crème."

"Are you serious?"

"Yup, the hotel is filled with them. Right on my own floor."

"Jeez, that's pretty impressive," Pete said with all sincerity.

"Lance, too—the whole U.S. Postal team. I hung out in the bar with Johan and this guy by the name of Steve Bauer."

"I know Steve Bauer. He's Canadian, an Olympic medalist."

"Well, they're super nice and we had a lot of fun. What a riot! You can bet I'm playing the Queen of France card big time. *Journaliste américaine*, too."

Pete laughed on the other end of the phone. Sort of a nervous laugh. Maybe he was a little jealous.

"I can't believe you're missing this. You should come over— this is all too exciting to miss." I thought I heard a sigh. *Better not rub it in too much.* Plus he was at work and I didn't want to disturb him long.

"Well, goodnight, sweetie. I'll give you another update soon."

"OK, be careful," he cautioned.

"Will do."

In comparison with the night before, all was relatively quiet the next morning at breakfast. And when I did spot cyclists or members of the support staffs, everyone looked pretty serious. On one of my elevator rides I asked George Hincapie (a key U.S. Postal cyclist who is also tall, dark and handsome with large features—just my type) if he ever gets nervous and he admitted that he was the day of the team time trial. He looked fairly cool today, though. I congratulated him and a few of his other teammates on their accomplishments thus far, and they responded in unison, "We haven't done anything yet. But it's all going to change today."

"Just do the best you can," I replied in a motherly sort of tone. All of a sudden, I realized that they seemed young and nervous and I felt very old. *Where had all those years gone?*

"Good luck on the climb," I said to Lance and Johan before emerging from our own private enclave. Hordes of people had already gathered outside the hotel, enthusiastic fans eager to sneak a peek at these supreme athletes and their managers.   My special press pass entitled me passage into the large parking lot where all the team buses and media were assembled before the start of the race. One of the best parts about attending the Tour de France is it gives you the opportunity—even if you don't have a special pass—to be up close and personal with the 180-some cyclists participating in the competition. Not many sports allow spectators within such proximity of the athletes.

As I walked up, lots of riders were just pedaling into this sort of immense holding pen after having taken a little warm-up spin on their sleek riding machines. I couldn't stop likening them to jockeys on their mounts, particularly since most of the riders are indeed small, extremely svelte and ride with the fury of a thoroughbred yearling. Their brightly colored, synthetic jerseys and shorts reminded me of jockeys' silks as well. But still, with these thoughts, I couldn't help considering that no one—neither man nor beast—endures such pain as these riders in the three weeks of the Tour de France.

A cavalcade shimmering with all the colors of the rainbow charged by at the start in Aix-les-Bains. I yelled out, "And they're off!" But nobody around me seemed to understand. Everyone clapped loudly and we all felt a cool breeze on our faces as they blew by. A whole motorcade of support vehicles and motorcycles trailed behind them, and in less than ten minutes, *le départ* was over. Yet it was just the beginning of the six to eight hours that the cyclists would spend in the saddle that day.

I felt a big letdown after they all left although I consoled myself with the idea that I'd be meeting up with the Tour again three more times. Still, I found it unlikely that I'd be lucky enough to stay in the same hotel as the U.S. Postal team a second time. I realized that what I'd experienced yesterday could be classified as a once-in-a-lifetime adventure. These thoughts eventually led to Pete, and, as I packed up my belongings in my hotel room, I couldn't help thinking that it was a shame that he wasn't here to share in all the Tour fun. The rest of this picture-perfect day was spent sunning on the beach of le Bourget, reading and occasionally wondering how the race was playing out in the mountains.

It was a race for me, too, at the end of the day to find my way to the station to pick up my train for Grenoble. The taxi finally arrived, and as I sat down on the back seat, I could hear the radio blaring with the commentary of the race. "What's happening?" I asked the driver in French.

"*Ça va être Armstrong.*" We both listened as Lance crossed the finish line solo at Alpe d'Huez, a good two minutes in front of Ullrich. He was the leader of the Tour de France for a third time; he'd now be wearing the coveted *maillot jaune*. I guess the guys did show their stuff. I looked at my watch and it read 5:08 p.m. They had left at 10:30 a.m. I suddenly felt guilty that I had spent the whole day on the beach.

The lobby bustled with activity at the Hôtel Europole in Grenoble when I checked in. There seemed to be a lot of media people but I don't think there was a single cyclist. I switched on the TV up in my room to check out the coverage of this epic stage win. From what I heard in the taxi, Lance had smoked his chief rival Jan Ullrich, the German, on the Alpe and I wanted to know more. "The Look" Lance threw back to Ullrich when he passed him on the climb was replayed numerous times. I listened intently to the commentaries of the French reporting team as everyone seemed to have a different opinion about "*Le Regard.*" Was it a dare, as in are you going to chase me down? Maybe Lance was just savoring the moment, looking back at Jan's face and his jaw clenched in pain. Or was that anger? Whatever it meant, it appeared to signify the apex of their duel, the crucial moment before a fierce competitor pierces the heart of his unrelenting opponent with his steely sword.

I changed quickly in front of the TV, then reluctantly turned it off. I had to meet Brigitte Roland from the Tourist Department of the Isère, the person who had helped me to plan this part of my trip, and who, above all, was going to help me to find my way up to the finish at Chamrousse tomorrow. (Generally it does help to have a car when following the Tour.) Over glasses of red wine and the regional specialty of *ravioles de Romans* (cheese-filled ravioli), we talked about the rich cultural heritage of Grenoble and the perfectly preserved beauty of the city today. Café de la Table Ronde, the restaurant in which we dined, served as an excellent example—it is the oldest café in Grenoble, founded in 1739.

Gaëtane, from the tourist office of Grenoble, picked me up at 8 a.m. the next day and we both expressed dismay about the driving rain that was yet again plaguing France. "It's really more like November weather outside," she said.

"Yes, I guess so. I'm wondering how I'm going to stay warm with my simple summer layers."

"You might have to do some shopping," Gaëtane teased, although I knew that this was no laughing matter. At the top of this modern ski resort, a huge village had been erected in addition to the existing structures. We made a run for it, after having landed a prized parking spot, and charged into an immense tent reserved for some 600 members of the international press. It was fascinating to see such a setup, rows and rows of long tables and chairs that made up the work stations of these journalists. The tables appeared dressed in laptops, assorted papers and publications, coffee cups and a tangle of cords. Most of the press was nowhere to be seen.

Brigitte was there though. "Please make use of this space as much as you want. Help yourself to all the free water, coffee and hot chocolate. It's provided all day long. It's nice to have a base since the cyclists aren't due in until the afternoon." I could tell already that it was going to be a long day, but waiting, as I found out, is all part of the Tour routine, since many spectators often claim their spots eight to twenty-four hours before the peloton passes through. (Most of the time, too, the roads are closed many hours in advance and don't re-open until after the finish.)

"Thank you for everything. It's nice to have such a refuge. Now I think I need to head over to the shops to buy some clothing." Every other person seemed to have that idea, too, which had all the boutiques going full tilt. Rain and cold-weather attire was snatched up faster than you can say cash or credit card. I thankfully was able to buy the last pair of rain pants in my size, along with a fleece jacket and a floppy hat that made me look like an English woman at a dreary garden party.

It was just after noon, so I decided it was time to claim my spot along the metal barricades with the rest of the spectators, 150 meters (about 500 feet) from the finish. I squeezed in between a German and a Frenchman, both of whom said they had already been waiting there for three hours. They were studying a newspaper in their respective languages that listed the general classification of the riders and their start times. It seemed more and more like the races, and people were also beginning to test hanging over the rails to check out the view.

Today was an individual time trial day with a unique mountain finish. The cyclists were departing at various intervals with the first one expected to arrive at about 1:15 p.m. Music and commentaries helped to rev up the crowd, which was already warmed up by the excitement of it all, despite the bad weather. Varying levels of enthusiasm rang out for each passing cyclist, however, all Tour participants were cheered on to one degree or another. My hands were numb after the first hour from banging on the barriers but like the rest, I hung on in order to acknowledge the athletes' super-human accomplishments. No one looked fresh at the finish of that thirty-two kilometer (twenty-mile) stage, which swiftly climbed to 1,730 meters (5,675 feet) from Grenoble. Foam was actually spewing from the mouths of some, others looked as though they had just passed through a shower, and virtually all had the look of agony plastered on their faces. It wasn't the rain that had caused that drowned aspect either, since by mid-afternoon, the skies were clearing, and the sun even dared to come forth.

Coverage on the big screen TV also appeared at this point, an added feature that made fighting the crowds at the finish line all the more worthwhile. The spectators went wild when Jan Ullrich zoomed through and Lance Armstrong—with a look of intense concentration but not exhaustion—motored up behind him. Lance had the better time and had won again. And I could have sworn that's when I heard the funny noisemakers whirl the hardest, the hands bang the most and the voices scream the loudest.

I only had to walk a little way down past the finish for the awards ceremony. I ended up behind a cameraman, a happy occurrence that placed me front and center from the podium. It was exciting to see Lance on stage twice, once for the day's win, the other for the overall lead.

The ambiance was great, even as the crowds pushed their way out. I made my way back to the press tent, which now was alive with activity. Clearly the heat was on. *I don't know how they work like that*, I wondered. *All the noise, cigarette smoke and togetherness—I couldn't do it. I like a nice, quiet, clean space all to myself. How exciting it is, though, to watch the reporters bang out their stories on their tight deadlines.*

"I've made arrangements for a taxi to come and pick you up to take you to your next destination," Brigitte said. "But you have to wait a while for the traffic to clear."

"No problem, I'm enjoying taking in the scene." I hung around some more and then after I had enough refreshments and my fill of smoke, I decided to walk around this specially installed Tour de France base camp to see what I could take in. Outside the tent, I noticed there was a special Tour truck that served as a portable business center. It was churning out photocopied pages of Tour results by the hundreds along with other kinds of information sheets for the press. Another truck served as the official roving post office for the Tour, while others encased portable boutiques for all the Tour merchandise. The podium and grandstands are quite mobile, as are the tiered boxes reserved for the officials, the commentators and other representatives of the media. All this and more folds up at the end of the day and travels to the next location. The mere logistics of this grandiose operation are mind-boggling. There is no other sporting event like it. More than 3,800 people work the Tour throughout this three-week period and all seems to come together with clockwork precision.

My taxi arrived shortly after my tour was completed. "*Bon Tour*," Brigitte and Gaëtan warmly extended to me as we said goodbye. I knew I would catch up with them in a couple of days, since we were hoping I'd be able to do some cycling around Grenoble. Now, however, it was time to make the pilgrimage to the renowned Alpe d'Huez, a ski resort high up in the sky, that cyclists made famous long before Lance's ride there yesterday.

"Do you want to take a shortcut from Chamrousse to Alpe d'Huez?" the taxi driver asked in French.

"Is it scenic?"

"*Oui, madame. Très.* Plus, it's best, since the major road leading off the mountain is all jammed up," he continued. "We won't have to go out of our way as much either."

"*OK, très bien.*"

"Do you have your seat belt fastened?"

"Yes, of course."

I had never been on such a serpentine trail—even in the Pyrenees—in all my life. We twisted and turned down the mountain through thickly wooded terrain where the width of the road measured not more than ten feet. Traffic signs and guardrails were practically nonexistent but the scenery—and the pitch off the side of the road—was stunning.

"*Ne vous-inquiètez pas,*" the chauffeur said, sensing my worry. "I know this route well." Thankfully, he did. His near-intuitive knowledge of each bend in the road and his exceptional driving ability helped to ease my fear. From what I gathered, we had taken the Col Luitel route.

After passing centuries-old farms and alpine fields, the road finally opened up onto a fertile valley that extended as far as the snow-capped peaks surrounding Alpe d'Huez. As the taxi began to weave up through the twenty-one *lacets*, or laces, of this renowned mountain, I imagined Lance powering up them just the day before. There's no doubt that I was arriving once the party was over. But for me, it was better to come late than not at all. (I had messed up slightly with my planning, which actually ended up paying off or else I wouldn't have hooked up with the U.S. Postal team in Aix-les-Bains.)

I had seen the infamous hairpin turns of the Alpe on TV but that was no preparation for the sharpness of their reality. Each switchback cuts through the mountain with surgical precision, beginning just beyond Le Bourg-d'Oisans and taking the traveler higher and higher up to the summit of this 1,850-meter (6,070 feet)—*hors catégorie* (beyond category)—behemoth. You have to love steep climbs to take this monster on because its punishing gradient leaves no room for Sunday riders. A different marker posted on each of the turns indicates the altitude and a name of one of the twenty-some-odd champions that have conquered Alpe d'Huez in the Tour. As I looked down at the roadway covered with the names and words of encouragement of the Tour riders, I could almost hear the cheering fans, known to go totally berserk at this stage.

A good number of camping cars and tents remained, along with tremendous amounts of garbage that had not yet been picked up. It was beginning to look more and more like the day after a big bash. "Approximately 20,000 spectators were here yesterday," monsieur said. "They come days in advance to claim a spot."

"I can't believe this is such a big event," I replied. "Even more impressive than on TV and I'm not even seeing it with the crowds."

"It's considered the most mythic climb of the Tour," monsieur replied proudly. I gazed out the window and could almost see all the crazies as we ascended, wildly enthusiastic fans, some dressed in nutty costumes, others content to just wave—or wear—their country's flag. There's almost always the red devil that feverishly roots on the cyclists by making wild gestures with his pitchfork. There's sometimes even a streaker or two. I'm sure the brouhaha in real life registers even higher on the entertainment meter than what is caught on camera.

"I'm always concerned that one of these over-excited fans will injure a cyclist," I said.

"*Ben, oui, ça arrive,*" the chauffeur answered, validating my concern. "There's not much to prevent them from having direct contact with the riders."

"I wonder if they'll change that some day."

"I doubt it—that's part of l'Alpe," he replied.

"Yes, I guess it is."

"Do you plan to do the climb?" he asked.

"You must be kidding," I practically shouted.

"Many people do. Many cyclists make the pilgrimage here from all over the world—particularly northern Europe—to ascend the famous Alpe d'Huez. Doing the climb is like joining a club."

"That sounds great. But my cycling isn't good enough for that."

"You go as slow as you want," he insisted. "You take a ticket from the little machine at the bottom and then give it to the tourist office up top, they record your time and present you with a special certificate."

"*Peut-être un jour,*" maybe some day, I said to monsieur, not wanting to disappoint him or myself.

The charm of the village of Alpe d'Huez exceeded all my expectations. Everyone had gone home or to follow the Tour to the next stage. Yet I felt content to experience it in such a tranquil fashion. The beauty of the jagged, sugar-frosted peaks was awe-inspiring and I was ecstatic to discover that the windows from my room at La Mariandre provided full coverage of this extraordinary alpine panorama. The warm chalet décor of this hotel further endeared me to this humble place of lodging. And when fresh ham and cheese sandwiches and fruit were brought to my room upon arrival, I nearly wept. After such a long day, I didn't feel like going out for dinner, and I was actually happy there was no TV. I didn't want anything to disturb the serenity of this heavenly retreat.

Marie-Hélène, from the Alpe d'Huez tourist office, met me on the deck of La Mariandre for coffee the next morning. Tanned and energetic, she exuded all the sportiness of this mountain resort. It was a sparkling day, albeit a bit crisp, so I decided that after my debriefing with Marie-Hélène, I'd activate myself even if I wasn't going to do the big climb. Instead, I took the gondola from the top to the little village below and hiked around enough to work up a light sweat. (The gondola ride back up the mountain provided a spectacular aerial view of the renowned switchbacks below.)

Lunch at Le Petit Creux was not only delicious but also warm and cozy, since red and green Christmas decorations still adorned much of this restaurant's old interior. (I had already noticed remnants from the holidays in other locations in the Alps, leading me to believe that many Christmas decorations are left up year-round. Red and green are also the traditional colors of the mountains.)

I enjoyed meeting up with Marie-Hélène later on not only because she brought me on a hike alongside pristine alpine lakes, but also because I found that she had a lot of spunk. "I'm busy promoting La Megavalanche—a mountain bike marathon," she told me.

"Wow, just the name of that sounds extreme."

"It is extreme. One of the most extreme competitions open to amateurs."

I could imagine Marie-Hélène riding in it herself in between her work responsibilities and caring for her husband and two kids. She made me think of almost every French woman I know. *How is it that they all seem so capable, so strong and free-willed? But at the same time, none of these women ever appear to compromise their femininity. Instead, in most instances, they exude enough sexuality to make a man put down his remote and pay some attention. That—along with their secret to thinness—remains somewhat of a mystery.*

Teatime is one of my favorite rituals, so I didn't object to waiting on my own for an hour before another taxi was to pick me up for my trip off the mountain. Sitting outside in a spectacular setting is not something I like to miss, either, so I selected my pastry at a nearby bakery and picked out my spot on a sunny terrace. I had said goodbye to Marie-Hélène and promised to return for at least one of her mega-atheletic events, hopefully for the Tour de France. I had seen enough of this great *station de ski* to know that it's a place to return to in winter and summer. No sooner did I take my last swallow of tea, then I heard the beep of the taxi's horn.

"Do you have your seat belt on?" the chauffeur asked. *Oh no, here we go again*, I thought. "It's quite the descent. Maybe you should sit upfront," he suggested. "That will make it easier on you." The drive started off with a smooth downhill where monsieur casually talked about yesterday's action.

"*Voilà, ma maison*," he said suddenly as he pointed to his house. "We can watch the whole race on television and just stand out on the balcony as it passes. That's what we did yesterday."

"That's fantastic—what a great way to take it all in."

"Yes, a lot of the roadside spectators have organized themselves like that— some have portable TVs that plug into their vehicle's lighters." My ears popped as we descended the mountain, which in many respects seemed more impressive going down than up.

"I'd like to be in on all this fun some day," I said.

"*Oui, c'est magnifique.*"

I was beginning to understand, too, why monsieur had suggested I sit up front since with every turn of a switchback, I felt like I was on The Scrambler, one of my least favorite carnival rides as a child. This, combined with the heady scent of this kind man's cologne, was beginning to make me feel sick. "Do they ever go down this in the Tour?" I asked meekly as I pushed my foot to the floorboard.

"No, never, it's too dangerous. But Lance Armstrong climbed this in only about thirty-eight minutes."

"That's all?" I asked, astonished by the time and also that this Frenchman was speaking so boastfully about one of my countrymen. By then, we had completed our descent and I realized that twenty minutes had passed, which seemed to be the same time it took the other taxi to ascend the mountain yesterday. "How long does it take you to drive up this mountain?" I queried.

"Twenty minutes, always twenty minutes, twenty minutes up and twenty minutes down."

"Now I understand why they say that pro cyclists typically live ten to fifteen fewer years than the average man."

It was downhill all the way into Grenoble, a good one-hour drive that seemed interminable. It would have been lovely were it not for the fact that my stomach was still doing flips and jumps. I checked into my hotel, then stretched out on the bed, making sure to keep one leg planted on the ground. How ridiculous that I still felt so nauseous from a ride down a mountain. These sensations made me appreciate the challenges of the Tour riders even more, because even though they didn't descend the Alpe, they did careen down many other hair-raising descents at average speeds of sixty to seventy miles per hour. The most I had ever cycled in one day was forty-five miles and I can remember that each time I was in a car a few days after that, I had the sensation of going up hill and down dale on two wheels. Whooo-eee! Can you imagine how it is after twenty-one days of riding more than 2,000 miles?

Always when I feel a surge in my mood—either up or down—I feel an added desire to be in touch with Pete. I realized, too, that I promised to give him an update on my Tour antics and hadn't yet followed up. Then I said to myself, on somewhat of a whim, that it was absurd he wasn't here and that he'd be crazy to stay away any longer. Nearly ten days of Tour mania remained, and we'd probably both always regret it if he didn't show up for some of it. I tried calling him numerous times but could only reach the answering machine. Then I finally decided to plead my case to an electronic telephone device and hoped that he'd see my logic.

I must have been pretty persuasive, since I received a call back from him the next day, expressing interest. "Really, will you come?" I exclaimed as he started to talk about wanting to make the trip.

"If you can get me a cheap flight, I'll come."

"That's great, but finding any kind of a transatlantic flight at the last minute in the dead of summer will be tough, let alone a cheap one. Why don't you call around to the airlines and check on-line to see if you can find something good? Sometimes you can get killer prices at the last minute. I can't make those kinds of arrangements from here. Plus, I'm really on the go."

Pete called me the next day and I learned that the plan proved to be a dead end. "Unless I'm willing to drain a huge amount from my savings, this isn't going to happen. It's beginning to sound like one big frivolous adventure anyway."

"No, no, wait. Let me think for a minute. Yeah, this is what popped into my head last night in bed. I have a contact at Nouvelles Frontières—not sure if she's still there. They specialize in inexpensive flights, particularly to France. I think they're charters." *Now where's her number?*

Miraculously, I managed to guide Pete through my sea of files at home to locate this person's essential information. "I think I found it," Pete said. "Yeah, here it is—it says New Frontiers."

"It's Friday afternoon in California—that's where she's based—I better move fast," I said hurriedly. I placed the call, leaving all the necessary particulars on her voicemail, and prayed that she would be able to work out something with Pete back in the States. It was late in France and I was tired both from all this mental juggling and from having spent much of the day in Grenoble battling the return of more rainy weather.

My cycling plans ended up being nixed here, so I did some sightseeing by foot and tram instead. I had lunch with Brigitte and Gaëtan at Le Jardin de Ville, a restaurant overlooking this romantic square of the same name. On clear days, many people do *cyclotourisme* in this town, often considered to be the epicenter of cycling for much of the Alps. However, I was learning to take life as it comes, and as with Pete's plans, turn it over with the knowledge that relatively little is under my control.

At breakfast the next morning, I received a fax from Pete which had arrived during the night. He would be flying into Paris the following Friday, time enough for him to attend the last two stages of the Tour! Best of all, my contact really pulled through for us by offering Pete a roundtrip ticket at an unbeatable discount. My prayers were answered, a sign not only of the power of my intention but also that clearly Pete and I were meant to be together.

I must have appeared radiant at breakfast from all this good news since a man across the room seemed to be drawn to me. He was American, perhaps recovering from a divorce or suffering from some other lassitude, as it seemed as though he yearned to make an acquaintance or at least strike up a conversation. I couldn't help thinking that perhaps I, too, would feel bereft by now had I not persuaded Pete to meet me for the tail end of my trip. We joined up and fortunately this man and I did have a fair amount to chat about. He, too, had been a follower of the Tour, but unlike me, he had actually tackled some of the insidious climbs in addition to being a spectator.

I learned that half the people in the room were part of this organized tour. Boy, was I beginning to feel lame. In my defense, I stated, "I'm staying another week in France and definitely plan to do a lot of cycling then."

"Oh yes, I recommend you do," the man answered. "It really makes you feel like part of the Tour." *Jeez*, I thought, *how much more exciting can it get?*

By the time I finished breakfast, the sun emerged and the temperature began to rise noticeably. Today I would finally be able to do some cycling, a welcome proposition since my pants were already feeling tight from too much eating with too little exercise. The plan was to spend the day at Lac de Paladru, near Charavines, a popular destination for the *grenoblois*. Being carless, I was forced to take a taxi for the approximate forty-minute trip northwest of Grenoble, a situation that was beginning to amuse me. It occurred to me that few people taxi around the Alps the way I had been doing this past week. In the end, though, it was far cheaper than renting a car, and for me, much less of a hassle.

I soon learned that V.T.T., or mountain bikes, are the bicycles of choice for cyclists in this area, news that chagrined me a fair amount since I prefer riding on the road rather than off. "Don't worry. I'll take care of everything for you," Patrice, a local bike outfitter and my guide for the morning, said. "We'll just change our itinerary."

"Also, I'm not very comfortable on mountain bikes. You wouldn't have a road bike, would you?" *There goes that travel writer card again.*

He noticed a look of distress on my face, then said, "We only have mountain bikes, but I might have a bike for you."

"That would be great, Patrice. Thank you."

We headed over to his shop where he dug up an old G.T., an American bike, as a replacement. "*Voilà*," he said as he wheeled out the bike and dusted it off. "You can use this one."

It felt like an old tank compared to Bella. The seat bounced so much because of its full suspension it seemed like I was on a hobbyhorse. It was better than the V.T.T., so after a few minor adjustments, we were finally off. It's amazing how accommodating the French can be, while at other times they're impossible.

As we approached the lake, we spotted many beach-goers making their way to the sandy shores of this beautiful, blue body of water. "It's going to be a hot one today," Patrice said.

"Yes, I'm glad we're cycling first. Maybe I can spend some time on this lovely lake later."

Patrice flashed his bright eyes, and with all the enthusiasm of a tour guide said, "Let's go all the way around the lake. That way we can take in the various views along the way."

"That sounds wonderful." The first part of the ride proved to be a bit hairy, but after that we traveled primarily on country roads that offered extraordinary views of this jewel-like lake and the rolling hills beyond. With little prompting, Patrice furnished a wealth of information about the history—geologic and otherwise—of this alpine oasis about which he is clearly *très passionné*.

This came as a surprise to me, since I first thought that Patrice was just into bikes. As is the case with so many of the French, however, he clearly possessed an excellent *culture générale*, and, in the case of Paladru, *culture régionale* as well. I couldn't help but consider how different the average French person is to your average American. Both in school and at home in France, strong emphasis is placed on history, tradition and culture, and from what I can tell from most of the French people I've encountered over the years, few let the information they gather lay dormant. So this is how I came to find out all the details of this glacier-carved lake that approximately one thousand years ago boasted three separate villages at different ends. (One of the villages has remained amazingly well preserved just below the surface of the water and is the site of an archaeological dig that may be visited during the summer months.) In all, Patrice and I cycled a seventeen-kilometer (eleven-mile), fact-filled ride together.

Still dressed in my bike attire (not exactly slinky Lycra but quite jockish nonetheless), I met Annie, from the local tourist office, for lunch. Clad in a pretty summer dress, Annie embodied the essence of a true Frenchwoman as much as Patrice appeared to be the quintessential Frenchman. Fortunately, her grace and charm put me at ease in my sweaty tank top and nylon shorts and we both seemed like two ladies doing lunch on the sun-filled terrace of the Hôtel Le Lac Bleu overlooking this pretty lake. Our conversation began with tourism but shifted over to health and aging and the challenges of staying fit at this juncture. Neither of us actually revealed our ages but it seemed as though there was not much of a difference in years between us. Annie appeared decidedly slimmer than I, an injustice I secretly attributed to her fine French genes and my more corpulent American ones.

"How do you stay so fit?" I asked Annie, now that we were feeling like two girlfriends; a bold move, since the French are usually more formal.

"*C'est le sport. Oui, oui, oui, oui.*" (This time it was four *ouis*.) "We have to do sports the rest of our lives."

"I agree."

"I love swimming," she added.

"Me, too. But really, Annie. How do French women stay so slim? What's their secret?"

"*Vitamines,*" was all she was prepared to offer up. "Yes, I take a lot of vitamins."

Hogwash, I thought. *With all this bread, wine, cheese and pastries, there's more to it than that—and we both know it.* I didn't say anything for a while, thinking that maybe Annie would pipe up about something else. But as I found out the hard way with recipe exchanges in France, they don't like to share "secrets." (French women do not like to trade recipes—they're too possessive about them. They don't want you making their special dish.)

Then it occurred to me that Frenchwomen seem to burn up more calories because they run on a lot of nervous energy. Whether it's the coffee, the smokes or just a more agitated approach toward life, they seem to function at a higher rate than most American women I know. I'm a snail compared to all of them. Plus the French eat quality, not quantity. And they don't snack between meals. Those are the biggest differences between French and American eating habits.

Annie explained that she had a number of activities lined up for the end of the afternoon but was happy to drive me out to the Château de Virieu for a visit of this castle and its gardens. It was worth the trip since I found the château to be among one of the best looking examples of its kind in the Alps region. Still privately owned, parts of this handsome, toast-colored stone structure date back as far as the eleventh century. Annie and I passed the proprietress and a friend sitting quietly in a corner of the garden as we strolled down through these immaculately trimmed quadrants of grass. Both of the women were beyond what the French term *un certain age* and upon seeing them I couldn't help remarking to myself how they looked as beautifully preserved as this magnificent château. *Ça ce sont les françaises.*

The lake beckoned, so after our informative visit, Annie dropped me off at Les Mélèzes, a glorified snack bar that also rented a variety of boats. Of course I chose the pédalo over the others, since pedaling seemed to be my preference these days. It would have been interesting to have an odometer to learn exactly how far I pedaled from one side of the lake to another, but for the most part, I just contented myself with the great feeling of being out on the water. I couldn't help thinking about the masses of tourists in the south of France as I gazed out onto this lake, which to me represented the epitome of summer fun, solitude and fresh air. The French often refer to themselves as sheep, so that seemed to be one explanation of why so many people follow so many others, even if the destination is bulging with tourists.

I decided to delay my taxi until early evening and took up a spot on the terrace of this lakeside fun center in front of a Kodak view of the end-of-the-day sun shimmering on the lake. It was Saturday evening and I couldn't believe the place wasn't jammed. To me, it seemed like a perfect get-away for the folks of Grenoble. I ordered an aperitif from my server and asked, "Where are all the people?"

"Most are probably home, tired out from the passage of the Tour de France." *I think they all foolishly took off for the Riviéra*, I said to myself.

"Tant mieux pour eux," I answered, which means "good for them."

"I'm happy to discover my own little piece of paradise without battling the crowds."

Almost Solo in the Loire

My relaxing day at Lake Paladru at the foot of the Alps served as a good transition for the short week I was to spend in the Loire Valley. From the look of my itinerary, this region promised to be a welcome respite from the Tour frenzy I had become caught up in for the better part of last week. I was not due to meet up with the Tour again until Saturday, so it seemed that this was the week for me to accomplish some cycling on my own terms.

I was thrilled to discover that my tourist board contacts had prepared a rather unencumbered program for me. It seemed as though the only real imperative I had was to do a good amount of cycling. That was great news to me, for after having followed the Tour so intently I couldn't wait to do some serious cycling (at least by my standards) myself. I was going to be on my own quite a bit—more so than in the Alps—so I considered the next four days as an opportunity to come even more into my own power. I had traveled solo in France extensively and enjoyed it immensely, but cycling alone would be more of a challenge.

It felt like I was in a good place. I was alone but not lonely. And now I was able to look forward to Pete's arrival in the region on Friday morning. I had reached an emotional arc last week with all the Tour hoopla, and more importantly, over the excitement of Pete finally meeting up with me again in France. So now I was ready to just put myself into smooth sailing mode until the adventure hit.

I thought about all this and more as I zoomed through the countryside once again on the TGV. It was such a joy to travel on this super-fast, super-stylish train, that I knew that even though I had a

212

day in the mountains for Lance. After a train change in Paris (which also involved changing stations), I arrived in Blois at about 8 p.m. There I was greeted by Madame Gallopin, a tall and welcoming French woman with flaming red hair. Madame also happened to be the new proprietress of the château where I'd be staying the night. We chatted throughout the half-hour drive to Hôtel Le Clos du Cher, the establishment in Noyers-sur-Cher that she had purchased just two months before with her husband.

I was ravenous and was delighted to learn that there was also a restaurant on the premises where Monsieur Gallopin served as the *chef cuisinier*. The dining room was in full swing by the time I entered, but despite such a busy scene, at least half the diners looked up from their plates and stared at me when I entered this large room. The looks continued a few brief moments after I settled into my place until I gave some of them a perfunctory nod as if to greet them. Fortunately, I'm accustomed to this odd custom, which falls somewhere between "checking someone out" and inviting the other person to meet their eyes. It happens in most restaurants in France and usually entails the person entering or leaving the establishment being surveyed from head to toe, whether they are alone or not. It's not that I looked particularly attractive or particularly unattractive, it's just that the French (and many other Europeans) don't view this sort of staring as an invasion of the other person's privacy. The notion of personal space is greatly reduced in Europe. Tonight I think I had even more attention on me because I was alone. I detected—in addition to the usual inquisitive looks—some more compassionate glances from my fellow diners, since I was the only person dining unaccompanied in the restaurant. This is not common in France, particularly for a woman, and especially in a country restaurant where clearly everyone there was on a vacation of sorts.

I pondered all this as I sipped my Kir Royale. The stares, thankfully, abated. There is much more of a notion of coupledom in France. People rarely go out socially without their significant other. Girls' night out is practically nonexistent. And I never knew any Frenchmen to "get together with the guys" for any reason whatsoever. I once held a bridal shower for some French women and they thought it was very odd that I had organized a gathering just for the ladies. I looked at my schedule and saw that I'd be dining alone for the next four days, so I sat up straight in my chair and decided to brave all the gawking.

"*Ça va l'Amérique?*" No sooner did I finish my first course, than I heard a man from the table across from me ask, "How's America doing?"

"Oh, did you hear my accent?"

"Yes, but not too much," the man responded with an accent of his own. I learned that he and his wife were Belgian and by the time my main course arrived, I heard all about his three daughters that had lived in the U.S., the two supermarkets he owned in Belgium, and, of course, his take on what I was doing in France along with his commentary of the Tour de France. "*Oh, ça va être Armstrong.*" It's going to be Armstrong, the man fervently declared as he voiced his enthusiasm for cycling, indisputably the national sport of Belgium.

It was nice to have this unexpected exchange. But by now, I was eager to eat in peace, so I was grateful when another table of Belgians chimed in, providing me with the opportunity to gracefully withdraw from the conversation. They were all genuinely nice, and had I not been so focused on my meal and all the research material I was reviewing, I might very well have welcomed their company. Tonight, however, I was in a solitary mood and was reluctant to break the spell.

I didn't linger at breakfast the next morning since I knew I had a big day of cycling ahead of me. Madame Gallopin seemed to be impressed by my program, which called for me to cycle about fifty kilometers (thirty-one miles) by the day's end. Her kudos buoyed me up some, which reminded me that I was indeed capable of doing this bike touring, even without the help of any sort of a support vehicle.

"A bike has been delivered for you," she informed me. I was happy to see that although it wasn't nearly as sleek and stunning as Bella, it looked pretty nonetheless. As I had suspected, I had been given a hybrid bike—of the most brilliant sapphire blue—so it seemed that it was more than sturdy enough to carry me over a variety of terrain. I had adjusted my cycling attire accordingly, having opted not to bring any of my flashy outfits—all of which are far better suited for road bike riding. Stretchy tank tops and baggy shorts (with padding, thank goodness) were de rigueur this time around, which I also figured would make me look more presentable for the château touring. "They even dropped off a helmet," madame said as she pointed to a very ordinary Easter egg-like magenta helmet which had been placed on a nearby table.

"Is there a bike lock?"

"*Non*, you don't have to worry about that—there's no theft in this part of France."

Monsieur and Madame Gallopin waved a cheerful goodbye. "Your luggage will be delivered to your next place of lodging sometime during the day," madame reassured me. I sped away feeling like one of the happiest persons in the world. It was a gorgeous summer day and I was pedaling through some of the prettiest countryside of France.

My first recommended stop was at Zoo Parc de Beauval in Saint-Aignan. I parked my bike out front and attempted not to worry about the fact that it might not be there when I returned from my little tour. I did, however, decide to take my special Tour de France water bottle that I had purchased from one of the Tour vendors in the Alps, since that was a souvenir I didn't want to lose. Even though this zoo had much to offer in terms of exotic birds and animals (a rather incongruous display of nature for this part of France), I didn't feel like doing more than a quick walk-through here. I felt like Pete. My bike shorts weren't bothering me, but I wanted to get back on the bike.

I was delighted to see that my bike was still there. So I pedaled off, ringing the little bell, freewheeling all the way down the hill into the medieval town of Saint-Aignan-sur-Cher. Here, too, I contemplated doing a bit of touring, but decided against it since I really wasn't in the mood and also because I looked at the map and realized that I had not covered much ground at all so far. From what I could tell, it looked as though I was going to be traveling on small country roads most of the afternoon. *I'd better stop and have lunch now,*

I thought to myself, cognizant of the fact that I was not one to fuel myself on energy bars and the like, particularly when there was a tasty French meal to be had. I pulled up to a shady terrace and ordered a salad with smoked duck and a variety of other savory ingredients. *"Voulez-vous du vin?"* my server asked.

After a three-second pause I responded, *"Oui, donnez-moi un quart de rosé, s'il vous plaît,"* asking for a quarter of a pitcher of rosé wine. Clearly I was in some sort of a celebratory mood.

I had just experienced my very first *kilomètres* of cycling alone in France and I was feeling more confident than ever. I was not with Pete, I was not on an organized tour and I was not with anyone else. I was finding my own way all by myself—I wasn't even on a bike path. Best of all, I was going at my own pace, so I didn't have to worry about keeping up with anyone. No one was there to yell at me to go faster, to change gears, to pedal nice round circles, or to tell me how to wipe my nose. I was having the time of my life.

As I sipped my coffee, I reviewed my maps and notes in an effort to plot out my afternoon. My last destination for the day was to be Chitenay, but I was not clear on how to find my way there; I was working from about three different maps, none of which appeared to reveal a choice route. The server at the café suggested I just follow the signs for Saint-Romain, Choussy, Feings, Fougère-sur-Bièvre, then finally Chitenay. I was grateful at this point that I spoke fluent French.

After refilling my water bottle, I was finally off. The road at first was a little nerve-wracking with all the traffic, but once again, I felt reassured by visualizing myself wrapped in pink light. Just as I'd had enough of the noise and pollution, I spotted the turnoff for Saint-Romain. From then on, I found myself on little-traveled country roads like those Pete and I had encountered in Burgundy (although much flatter—praise the Lord). There was absolutely no one around; the only company I had was provided by nature. I was thrilled to finally pass by mile after mile of sunflower fields, the quintessential French landscape for cyclists. When Pete and I cycled together in France it was too late in the season to see their glory. Today, though, I admired their golden faces turning toward the sun as that blazing ball of light inched its way across the sky. It's no wonder the French call them *tournesols* (as in turn toward the sun). As in Burgundy, just as I was beginning to feel faint from the fierce heat of the day, my little route passed through a forest that cooled me with all the freshness of a summer morning.

Maybe it was partly due to the storybook-like eeriness of the forest or perhaps it was because no one had passed me for over an hour, but I began to wonder *what if something happened to me out here?* I didn't think I was going to expire (although it was incredibly hot by now) but I did think that something as basic as a flat tire could occur. *Or what if a storm blew in?* I looked up and realized that was impossible, since there wasn't a cloud in the sky. *Stop spooking yourself,* I told myself. *Don't doubt your self- confidence.*

I was somewhat reassured a half hour later when an old Citroën puffed by me. It helped to bring me out of my head. Up until my little forest scare, my mind was, thankfully, fairly blank—an unusual happening of sorts. My thoughts switched to Pete. *He'd be really proud of me today. I can't wait to tell him all about my cycling.* Then I began to feel really connected with him, almost in a hauntingly familiar way. It was amazing how I could feel his presence, especially on the bike. "Keep pedaling even when you're going downhill," I could hear him say, as I descended a particularly steep grade and felt perfectly content to just sail down instead of powering forward. In an effort to heed his advice and to improve my cycling ability, I gave my little chug-a-chug bike a few good pedals.

As I reached down to grab my water bottle, I remembered in the beginning of my cycling days how I was afraid to do that while riding out of fear I'd lose my balance and topple over. That seemed so silly now. But still, I was far from an expert bike handler and wouldn't even attempt to ride without at least one hand firmly on my handlebars. "Pedal!" I could hear Pete yell as I slogged up a hill. "Shift your gears!" He was my coach and his words still echoed in my mind; I sensed him with me on my adventure.

At Fougère, I stopped at an outdoor café just across from the château in this little village. I had calculated that I was only five kilometers (about three miles) from Chitenay, but I still couldn't go any farther feeling so parched. I practically chugged an ice-cold bottle of Coke and then refilled my water bottle for probably the fifth time of the day. It was a welcome break, and I totally appreciated the tranquility of this small country town.

I was exhausted by the time I rolled up to the Auberge du Centre in Chitenay. I didn't have an odometer on my bike, but according to my calculations, I had pedaled over thirty miles. In many ways it felt like I had cycled even more than that since the sun shone so intensely throughout the whole day. It made a big difference, too, not to be on Bella, my beautiful Bianchi. With this other bike, I was convinced I had to work at least twice as hard. Thankfully, it felt as though I had landed in the right place. After I checked in at the reception, I was instructed to wheel my bike around to the back where I would also find my room. I was thrilled to discover a wonderful country scene that included a large stone terrace and sprawling lawn replete with a little water well surrounded by an array of outdoor furnishings. There were tables all over, all neatly dressed with fresh white linens. Planters and pitchers filled with colorful flowers of the summer season were also scattered throughout this garden party scene.

It seemed, too, that many of the guests in this country inn were cyclists. A huge number of bikes of all shapes and sizes were lined up alongside the two principal buildings of this establishment. I wedged mine in there, too, hopeful that it would not be lost in the jumble. Not a one was locked.

My room was also lovely. As I looked around assessing my surroundings, I was pleased that I was to spend two nights at this auberge. I was about to do some lolling on the bed when the phone rang. I was expected a short while later to have a drink and dinner with Monsieur Martinet, the owner of the Auberge du Centre and Monsieur Genies, one of the officials from Cheverny. I took a deep breath and told myself that it was time to shift from my solitary mode into a more sociable way of being. Travel writer duties were calling.

The whole garden area was filled to capacity by the time we were seated at our table, a pretty summer scene that offered the perfect ending to a great day. It was still light out at 9:30 p.m. when we were served dessert, just another one of the perks of visiting France in July. There wasn't a single bothersome bug and (thank goodness) none of those ghastly zappers, either. Sounds of chirping birds mingled with the polite din of the diners—it was truly a marvelous evening overall.

As is often the case in France, the gentlemen were charming, and each was happy to have the opportunity to tout the high points of his area to a visiting *américaine*. "I love the cycling here," I said right off.

"The Loire is a marvelous region for cycling," Monsieur Martinet added. "Many plans are in the works to further develop this activity in the region."

"That's wonderful, since the terrain is gentle and there's so much to visit."

"The goal is to link all the châteaux with bike paths and also to create a bike path across the Chambord forest," monsieur explained.

"For me, just sticking to the rural roads is wonderful. As long as I don't get lost." We all chuckled and savored our delicious French country fare.

Monsieur Genies filled me in on the famous *chasse à courre*, or hunt, that takes place at Château Cheverny twice a week—on Tuesday and Saturday—from October through March. "The dogs chase after the deer and then people follow the hunt across the countryside in cars and even on bikes." *I'll stick to cycling around the quiet roads of the region*, I thought to myself, grateful we were in summer and there was no chance of me encountering the hunt. We said goodnight to each other and I retreated to my room, disappointed I had missed most of the Tour coverage on Eurosport for a second evening in a row, but content that my day and evening had been such a success.

I found it ironic that I hardly did any visiting yesterday, even though it was the first time I was off cycling alone in France without Pete. I knew I would more than make up for that, since today's little slice of France would be particularly rich in châteaux. Monsieur Martinet sent me on my way in the direction of Cellettes, where just beyond I found Château Beauregard. I had never heard of this château before even though I was familiar with the châteaux of the Loire, so its beauty and enormity came as a surprise to me. What a switch from the untamed fields and forests of yesterday. The panoramas surrounding this château were decidedly more cultivated and refined. It appeared as though the sea of green that surrounds the park is maintained with hand clippers and that the gravel paths leading up to this stately castle are raked daily.

The château dates back to the beginning of the sixteenth century, and not surprisingly, was built as a hunting lodge. Originally inhabited by King Francis I, today it's privately owned by Countess Alain du Pavillon. My favorite room was the portrait gallery—the largest in Europe—where at least several hundred paintings, mostly of men, hang on display. Kings, princes and prominent leaders of the church—most of which appeared very self-important in their high, starched collars and ruby red vestments, stared out at me as I walked before these centuries-old walls of fame in my bike shorts and a tank top. I liked its sixteenth-century kitchen as well, especially its plethora of shiny copper pots and dual fireplaces. *Boy, what it must have been like to cook here centuries ago.*

It felt even hotter when I stepped outside and I could tell already that today was going to be more sweltering than yesterday. I decided to conserve my energy and not walk around the park more than I needed to in order to return to my bike. I knew it was going to be a long ride to Cour-Cherverny, my next stop, so I decided to shove off right away.

The crowds mounted as I approached Cour-Cherverny, an indication that this was one of the stellar castles on the Loire Valley tour. I decided to stop and have lunch before becoming caught up in the hubbub within the walls of the château. How I love the French terraces. There's always a shaded spot to be found that serves a good meal at a reasonable price. I pulled up to the Hôtel-Restaurant Saint-Hubert where I delighted in two refreshing appetizers: melon with smoked ham and a tomato and mozzarella salad. No wine today—it was way too hot. I realized, too, that these little pit stops were essential since they provided me with the opportunity to replenish my water supply. (I couldn't quite bring myself to fill up at the local cemetery the way we did on our group ride in Languedoc.)

I felt OK after lunch. My legs weren't too heavy but the fiery sun was pelting down. Long rows of tour buses and signs in English indicated the importance of this world-renowned site.

I was a little put out that visitors had to snake around through the souvenir shop—weaving in and out of displays of swords, tapestries, goblets and every imaginable type of picture, postcard and book on this château and all the others—in order to finally arrive at the entrance of this grandiose estate. "Would you like a brochure in English?" the ticket lady asked before I even opened my mouth.

"*Merci*," I responded rather sheepishly, suddenly feeling underdressed for such a grand affair. I entered the castle and found myself herded along through the series of well-appointed rooms with legions of other casually clad tourists speaking every imaginable language. Kids were seated Indian-style on the floor listening to their group leaders' descriptions of the eccentricities of the rich. Busloads of people shuffled through one exquisitely decorated room after another, making sure not to miss peering at the pictures of the current owners, the Count and Countess Hurault de Vibraye and their lovely brood.

I was probably most impressed with the kings' room, an ornately decorated bedroom whose focal point was a fifteenth-century silk bed covering from Persia, embroidered with gold. The tour guide announced that no king had ever stayed here, so I couldn't help wondering if that meant that the bed had never been slept in. I would have asked, but I wasn't part of that tour—I was just eavesdropping.

I peeked in at the Orangerie—the place where the orange trees were once kept during the cold weather months—and was disappointed to see more medieval schlock crammed into this beautiful space. Clearly the château business is big business, which I suppose is understandable considering the exorbitant costs involved in the repair and upkeep of such a magnificent place. I pondered this as I passed a gardener on a huge mower. His machine seemed to be trimming the tips of the blades of the grass ever so slightly. *What a job it must be to maintain that fresh-cut aspect of the grounds all season long.*

After a short stroll over to the pond and the canal that splices through this vast property, I decided that I had to make an obligatory visit to the *muette,* the small building that housed the pack of prized hounds reserved for the hunt. The dogs were much bigger than I had expected. I couldn't help looking at them with some reserve as I considered the main purpose they served here at the château. "They give the entrails of the poor slaughtered beast to them after every catch," I overheard a woman next to me say. I breathed a sigh of relief that a large fence separated them from me, since who knows what they would do to an errant tourist?

I exited through the souvenir shop and was glad to find myself breezing along once again on a little country road with nothing but gentle pastoral views to stir my senses. The fairytale-like châteaux of the region are extraordinary and definitely a must-see, but there's no doubt that I was in a more down-to-earth frame of mind. I was wishing that Pete was there to see them because pictures and postcards cannot fully capture the majesty of these historic sites. Being the history buff that he is, I'm sure he would have appreciated some of the visiting—at least for a little while.

An entirely different experience awaited me at Château de Troussay. The name of this type of château—a Gentilhommière Renaissance—delighted me in and of itself. Gentilhommière actually means small manor house but I found it interesting that it is a derivative of the French word for gentleman. There were absolutely no crowds here; in fact, I had to wait a while for enough of a group to gather for a tour. I loved this château's proportions. I found it to be totally livable—of course after a good freshening up—and the intimate size of its rooms pleased me considerably.

Finally it was time to call it a day. I had heard enough talk about Henry II, François I, all the Louies and the Regence for one day. Fortunately, I had studied art and art history in college and become familiar with the French decorative arts during the time I lived in Paris. What did people do who had no background in this whatsoever? Not once did I hear a guide talk about the particular characteristics of a style. I guess they assume that people should know about these things. At Cheverny, I remembered hearing a guide tell a child that a certain piece of furniture was a *gueridon anglais*, or an English pedestal table, without any explanation whatsoever. And the child seemed to get it, right away. It probably was a good idea that Pete wasn't with me for this part of my journey because he likely wouldn't have had much patience for all this fussiness after all.

I was told I had only six kilometers (about four miles) to go to reach Chitenay. Thank God, because I could hardly sit on my bicycle seat a moment longer. I have no idea how much I pedaled that day in all but I know it was a lot. One Lycra-clad cyclist passed me on my way home. It occurred to me that he was only the third serious cyclist I had seen in two days. I was in some kind of a mental stupor (perhaps due to my physical exertion and the cultural and historical overload of the day), because suddenly I was fixated on how none of those cyclists seemed to be wearing socks. Is that a French phenomenon to wear cycling shoes without socks or is it that they wear teeny-weeny socks that I can't see? *I'll have to ask Pete. I think the heat is really beginning to get to me.*

I collapsed on the bed as soon as I arrived back at my room. Excellent—I was just in time for some Tour coverage on the French television station, Antenne 2. They were interviewing a cyclist that had nearly passed out from hypoglycemia that day. "I immediately downed three Cokes at the finish," he said. Then the reporter showed other riders eating a big macaroni and cheese dinner. With that report, I felt even more deserving of the little feast I had laid out before me which included one apricot, two nectarines and a Crunch bar. I ate with glee and couldn't help wondering if perhaps I was hypoglycemic. There's no doubt that I was suffering. My legs were sore. *Was that from all the riding or the sunburn? I desperately need some rejuvenation.*

Thankfully, I could take my time and not have to worry about meeting up with anyone for dinner that night. After lots of TV viewing and some telephoning, I took a leisurely shower and prepared for dinner. I did a double check in the mirror because it looked as though my butt appeared tighter. *Wow! I'm finally beginning to see results. Or is it just this mirror? Too bad my belly is so bloated from all the water consumption. I doubt this happens to the Tour riders.*

Dinner on the terrace of the auberge was again delightful. I was alone, so the parade of looks recommenced much like they had a couple of nights before. Tonight, however, I think that many thought I was some sort of a VIP, perhaps because some had seen me the night before with the hotel owner and the tourism official. Also I received several phone calls; each time the phone was brought directly to me at the table which was, in truth, rather bothersome. The stares increased, but I paid them no attention. Instead I focused on my note taking (which had also increased the curiosity factor, I suppose), my succulent salmon and its accompanying Sauvignon Blanc. I continued to consume copious amounts of water until I fell asleep. Not surprisingly, I was up half the night going to the bathroom, but at least I no longer felt bloated in the morning.

As much as the heat and the cycling were beginning to tire me out, today I felt extra perky because I knew that Pete was arriving tomorrow. It was hard to imagine he was actually joining me in France. What made it even more incredible was that we were not rendezvousing in Paris. Instead we had planned it so that he would meet me in the Loire Valley, then we would attend the start of the penultimate stage of the Tour together in Orléans before we moved on to Paris for the big finish on Sunday. This way Pete would have another taste of the provinces, which he liked so very much. But even more importantly, he'd be able to attend two stages of the Tour instead of just one. The more I thought about all this, the more excited I became.

I prayed that it would all go smoothly. Pete was to arrive early the next morning—Friday—in Paris, then find his way from the airport to the train station to pick up a train for Beaugency. For Pete, this sounded like a Herculean task. If it wasn't for the fact that he wanted to attend the stage in nearby Orléans, I'm sure he wouldn't have dreamed about attempting such a program. He had already voiced (over the phone) his concerns about finding his way around the airport, the city of Paris and the train station without me. *I knew he should have done at least a test run to the corner café on his own the last time we were together in France.* No sense in worrying about this now—there was nothing I could do short of hiring a car to provide him with door-to-door transportation. I felt confident that it would all work out, particularly since we had lucked out so well with our last-minute plans thus far.

I had my own program to follow within the next twenty-four hours. I packed up my luggage once again and left it for the baggage transfer person that was to take it to Beaugency, my next destination. I said goodbye to Monsieur Martinet and set out for another day of cycling and touring, the last I'd spend by myself in a while. I didn't think it was possible but today it seemed even hotter. It was definitely more humid, and as I pedaled off in the direction of Chambord, I noticed that the sky wasn't nearly as blue. *Well, maybe it's good the sun isn't shining so brightly because today is to be my biggest day of riding on my own.*

Chambord, my first stop, was more than twenty kilometers (twelve miles) away. I felt as though I could identify even more with the pain and suffering that the Tour riders endure during their three grueling weeks of cycling—ha! Today was the first time in a while that I had cycled for so long, three days in a row. Already my legs seemed made of concrete. My bottom felt so tender that I had to constantly stand up in the saddle, particularly when going over bumps. This already would have been tiresome for me on Bella, a streamlined road bike designed for such a maneuver, but on the hybrid I was riding it turned out to be quite the feat. How did the Tour riders possibly push themselves to such limits for six to eight hours a day over the course of this long race? No wonder they needed their nightly massage. *Hmmm, a massage—that would feel pretty good right now.*

I was jolted out of my reverie by a group of German guys in a German car barreling by me just outside of Chambord. "Hut! Hut! Hut!" or go, go, go, they all hollered. I must have looked as though I was dragging myself along. I considered yelling back—some sort of a dig about Armstrong whipping Ullrich (the German contender) in the Tour. But they were already long gone. Their catcalls served as a motivating force for me, since after that I found myself blowing into Chambord at nearly twice the speed.

I felt stupefied standing in front of Chambord gazing at this colossal castle. I had been here some twenty years before, but I didn't recall it being so spectacular. I hadn't remembered there being so many turrets, towers and spires. It looked like the most outstanding movie set you could imagine. *Oh, how I wish Pete could see this with me right now.*

Even though I didn't feel like going on a full-fledged tour, I did want to take a peek inside. I was also seeking relief from the heat since the sun was high in the sky and I was certain it would be cool within the thick, stone walls of this monolith. The crowds were beyond belief, but here—where everything was conceived on the grandest of scales—there was more than enough room to accommodate all the people. I did my own mini guided tour in twenty minutes, which was still exhausting. I trudged up the famous double spiral staircase, zombie-like, my legs aching with every step and took a cursory look around this sparsely furnished château. I passed a few fellow cyclists, we exchanged nods and I wondered how they were feeling in their chamois-bottomed shorts.

I had contemplated taking a ride on one of the boats you can rent on the premises but decided not to become too sidetracked. Plus, the moat looked awfully murky. At the boat and bike rental, I sought out Jean-Marie, the kind man that had delivered my bike to me a few days ago at Noyers-sur-Cher. We sat and had a bite to eat together on one of the many terraces in the little hamlet across from the château. "I don't remember all these shops, restaurants and ice cream vendors here twenty years ago," I said.

"They weren't here then," Jean-Marie replied. "Much has been developed around the château over the past two decades. I started my boat rental business here six years ago. The bikes, four years ago."

"It looks like you've followed one of the golden rules of starting a business," I exclaimed.

"Which one is that?"

"Location, location, location."

We both chuckled and in his wonderful, warm accent reminiscent of the south of France, this *marsellais* replied, "Yes, but I do miss the sea."

After chit-chatting about the many pleasures of cycling in the *parc de Chambord*, our discussion turned to a more serious matter as we heard rumblings off in the distance. "I think there's a fifty-fifty chance of a storm," Jean-Marie said. "No, make that seventy-thirty. The Loire acts as a barrier, though, so maybe we won't get the storm."

"The problem is that I'm crossing the Loire soon after I leave here," I added. Jean-Marie shrugged and then provided me with a bike lock (finally) and some vague directions about how I might best avoid the storm.

The old me would have found a way to hole myself up at Chambord until the storm blew by. Or I would have located a taxi that would have transported my bike and me to Beaugency for a small fortune. Surprisingly enough, I didn't even think about these alternative solutions—I just decided to go for it.

I rode away from Chambord, legs heavier than before. The heat was really bearing down now, even though it was more overcast. The views on the other side of the *parc* intrigued me. I peered into the woods to see if I could spot a recognizable beast through this veil of green. A carpet of ferns lined the forest floor and all was extremely quiet. The only sounds I heard were the tweeting of the birds, the clicking of my bike and the engine of an occasional passing car. The tranquility of this place and the repetitiveness of this vast forest lulled me into a meditative, almost trance-like state.

I hit a bump in the road and was brought back to my current reality. The combination of these dense woods and the ominous sky was foreboding. Suddenly I felt scared. I was surprised, too, that there weren't many cars on this route. I could tell that my emotions were beginning to get the best of me. I heard a rustling off to the side of the road and swerved out to the middle of the lane thinking that my life-long fear of encountering a wild boar in France was finally going to become a reality. (I had heard and read about many wild boar-charging stories in France, so I figured that if it was going to happen, the *parc de Chambord* would be the place.)

Finally I emerged from the forest. I began to feel more reassured about my decision to brave the storm. I could always take cover in some little café or boutique. I re-entered civilization at Muides-sur-Loire but missed the turn where I was supposed to cross the Loire. I twirled around a while until I located the designated bridge and gulped when I saw the busy traffic that passed over it. There wasn't any sort of a shoulder for cyclists. "Claim your lane when you go over a bridge or any other narrow roadway," I heard Pete saying. It felt gutsy in this instance, but I did it anyway.

I took the first turn off to the right of the bridge per Jean-Marie's suggestion. Here, supposedly, I would find the road that borders the Loire that would lead me all the way to Beaugency. I kept trying to trust that I was in the right spot. I circled around to avoid huge sand banks and a sort of quarry, all of which made up some kind of a large sand and gravel outfit. At one point, I found myself sharing the dirt road with mammoth trucks. I darted in and out of all the branches off of this hellish thoroughfare in an attempt to find the one that I was supposed to be on. I did this turn, then that turn, until I finally saw no one anymore. I detected no signs of human life except for the distant roar of work vehicles digging along the banks of the Loire.

My dirt road, which had become a path, suddenly ended. I was lost. I decided to pedal a stretch over cut hay, thinking that maybe I could find the path again elsewhere. I so hoped that all the distance I had already covered was not for naught. Soon I found myself in cornfields much taller than me. Then I found myself navigating alongside a very stagnant-looking creek. I felt sure I'd see a snake or some other type of critter. The storm loomed. I felt panicky. It seemed like I was back in Burgundy but this time without Pete. I had to get off my bike and walk it since I could no longer move forward even an inch in the sandy soil. It all seemed even more eerie when I spotted the chimneys of two nuclear power plants way off in the distance. I was sure I was about to cry.

My prayers were answered and I finally found my way out of the labyrinth of muck and sand when I located a nice gravelly path. It didn't provide the smoothest ride for someone that has a sore bottom, but I took it at a slow pace. I found myself riding almost directly toward the nuclear power plant. I couldn't help feeling a strange, menacing presentiment. Was it because of Three Mile Island, *Silkwood* or Chernobyl? Or was it the unfamiliarity of it all? As I advanced, I heard a loud hissing noise, almost like rushing water. But the Loire was so placid here. I had passed by nuclear power plants before in France but never noticed the noise. It's amazing how much more you pick up on a bike. You're so much closer to everything, and you can see and hear far better than when you're in a car.

I passed by this immense plant easily enough. Thankfully it was on the other side of the river, which gave it the illusion of being a safe distance away. The scene in front of it provided an interesting contrast: a large flock of birds paddled about in the water beneath the plant, creating a peaceful landscape incongruous to the mighty reactors beyond.

As I pedaled past the plant, the vistas became even more spectacular, providing wild and wonderful panoramas for which this part of the Loire is renowned. I passed a fisherman, then a cyclist, both of whom were the first people I had encountered in an hour. The cyclist and I confirmed our directions, reassuring each other that we were both (basically) headed the right way. The riverscape became even more extraordinary and with each short distance I traveled, this magnificent expanse of water revealed its many characteristics to me. It was wide and wily, calm in some places, whirring in others. The infamous current here has been known to be the demise of many a visitor to this river's shores. Cornfields bordered one side of me, marshlands another. I thought about the striking contrasts with Chambord. I mentally compared the beauty of this untamed river with the manmade grandeur that is Chambord. Both are disarmingly spectacular, both are stunning in their own right. How blessed I felt to be able to experience and appreciate them together in one day.

Despite my river rapture, I couldn't ignore my pain. The ruts on this road were doing a number on my tush. My fingers had gone numb—I suppose from holding the handgrips so tightly—and my head was pounding. I desperately needed water. Even with all my rationing, my water bottle had long gone dry. My throat was parched, and all my perspiring wasn't enough to keep my body cool. Just when I was truly growing weary, I passed a man with his young child and asked if Beaugency was far. *"Non, à deux kilometers."*

"Merci, monsieur," I responded most gratefully, since even in the state I was in, I knew that two kilometers was manageable.

Shortly after that, I pedaled onto a paved pathway, a delightful little road with flowers and trees planted at the river's edge. I wended my way up the hills of Beaugency toward the hotel where I was to spend the next two nights. It was 6:30 p.m. and I was whupped. The last leg of today's ride had taken two hours, as Jean-Marie predicted. I didn't know how many miles I had logged in all today but I know it was a lot. I said a prayer of thanks that the storm was kept at bay.

The exterior of the hotel where I was to stay was charming. Inside, however, told a different story. It's never a good sign when a hotel has carpeting on the walls. The interior didn't smell fresh, and in addition to a pervasive mustiness, I was sure it also reeked of hashish. (Hash is more prevalent in France than marijuana.) Sadly, my room upstairs wasn't any better. Here, the walls were not carpeted, however, the bathroom was—in a deep-pile shag of the muddiest brown. Little pieces of fabric were strewn about the room as doilies in an attempt to hide the ugly furnishings. This didn't at all look like the love palace I had envisioned for my sweetie and me in which to hold our special reunion.

My heart sunk with disappointment. I couldn't imagine us spending our first romantic evening in this dump. As tired as I was, I knew that it was my duty to go out and search for a better place of lodging. I rode my little bike all around this hilly town in the hope of finding an appropriate love nest—or at least something more palatable. I looked dreadful. I'm surprised I wasn't turned away at half the places. I was disheveled and sweaty and covered with bugs from the Loire Valley. I was on a mission, though, because already all of the places I had visited told me that they were fully booked since Beaugency was only a short distance from Orléans, the start of Saturday's stage of the Tour.

Finally I found what I'm sure was the last room in town (aside from mine back at my hotel). It was at L'Ecu de Bretagne, a lovely country inn much like the place I had pictured in my mind. Its last available room was grand in an old château-like kind of way, the perfect romantic hideaway that I reserved for sweetie and me for the next night. (I would have moved right in but it was not available that evening.)

Yippee! We were back in business. I practically danced back to my hotel on my little bike. Pete often said that when riding, you sometimes have to go through some tough stuff to arrive at where you want to go. That's how I viewed my night in this first hotel.

After I had a nice dinner out with Mikaël, one of the representatives from the regional tourist board, I tiptoed back to my room and fell into bed without much looking around. The next morning was more of a challenge since the proprietor had learned that I'd be moving out a day early, and as a result, he acted rather bristly toward me. I decided not to let it bother me. In fact, not much could disturb me at that point because Pete was due to arrive in a few hours and we were going to check into a charming French country inn together. I just sipped my tea and gathered my thoughts until it was time to depart.

Once I had deposited my luggage and bike at L'Ecu de Bretagne, it was time to meet Pete at the train station. I arrived a good fifteen minutes in advance just in case his train was early. My heart was pounding. I couldn't believe that soon a train would pull up in a little town in France and he'd step off of it. I couldn't wait to see him. It seemed as though we had been away from each other for three months—not just under three weeks. I was all a-twitter. I had sweaty palms and a shortness of breath. It actually felt good to feel this kind of nervousness. My love for Pete felt really alive. Physically, too, I was feeling great and there's no doubt I was looking better than I had all summer. I was tanned and also trimmer than when I left. And thanks also to my recent cycling exploits, I'm sure I looked more relaxed and confident despite my schoolgirl jitters.

Pete was the last one off the train. My heart stopped for a moment or two when I thought he had missed his connections. But when I finally saw him descending the steps of the train—flashing his wide grin and big brown eyes at me—I ran to meet him. He dropped his luggage and we hugged each other and laughed and then kissed and laughed for a long while. "I can't believe you're actually here," I almost shouted.

"Yeah, I made it without a hitch, too. I was even bumped up to business class on the plane."

"Really?"

"Yeah, one of the guys in charge at check-in knew you."

"No way! That's great! I'm so glad you're here. I'm so glad you had a good trip."

"I'm glad I'm here, too. And you look great! How's the cycling going? Have you lined up anything for us with the Tour?"

We were so excited about seeing each other that we could hardly contain ourselves. Pete was weary from his night of travels but that didn't dampen his enthusiasm about us finally being together. I detected, too, his contentment about having made such good connections all the way to Beaugency.

"I'm so proud of you!" I yelled as I gave him another big hug. "Now that you have a taste of being on your own in France, you'll probably be looking to take off on me."

"No way, I'm not going anywhere without you!" he teased. Our short walk to the hotel—wheeling Pete's luggage over cobbled roads and bumpy sidewalks in the already beastly heat of the day— was made more than bearable by our excitement about being together. In between brief snippets about all that had transpired for us during the time we were apart, we bubbled over with happiness about our reunion. I don't think either of us had imagined how good it would feel to find each other again. And it was clear we both had much more than cycling and the Tour on our mind.

"We can't check into the hotel just yet," I announced. "The room won't be ready until early afternoon."

"Well, I'm pretty hungry anyway," Pete admitted. "So maybe we can have something to eat first."

"That sounds good to me. Actually I noticed the perfect place just a few doors from our hotel," Just a short while later, we found ourselves settled onto the terrace of a pizzeria where we sat beneath a brightly colored umbrella, amply shaded from the mid-day heat. I'm sure we both felt as though we were experiencing one of those moments we'd never forget.

"I can't believe I'm here," Pete said. "And at the same time, I feel practically at home. I love how the French take time to enjoy a meal on a terrace like this."

Whoa—could this be the same Pete? He must have missed me. And France, too.

Our lovemaking after lunch was sweet and full of passion. It was obviously much anticipated by both of us and it didn't disappoint. It was the ultimate confirmation of our love for each other and our eagerness to be together.

Pete looked like a god to me. He was right up there in the ranks with the pro cyclists I encountered last week. (Actually, I find him even more attractive, since he's more filled out.) He'd been cycling hard since I left and it showed. It was such a turn-on to see him so strong and svelte. I was feeling pretty good about myself, too. Yes, that made a difference as well. I was exuding a sexiness that made it better for us both.

After basking in an especially nice afterglow, I got up and began to prepare myself for an outing. Pete was fast asleep by now, so I decided to head out and take one last spin on my bike. It felt funny to be doing such a thing, particularly in the heat of the day, and especially after making love. I was surprised by myself. Normally I would have laid on the bed reading, while Pete slept soundly by my side. That would have been the old, less adventuresome me. Today, I didn't think twice about suiting up in my bike clothes and heading out for a ride. The fact that I had just had a passionate romp made me feel all the more revved up and daring.

I zipped down the hill at Beaugency in search of the water's edge. I was drawn to the Loire and I relished the idea that I had one last chance to pedal alongside of it. This time I headed farther north toward Meung-sur-Loire. I felt myself sink into a state of deep relaxation as soon as I was cruising alongside this vast and mighty body of water. It was beastly hot, but my proximity to the river helped to cool me off. I felt so happy and free, so fulfilled and grateful. Pete had made it all right and here I was out cycling while he slept gently back in our room. Tonight we would have a romantic dinner together. Tomorrow we would attend the Tour; then we would find ourselves back in Paris. I thanked the heavens above for how this had all worked out.

It seemed to me that my time away from Pete had served a purpose. It had given me another opportunity to grow as a person and also to become a more confident cyclist and Tour aficionado. Our separation had helped us both to reflect on our relationship and what we really meant to each other. In many ways, this separation was even more significant than the two-month one we had experienced when Pete went to Montana. I thought about all this as I rode alongside the Loire and concluded that it looked as though Pete and I were in it for the long haul. I chuckled when I thought of this, knowing that this meant that I'd have to learn how to handle him better. In the name of peace and *bonne entente*, I'd have to respond in a more detached manner to his grumpiness and lack of patience; I'd have to learn how to let so much more go. I'd have to allow his yang to balance out my yin.

Sure I was less of a girly-girl than when we first came together, but I was still impossibly feminine in many ways. Pete was trying to understand our differences more. But he was still such a guy; he didn't show his warm and fuzzy side as often as I would have liked. There would probably always be a gulf of misunderstanding between us. We were both made very differently and didn't always think alike. *Vive la différence!* He was a sweetheart, though—there's no doubt about that. Don't opposites attract anyway? We still had a lot to experience together, we still had much to learn from each other. There's no doubt, too, that as much as we were different, we both felt a real connectedness to each other, a deep resonance that kept bringing us closer to each another both physically and spiritually. *Live the mystery of this love,* I told myself. *Let it be what it is. Savor all that is wonderful about it.*

My river contemplations made me feel even more dreamy about Pete, and consequently, more hopeful about our future together. I envisioned us with a child. He'd be a great father. I was almost sorry I was already coming up on Meung-sur-Loire. Then I told myself, *That's a good thing. You need to get out of your head more. Just go with the flow.*

It was recommended to me to take a tour of Château de Meung-sur-Loire, the small, medieval treasure of this village of the same name. I joined in on a guided tour with a jumble of foreigners; together we nodded approvingly over the various appointments of this historic dwelling as well as the scope of its history. "It served as the residence of the bishops of Orléans during the eighteenth century. Parts of this château actually date back to the twelfth and thirteenth centuries, a time commonly referred to as the Dark Ages," the guide informed us. Then she recounted grim stories about this era, telling us about the atrocities committed at—or rather beneath—the château throughout the centuries.

We all descended a very steep and narrow staircase into the bowels of the earth, way below the château, where we could see for ourselves the underground prison and torture chambers that were once a very real part of this château's history. At first we felt refreshed by the chilliness of the air below, but after hearing some of the horrific tales and methods of torture, it seemed as though most of us regarded the underground as just plain chilling. No one walked away, though. The last stop on our tour was outside beneath the château. All of us peered down into a ghastly hole in the ground and discovered the oubliette, the place prisoners were thrown away and more or less forgotten. (*Oublier* means "to forget" in French.) We dispersed after that, grateful, I imagine, that we now live in more civilized times.

I was thirsty, so I decided to sit on a terrace in the center of town and enjoy a refreshing Coke. Everyone else was paired off, which didn't disturb me since I knew my other half wasn't far away. Despite the gruesome château-life stories, I shifted into my happy-go-lucky mode and just sat there watching people and the world go by. When I went inside to *les toilettes*, I noticed the Tour was blaring on the television and a crowd was gathered round cheering on the riders. I stopped and took it all in, reassuring myself that Lance was still the overall leader, and that he remained unstoppable. *"Vous êtes américaine?"* one of the men asked, inquiring if I was American. (It must have been my sporty attire once again.)

"*Oui*," I responded. Then a group of men gathered around me and praised the accomplishments of the U.S. cycling team and Lance's outstanding performance. I felt proud and delighted that I was standing there in this little café in France, having such an enthusiastic exchange with a group of French men. "Sports can really bring people together," I could hear Pete say. This was certainly a good example of that. Too bad he was back in bed sleeping since I think these guys would have enjoyed his company.

My ride back to Beaugency flew by. I think I pedaled doubly fast because I was really anxious to be back with Pete. I hit a bakery once I arrived in town and purchased some croissants and *pains au chocolat* for Pete and me. He was just beginning to stir when I entered the room, so my timing was perfect. We gobbled up our goodies with copious amounts of Evian, not bothered at all by the crumbs in the bed. "How was your ride?" he asked.

"Oh, it was great—I really love that river."

"How many miles did you do?"

"Oh, I don't know—I've stopped counting. I don't have an odometer on that bike and I've stopped trying to figure it out. It doesn't seem to matter much anymore." Pete looked at me quizzically and I knew he wouldn't understand that comment. I knew he couldn't grasp what it meant to me to just ride for the ride, not for the sport of it all. We were still as different as ever, but it no longer seemed to matter as much.

He gave me a little wink after some reflection and said, "I know what you mean. It's probably just as well that I wasn't with you on this trip. It sounds like your rides weren't very challenging. It's good that you had fun, though."

We finished our treats while watching the day's wrap-up of the Tour on TV. We felt like two old chums and it definitely seemed like this relationship was on track after all.

That evening we shared in an enchanting meal in our French country inn. Our table was next to a large window that opened wide onto the *place* of this darling town. We dined at a table set with neatly-pressed linens and fine china. Candles and flowers further accented the romance that danced in the air. We delighted in a wonderful meal that would rival the best of those experienced stateside. The service was excellent and practically imperceptible. Pete and I were charmed by our surroundings and by each other. "You look more beautiful than ever," Pete said. I smiled back and prayed that the magic we had been feeling all day and night would last forever.

We both woke up easily the next day, extremely excited about joining up with the Tour. I was more than ready to get back into the thick of this electrifying event and Pete was anxious to have a taste of it for the first time. We chatted at breakfast about how we thought the morning would play out over big, steamy cups of *café au lait* and a basket of buttery croissants. "Since we're going to the departure at Orléans, you should have plenty of opportunities to see the riders," I told Pete. "It was really thrilling when I went to the start at Aix-les-Bains. The cyclists were actually quite approachable. They were just hanging out before they headed out for the day."

"That's what's so great about cycling," Pete said. "There's no other professional sport that provides such opportunities to be so close to the riders and so close to the race."

"Yeah, that's probably the biggest reason why cycling fans should attend the Tour de France at least once in their lives. As much as the TV coverage is great, being at the actual event is even more exciting. I still can't believe how small so many of the riders look."

"You'd look that way, too, if you burned all the calories they do in a day," Pete replied. And upon hearing that remark, I decided not to have a second croissant after all.

Mikaël, my contact from the tourist board, came by a short while later to pick us up. It turned out to be a real chore squeezing Pete and me and our abundance of luggage into his mini compact car, but somehow we managed. (My bike was left behind at the hotel for Jean-Marie to retrieve later that day.) You could tell something big was about to take place because there was already a lot of traffic at Beaugency, and it only increased as we approached Orléans. We were told that many streets in Orléans were blocked off for the Tour, so we parked a distance away from the city center. It seemed as though this start of the Tour was going to be much more hectic than the one I attended in the Alps.

That thought turned out to be an understatement because soon we found ourselves caught up in throngs of spectators and curious bystanders the likes of which you'd see at a visit from the Pope. "Where'd all these people come from?" I asked.

"I think they have come from the whole region," Mikaël proudly declared. I quickly designed a plan (and a plan B) about what we all should do in case we were separated.

We arrived at the center of town—by the cathedral—in time to see the beginnings of the publicity caravan. The atmosphere was super lively and carnival-like. Loud music, horn blowing and colorful people and vehicles galore put the crowd in a festive mood. A twenty-foot tall stickman operated by some poor fellow beneath him gyrated over the cobbled *place* accompanied by a two-man band that played about seven different instruments."I can see the start line," I yelled. "But we want to find the place where the cyclists congregate ahead of time." Thank goodness I knew about this, since with all this confusion, we might have just stayed there in the hope of garnering a good spot for the start.

"Some of the riders are up there signing in at the podium," Pete added, all wide-eyed about finally catching a glimpse of the Tour.

"Let's find the information booth," Mikaël shouted over the clamor of the drums. "That's where we should be able to obtain the pass that will let you into the village, the place you want to go." Another fifteen minutes of weaving in and out of the crowds passed before we reached the so-called information booth. I could tell Pete was becoming antsy—he was fearful that this searching around was going to make him miss the real action.

"Just bear with us," I said to Pete in a semi-pleading voice. He was ready to bolt off toward the start and I was hoping he wouldn't. After much consternation with the person in charge, we learned that despite our persuasive pleas, only one press pass would be issued, only one right of passage to the area where you could freely mingle with the riders. "You take it," I said to Pete. "I've done it already—I want you to experience this."

Pete immediately took off in the direction of the area where we were told the riders would congregate. It was too late to go to the village, a sort of roving trade show-like center where there's always a chance you might bump into some cycling notables. So as Pete attempted to find his way to the stable of the world's greatest cyclists, Mikaël and I wended our way all the way around the back of the cathedral to the other side, where we hoped to check out riders from the sidelines. Sure enough, by the time we made our way to the long avenue that extended out from the cathedral, we began to see the big, multi-colored team buses pulling up one after the other in this special area. Long rows of metal barriers and vigilant policemen kept Mikaël and me from entering this space, but we were so close to the scene from the sidewalks that we knew it was worth our trek over here. Just as the squadron of team cars approached and more crowds gathered both inside and outside this arena, Mikaël and I spotted Pete.

"Heeeyyy, Pete!" I yelled, waving from across the street, half expecting he might ignore me since he looked so caught up in the excitement of this vast assemblage of cycling talent. Instead he turned and waved, flashing me his big toothy grin, unable to contain his happiness about being in on such action. Little by little, the cyclists emerged from their buses, greeting the privileged fans and sponsors that had access to this reserved area. Clearly, many interviews were also being conducted there, and these reporters—along with their photographers and the multitude of other camera-toting people—only added to the celebrity-like atmosphere of the whole scene. Pete had my camera in hand and I could tell he was positioning himself for shots of his favorite athletes. Suddenly I remembered how Pete often mentioned that most of the top cyclists are treated like rock stars in Europe.

"Hey, there's Ja Ja," I yelled and pointed to Pete, referring to Laurent Jalabert, one of France's most talented and beloved cyclists. Pete had already seen him and was inching his way over for a shot. Ja Ja was busy signing autographs. I had given Pete a polka dot jersey from the Tour's collection, just like the one Ja Ja was wearing in honor of his standing as King of the Mountains (best overall climber). Before we separated, I suggested to Pete that he take the jersey because he'd brought it with him on the outside chance he'd have the opportunity to ask Ja Ja to sign it. "Here, take this," I gestured to Pete from the sidelines. He hesitated, but after a bit of insistence from me, grabbed it and headed back to France's darling. Darn—just as Pete approached, Ja Ja made a sign that he was through with signing autographs and pedaled off to join some other teammates. Pete and I shared an expression of disappointment from across the crowds.

Suddenly I realized that the U.S. Postal team bus was pulling up not far from me. Wow! It seemed as though I'd have a better vantage point for them than Pete. A huge crowd gathered near the bus because by now even those not in-the-know, knew about Lance Armstrong. As we all stood there with eyes fixed on the door of this splendid rig—not wanting to miss the moment it opened—Pete continued to bop around taking in the scene, snapping pictures of world-renowned cyclists such as Tyler Hamilton, Kevin Livingston, Jackie Durand and Jan Ullrich. It was all very exciting.

Finally, after what seemed to be an interminable amount of time, the U.S. Postal team cyclists emerged from their deluxe air-conditioned vehicle. The crowd—most of which were French—whistled and cheered as if these cyclists were their own. *"Bravo!"* they yelled, which I thought was sweet, but I was even happier to shout out my words of encouragement in English. Lance was the last of the team to appear, which, not surprisingly, made the mob go wild. He seemed quiet and reserved—almost shy—and decidedly quite modest about his huge celebrity status. I waved to Pete, indicating to him that Lance was there. He was just able to catch him as he sped away.

That seemed to be a sign of an imminent departure and everyone took their cue from Lance. The spectators—which included an array of people from fans, to local merchants, to a couple of old ladies hanging out of their balcony—waved a last goodbye to this rainbow-colored parade of cyclists. No one walked away disappointed from this show. Mikaël and I scurried to the start line. Pete had suddenly disappeared. We watched it from a street corner, striving to see over and between the heads of the thousands of people that lined the *départ*. The heat pounded down again today, but that didn't matter since we knew we wouldn't be standing there long. As in the Alps, they were off in a flash. I couldn't help thinking we'd given them a nice send-off for the 149.5 kilometers (ninety-three miles) they were to ride that day beneath a blistering sun.

"So, how was it?" I yelled to Pete as I spotted him at our designated meeting spot. He only smiled—a particularly big smile—and that said it all. We both had Tour fever and just being able to attend this rousing event made us even more stoked about it. It brought us together even more. It was so much fun to share this passion.

"Oh, and I saw Bob Roll, too. You know, the former pro cyclist who is now the commentator for OLN (Outdoor Life Network)," Pete added.

"I think most of the world's cycling greats were there on that avenue today," I said.

"I know," Pete replied. "I'm so glad I didn't miss it."

"Did you by any chance see Phil Liggett and Paul Sherwen in the commentator booth? Those guys are so suave—I'd love to meet them."

"Nah, they were probably parked at the finish."

"Oh, that's right. I forgot about that. I guess I don't know everything—yet," I said with a crooked smile and a wink.

"No, but you've come a long way."

"Haven't we both, it seems."

Paris and a Triumphant Finish

Less than an hour after the start in Orléans, Pete and I found ourselves whizzing toward Paris in the air-conditioned comfort of a French railcar. "It's fun to be traveling together again," I said. "Here we are sailing along on this marvel of French technology without either of us having to worry about the responsibilities of driving or navigating."

"It's nice just to relax," Pete said.

Of course we were both still high about our Tour experience. Much of our conversation centered around that, as well as our own joy at having participated in such a world-class event. The ride was made even better by the little picnic I had set up, which included sandwiches and drinks purchased at the station.

"You know what," Pete said. "I've actually missed these bready sandwiches. There's never much meat and cheese—and no mustard—but what's there tastes good. I've missed the Orangina, too."

"You can get Orangina in the U.S."

"Yeah, but I guess I've missed having it here in France with you."

"Ooooh, that's so sweet. You're sounding so sentimental," I said, half teasing.

"It's true."

"I think the sandwiches and Orangina bring back memories of our last trip to France," I said. "That's part of what I love about food—all the associations attached to a particular dish or snack. I experienced that a lot when I lived here, especially in the beginning

"What'd they sell?"

"They had Tex Mex, barbecue sauces, American mayonnaise—they taste different from French brands. And you'd find other random items such as Almond Roca and Velveeta cheese."

"Velveeta cheese?" Pete queried.

"Yeah, can you believe it? I'd hate to think that's American 'gourmet,'" I replied.

"What kinds of things did you buy?"

"Cranberry sauce, pecans—that sort of thing. I'd mostly go for Thanksgiving. But I'd sometimes buy Hellman's mayo and Toll House chocolate chips, too."

We munched in silence for a while, and then suddenly Pete asked, "Have you made plans for tonight?"

"Not yet, but I promise we'll have a good meal."

"Oh, I have no doubt about that."

"So what do you think?" I asked.

"About what?"

"About France. Have you fallen in love with France?

"Well, a country that holds cycling and fine dining in such high esteem *is* pretty fantastic."

"I think so, too."

The gradual slowing of the train gently awakened us as we pulled into the train station in Paris. We both felt beyond relaxed at that point—so much so, in fact, that we were still in a sleepy state when we dragged our luggage onto the platform. We strolled casually through the station despite our load. Right off, it seemed this trip to Paris was going to unfurl differently from our last. Our connections ran like clockwork, and even the taxi driver that drove us to our hotel was perfectly charming. It was still beastly hot but the summer heat wave only seemed to add to the festive mood of the city.

I had arranged for us to stay at the Hôtel du Louvre, right across from the Louvre on the rue de Rivoli. To me, this location seemed pretty ideal for attending the Tour, since the Champs-Elysees, the avenue where the finish is held, is only a brisk walk away. The hotel had also been recently refurbished, so I was also interested in checking that out. Aside from perhaps the Hôtel de Crillon—where you can actually watch the Tour from their balconies—Pete and I decided we were at one of the best locations for the last stage of the Tour.

"Oh, look at this," I said to Pete as I waltzed around our smartly decorated suite, done up in rich earth tones and elegant furnishings. "It's time to slip into Parisian high-styled mode," I cooed.

"Yeah, pretty different from the provinces."

"I'm sorry I didn't bring my silk peignoir. Had I known you were going to join me, I would have."

Pete clicked on the TV with the hope of catching the replay of the day's race. For once I didn't protest about the TV being the main focus. I slipped into one of the plush robes supplied by the hotel and eased into relaxed mode. I poured two glasses of Pouilly Fuissé from the bottle we'd found chilling in our room upon arrival.

"This feels like a dream," I said as we clinked glasses. "I still can't believe you're here."

"What'd he just say?" Pete yelled while watching and listening to an interview with Laurent Jalabert, which was entirely in French. *I guess this isn't a good time to be romantic,* I thought. "Tell me what's going on," Pete said, all rammy.

Translating this all-French coverage became a challenging task. The translation needed to be as rapid fire as the interview and I had a hard time keeping up, especially since Pete kept wanting to know what was just said before I could even get the words out. I could barely follow the TV reporting at all. "I know you're not telling me everything," Pete barked.

"I'm trying—you keep interrupting my train of thought."

"Your French is excellent—just tell me what they're saying. Don't just give me bits and pieces."

"Well, you know I'd never be able to work at the U. N.— simultaneous translation isn't my strong suit." Fortunately Pete chilled before we had a blow-up. It was all so perfect that it didn't need to be ruined by my half-assed translations and his impatience.

We each finished a couple of glasses of wine before feeling satisfied with the Tour recap of the day. Finally it was time to put the focus on us, to bathe, cuddle and think about plans for dinner. By now, Pete was beginning to feel the effects of jet lag, heat and the excitement of the day, so I decided I'd better pick up the pace or else our plans for a romantic evening in Paris would once again be thwarted. "Let's go to some place really fun and hip," I suggested.

"Sure, whatever you think would be a good choice sounds fine with me."

A half-hour had passed and the concierge still wasn't able to reserve a table for us at a reasonable hour at any of the "in" places I had in mind. "OK, it's Saturday night, but it's also the dead of summer. Most Parisians clear out of town by now. I can't believe it's so hard to find a cool place in the area, especially here on the Right Bank," I declared from the bathroom.

"I'm sure whatever you find will be fine."

"Oh, I just thought of a place where we can have a fantastic meal in an intimate setting. It's considered to be pretty happening, too, in its own quiet way. It's Asian and also one of my favorites. I'm sure a reservation there won't be a problem, either."

"Great," Pete yelled back.

I wrapped up my beautification and found Pete in an obvious quandary back in the bedroom. "What's wrong?"

"I forgot my loafers."

"Well, what shoes *do* you have?"

"My Birks and my sneakers."

"You mean your Birkenstock sandals are the only type of nonathletic footwear you have?"

"Yeah, I can't believe I forgot my loafers. I have my suit jacket, though. I had such a hard time packing—I wasn't sure of what to bring," Pete continued.

I gulped hard since I didn't want to make a comment that would make him feel bad, or even worse, start a fight. I didn't want to spoil our evening. Paris became even more casual since I'd moved back to the States. But this kind of footwear was hardly *acceptable*.

"We'll just have to go with it," I said. "There's nothing we can do about it until Monday when the stores open anyway."

We chuckled and I couldn't help rolling my eyes and shaking my head as we stood in front of the elevator assessing each other's attire. Pete had on an Oxford-type shirt, khakis and his very pedestrian-looking Birks. I was dressed in a colorful silk jacket, slim pants and the season's big rage, a pair of sexy mules. "At least you can walk," I laughed as we headed over to the restaurant. "I feel like I'm just teetering along."

Once settled into Davé, our little shoe crisis was forgotten. True to himself, Davé, a slight, effeminate-looking Asian, presented us with no menu and instead rattled off a few of the house specialties. Pete deferred to me since I had been to this little restaurant before, each time feasting on the best Chinese food I'd ever tasted.

"I saw Beck over there," Pete said in a low voice.

"Who's that?"

"He's a well-known musician. Great guitar player."

"Well, I guess I'm out of the loop. I've seen lots of people from the fashion world here, though—it's one of their favorite haunts. I always see someone famous here."

"No wonder, since it's so discreet," Pete replied.

"Yes, very hush-hush," I practically whispered.

"It seems like Davé was trying to figure out who we were when he greeted us," Pete said.

"I know, I got that impression, too. Just keep your shoes hidden underneath the table and maybe we'll eke by without too many questions," I kidded.

The meal couldn't have been more perfect. The dim sum (*les vapeurs*), the egg roll-like *rouleaux vietnamiens* and the shrimp in black bean sauce were as delicious as I had remembered them to be. All was washed down with a Tavel, a clean, crisp rosé from Provence. Pete and I were both conquered. Our evening in Paris was a huge success.

As I made my way back to the table after a short visit to the ladies' room, I spotted Pete with a devilish grin on his face. "Whaaat?" I asked.

"You'll never believe what happened."

"Whaaat? Tell me."

"Well, right after you left to go to the restroom, Davé came over and was pointing at my shoes. I had my legs crossed, so one of my sandals was sort of up in the air—in plain view. I put my foot down real fast. It almost seemed like he was going to scold me about my shoes. Then I realized he wanted to look at my shoe—UP CLOSE. So I took it off and handed it to him." My eyes widened. I couldn't imagine what Pete was going to tell me after that. "Next thing I knew, Davé was handling my Birkenstock and examining it very closely. I was mortified and I kept thinking—particularly after your comments—that he was going to say something for wearing this kind of shoe in his restaurant." My mouth dropped and I had all I could do not to burst out in laughter. "Then Davé asked me where I bought such wonderful shoes."

I lost it on that remark and started to howl. "You're pulling my leg."

"I swear—I'm not." And as he said it, I knew Pete was telling the truth. He has a good sense of humor but he's no jokester. "Then he asked me where he could buy them and I told him they come from Germany, but I bought mine in the States," Pete trailed off until we both began to laugh almost uncontrollably. (About six months after this happened, I saw a picture in a newspaper lauding Gwyneth Paltrow for wearing Birkenstocks with a Chanel suit. I guess Pete was ahead of the fashion curve, after all.)

We laughed more about that little episode at breakfast at the Hôtel du Louvre the next morning. "There's probably a lesson to be learned in all that," I said. "But please, let's find you a nice pair of dress shoes before we have dinner at the Plaza Athenée."

"Hey, there's Pedro Delgado," Pete interjected.

"Who's that?"

"He's a former pro cyclist. He actually won the Tour de France once. I bet he's here commentating on the Tour for Spanish television." Suddenly we shifted back to talk of the Tour.

"It's hard to believe the boys will be pulling into town today. After having watched them cycle throughout the countryside of France, it's difficult for me to imagine them zooming through the streets of Paris."

"I think a lot of people are here for the Tour," Pete said as he sized up the crowd in the sunny breakfast area of our hotel.

"So do you think you want to check out the Louvre?" I ventured.

"I'd like to check it out as long as we are on the Champs-Elysées in plenty of time for the arrival of the Tour."

"Oh, absolutely. I want to be there for all the doings, too."

It was another hot day in Paris, so it seemed like a good idea to while away the morning within the cool interior of the Louvre. As we approached the glass pyramid that marks the visitors entrance, we spotted a serpentine line that indisputably represented an interminable wait. "I'm not waiting in that line," Pete protested.

"No, I don't do lines like that either. Come with me—I've got a better idea."

We entered the vast area that lies beneath the pyramid from the rue de Rivoli, and after a couple of shots of each other posing in front of the inverted pyramid below, I proceeded directly to the counter at Virgin Megastore.

"What are you doing?" Pete asked for about the third time.

"I told you—I think we can buy tickets here for the Louvre and just enter down the hall without waiting in line."

"That can't be—you're crazy," Pete insisted.

"I know it's hard to believe. But I heard that somewhere, so I think it's worth a try." By the time I finished that sentence, a woman at the counter offered me help and then promptly sold me two tickets to the Louvre. I still couldn't believe it was that easy. "You mean there's no line anywhere here?" I asked.

"*Mais non, madame.*"

"Well, how come there's not a sign or anything else indicating that people can buy admission tickets to the Louvre here?"

"Because we don't want the crowds," the woman flatly responded. I held up my hand for Pete to give me a high-five and we breezed into the Louvre widely content with ourselves. This was at least the sixth time in three days that all worked out beautifully. *La vie est belle, quoi.*

Two steps into this massive collection of art and antiquities, I began to regret that I didn't have one of those little pullouts that I'd seen in so many travel magazines, the ones that feature touring the Louvre in an hour or less. Pete was already in fifth gear, darting about taking a look at this and that, then giving a quick tug of my hand, saying, "C'mon, let's go." We did the "c'mon, let's go" routine through about fifty rooms of the Louvre which probably spanned nearly ten different floors, Lord knows how many separate buildings and countless centuries.

"How can you absorb anything like this?" I finally asked, doing my best not to whine.

"I just want to get the general feel of things. I think I've got it now, so c'mon, let's go."

It's a good thing we decided to leave when we did because by the time we hit the streets, Tour mania was in full swing. It was not nearly time for the Tour to arrive but the crowds had gathered in driving force. We knew we didn't have far to walk from the Louvre to the bottom of the Champs-Elysées, the spot from where we figured we'd best view the Tour. But with so many people and so many roads blocked off, this jaunt proved to be a major challenge. I could tell by the look on Pete's face that he was becoming panicky. "Let's just stand here," he practically shouted, indicating a spot on an already crowded street corner where I figured we'd be lucky if we caught an ultra-quick glimpse of the riders as they sped by.

"No, let's try to go to the grandstand as planned."

"No, here is good, it's right outside the tunnel," Pete insisted. "This is a decisive part of the race. I recognize this from the TV coverage."

"C'mon, sweetie," I implored. "Just trust me."

We had talked about a scheme to gain special access to the VIP area at breakfast, however, now Pete appeared less sure of my plan. I suggested we try to find one of the Tour information booths where I'd see if I could obtain a press pass the way I had in Orléans. I suspected this would be harder to do in Paris, so I had devised a plan B, the plan that made Pete the most uncertain. "Let's just try to gain access to the reserved area with our press passes from the other stages," I had suggested earlier.

"That's pretty daring coming from you, Miss Goody Two Shoes."

"I know, I've always prided myself on being extremely honest. But this isn't much of a stretch. Look at all I do to promote France. And after this summer, I'm sure I'll be touting the Tour. So if we can't find the information booth, let's just squeeze in on the sly."

But as we stood outside our hotel in the thick of all kinds of barriers and officialdom, Pete seemed more reluctant about my plan. "How come you didn't arrange this ahead of time?" Pete stammered. "You did, after all, meet Lance."

"OK, let's not go there—let's just hurry or else we won't be able to make it through." We zig-zagged through the streets of Paris behind the rue de Rivoli and the place de la Concorde. "Look as though you belong here," I whispered to Pete as we approached the first security checkpoint. He looked as though he was about to bolt or at least have some kind of a fit. "Just let me do the talking," I said in a hushed voice.

Thank goodness we both breezed through without a hitch. There were so many people filing through that it was virtually impossible to closely look at each pass. I turned around in time to see Pete's wide grin. Clearly his confidence was greatly restored.

We practically skipped across the place de la Concorde, reveling in the fact that within this cordoned off area the crowds were far more manageable. "Let's head over to the grandstand section," I said to Pete, grabbing his hand as I began to veer off in that direction. From a distance, however, we both spotted one lone security person standing at the entrance to that separate area. Pete looked at me with an expression that said, Oh no, we're not going through that again.

"C'mon, let's try—we have nothing to lose. It would be great—plus we can sit down in that area." The look on Pete's face turned to one of resignation; he could tell I had my mind made up. He also knew I was good at pleading my case. So he probably figured I could talk our way into this special VIP section if need be.

Amazingly, that wasn't even necessary. It seemed as though it was enough for security to see some sort of official pass around our necks, so no questions were asked. Pete and I made our way to the middle section of the grandstand in front of the Champs-Elysées, ideally situated beneath the shade of an enormous chestnut tree, directly across from the big screen TV. We were ecstatic. We joked about pinching ourselves since we still couldn't fathom we were really there, ready to watch the final stage of the Tour de France together on the Champs-Elysées. We were in a great place to people watch, too, which we did enthusiastically as we observed the diverse range of spectators filling the stands. "Some of the friends and family of a few of the Dutch cyclists just sat down behind us," Pete whispered. Indeed, people from all over Europe and beyond claimed seats around us.

"This is truly an international event." I said. "I still can't believe I missed this all the years I lived in France."

"I can't believe it either," Pete said, shaking his head.

"Oh well, I'm making up for it now, aren't I? It's nice we can share this big, first-time event together," I said as I gave him a squeeze.

Once the grandstand became almost entirely filled up, Pete loosened up even more. "I'm glad I can finally relax," he admitted. "I kept thinking we were going to be booted from here."

"You just stick with me," I teased. "I feel like I've come to know my way around the Tour scene pretty well." Just then we spotted a woman descending the aisle distributing ice-cold Cokes.

"It looks as though they're free," Pete said.

"Yeah, and that other person is passing out sandwiches. Our luck is doubling by the moment."

Halfway through our most welcome yet unexpected picnic, the giant TV screen was turned on revealing the race in full Technicolor splendor. The Tour riders were approaching the capital. I could sense the excitement mounting around me with each kilometer that brought them closer to the Champs. The publicity caravan blasted in with all the hoopla of a fast-moving circus coming to town. The fanfare surrounding this colorful cavalcade of promotional vehicles provided an excellent distraction as we sat on the edge of our seats in anticipation of the cyclists' arrival. If the pretty girls that touted the sponsors' products were tired out from three weeks of being on display, they didn't show it. Each was fresh and smiling, waving from the many vehicles like beauty queens at a pageant. They knew what it meant to parade up and down the Champs-Elysées.

"Look, that colossal shopping cart with the giant cup of steaming *café au lait* even made it to the end," I said. "This is a triumphant finish of sorts for them, too," I laughed.

"Yeah, but that's nothing compared to the more than 2,000 miles riders log across France during the three weeks of the Tour."

"Belgium, too. Remember they also rode through Belgium," I added in a know-it-all kind of way.

As the caravan continued to do laps up and down this grand avenue, our attention shifted to the Jumbotron across from us. "There they are," Pete shouted. And when I looked up I saw that the cameras had captured the riders cruising alongside the Seine with the Eiffel Tower perfectly positioned in the background.

"The whole scene practically gives me goose bumps," I said.

Not long after the publicity caravan dispersed, a whole squadron of motorcycles buzzed by in front of us. Pete and I—and apparently the rest of the spectators—knew that this pack of *motos* indicated the imminent arrival of the cyclists. We all craned our necks toward the place de la Concorde as we followed the action out of the corner of our eyes on the Jumbotron. As everyone jumped to their feet and began to cheer wildly, the peloton zoomed into view and barreled up the Champs-Elysées with the force of a fierce wind. After the initial big swoosh, I realized the cyclists were traveling as fast—probably about 25 to 30 mph—as the motorcyclists that rode ahead of them. It was a glorious sight. As fast as it all happened, I could see that the U. S. Postal team lead the rest of the Tour riders into Paris, as is the tradition for the winning team.

It was great to be across from the big screen TV. As the cyclists made their way up and down the Champs-Elysées and back down by the place de la Concorde, along the Seine, through the tunnel, and up part of the rue de Rivoli, we could follow every bit of the excitement. "This is the best," Pete said. "The riders don't just blow by once. Here—along this loop—they pass ten times."

"Yeah, it's really impressive. Each time the peloton whizzes by, you feel a big rush. I'm over the the moon," I said to Pete. I had viewed the workings of the peloton—a group of approximately 150 cyclists—in action before on TV, but being here in person provided a whole different experience. You could feel the thrust of their combined efforts as the riders pushed the air before them. Everything I had learned about the power behind the peloton was playing out before my eyes. All the principles of drafting were revealed to me in full force. I could see how the riders could race faster for an extended amount of time when they were part of one big, powerful train. Lone riders were at an obvious disadvantage; they had no one to break the wind for them, no one in front of them to create a draft.

Like a colorful swarm of bees buzzing by, the peloton fascinated me both by its sight and sound. *The sound of grace in motion*, I thought to myself as I watched and listened as each swoosh passed before me. Even I could tell that the pitch on this sprawling avenue only enhanced the beauty of the workings of this massive assemblage of athletes. The conditions were ideal for all the cyclists to work together. "Whoa! There goes someone," I yelled as I spotted a cyclist break away from the main field on the giant TV.

"Oh, you wait and see," Pete said. "They're all vying for their moment of glory on the Champs-Elysées." And sure enough, true to Pete's prediction, one daring cyclist after another pedaled forth with all his strength in an attempt to separate himself from the mighty peloton. Little groups of intermittent breakaways formed throughout the course. But it seemed as though big gaps turned small again, until finally even those daring souls were gobbled up by the mass of cyclists moving ever faster. Surely it was a challenge for even the best riders to do much work on their own after so many miles *and* days of racing.

"This is a sprinter's dream," Pete declared. "This stage always is. You wait and see—it's going to come down to the wire. It's all about positioning and sheer strength in the end."

"What about Lance?"

"What do you mean?" Pete asked.

"What if he were to crash?" I asked as I looked out at the peloton bombing by at a high rate of speed. "I have to squint to spot the yellow jersey in that pack."

"He's OK once he's inside the last k," Pete responded.

"For some reason that doesn't reassure me."

"Don't worry. They pretty much take care of each other out there."

"Let's hope so," I said rather nervously.

The men in blue—the U. S. Postal team—did fortunately seem to do a good job of surrounding Lance each time they careened around the circuit and zoomed along straightaways of this elegant avenue. The laps ticked by and soon we could tell that many of the riders were jockeying for their best position as they headed down the home stretch. "This is one of the most prestigious stages to win," Pete said. "It's going to be an exciting finish—the sprinters love this." The fans roared as the cyclists whizzed by for the last time of the race. Before the remaining stragglers passed in front of us, we watched the heart-stopping finish on the Jumbotron across the way. It was indeed a sprinter's finish. And the biggest bike race in the world—the Super Bowl of cycling—came to an end.

As at the other stages, the award ceremony would soon begin. And this one promised to be bigger than ever. Pete and I kept looking up the avenue to see where the giant podium was installed. It seemed as though before you could say "finish"—the stage was set up in the middle of the avenue near the rond-point des Champs-Elysées. "Do you want to run up to check it out?" I asked Pete.

"No, I think it's better to watch the action on the Jumbotron." That was a good move since the winners were up on the podium in a flash. First came the stage winner, then Lance, the Tour winner, then the jersey winners which included best overall sprinter, climber and young rider. I'm sure Lance made many Americans proud.

"Look at all this," I said. "What a sight against the sweeping panorama of the Champs-Elysées with the Arc de Triomphe in the background. It's truly superb."

"What a gorgeous day, too."

"This is the ultimate culmination of our own tour de France as well," I said to Pete, which made him nod some more. It did feel like a triumphant finish for our relationship. Yet I refrained from saying this to Pete. It didn't seem like the right time. *We had climbed many mountains, and in the end, we crossed the finish line together. Sure, there was much we hadn't accomplished. Pete never did one of the major climbs in the Pyrenees. I still hadn't lost the weight I'd gained during our first trip to France and my cycling didn't improve a whole lot since then either. I still wasn't sure what kind of a form this book — our story — would take. But none of that seemed to matter so much. We had taken our relationship to a higher level — that's what was most important. We shared a passion for cycling and the Tour de France. But more importantly, our love had deepened. I think Pete would have the same take on "us" as well.*

"C'mon, let's go," Pete shouted, jolting me out of my thoughts. "Let's go down to the barrier. They're going to start the parade lap soon. Let's get up close." Just seconds after we situated ourselves at the barrier, the men in blue soft-pedaled by. Lance was out front gently waving the Texan and American flags. The crowds cheered wildly. A picture of the White House was beamed on the giant-screen TV before us.

"It seems odd to see *la maison blanche* projected onto this famous French avenue," I said.

"It's probably the most recognizable symbol of the U. S.," Pete replied.

"I guess you're right." And then I added, "Today's a good day to be an American, especially in Paris."

By the time the last team pedaled by, the crowd was beginning to disperse. Pete and I headed over to the place de la Concorde. Here we encountered some of the teams breaking up, veering off into different directions. It was great to see all the cyclists tanned, relaxed and elated that their three-week endurance test had finally come to an end. "What now?" Pete asked.

"Hey, there's the U.S. Postal bus parked outside the Crillon. Let's head over there and see if we can get in on the action." We stood outside of the bus with a bunch of other groupies until it had become apparent that nothing was going to happen there.

"You should have tried to line up something for tonight," Pete said, half accusingly.

"What do you mean?"

"Well, you were hanging out with all those guys. I thought maybe they'd invite you to their after-the-race party."

"Well, aren't you the wannabe hobnobber," I teased. "It actually didn't even occur to me."

"That doesn't sound like you," Pete replied.

"No, I guess not. I guess I'm not so perfect after all," I said wryly as I slung my arm around his shoulder.

We scuffed down avenue Gabriel, the street in front of the American Embassy, which was surprisingly quiet. "There's George Hincapie," Pete said as he spotted one of Postal's prized cyclists, pedaling slowly by, carrying a half-drooped American flag.

"Hey, George!" I yelled. He looked up in an inquisitive manner. "You did great—congratulations!" He gave me an appreciative wave and then pedaled off.

Pete laughed. "What's so funny?" I asked.

"Nothing."

"No, really—what are you laughing about?"

"Just you—you're something else."

"Me—why? Was it because I made a half-hearted attempt at chatting up Georgie? I'm thinking he might have recognized me," I said with a giggle.

"Of course he did. You're the Queen of France."

"Yeah, and you're the King of the Road, King of the Road Bike, that is," I teased back. "Make that King of the Tour, too."

Pete laughed at my silliness and practically bumped me off the sidewalk. I bumped him back and said, "Aren't you glad we combined our talents?"

"I really am," he said, now in a more serious tone. "And I'm glad you talked me into coming over a second time."

"It wouldn't have been the same without you."

Epilogue

Peter and I moved out West almost six months after our time at the Tour. After 9/11 we felt even more drawn to the open spaces and rugged landscapes of the Rockies. We did a three-week road trip in October 2001, traveling from Bozeman, Montana, down through Salt Lake City, Park City and Moab, Utah. We soaked up the healing power of the mountains and red rocks across these vast spaces of the West. It was a journey that seemed to have a greater purpose for us. We dipped farther south to Prescott, Arizona, then headed north again to Flagstaff.

When we crossed the border into Colorado, we finally felt the "ahhhh" sensation we were hoping to find during our search for where to settle in the West. As we traversed this southwestern corner of Colorado on our way to Durango—amid all the towering evergreens and verdant alpine landscapes—it felt almost like coming home.

We returned to Saratoga, wrapped up our lives and prepared for a big move. I sold the diamond from my engagement ring from my French husband to offset my share of the moving expenses. (I knew that wearing it as a pendant around my neck no longer fit my manner of dress in any event.) We flew out to Pagosa Springs, Colorado—the place we'd liked the most just an hour from Durango—early in December to line up a place to live. On January 1, 2002, Pete commandeered our big Ryder truck, filled with most of our possessions—including my prized armoire—over Wolf Creek Pass (at the Continental Divide). It was a white-knuckled ride that made him break a sweat. Indeed, we were embarking upon an entirely new journey.

Both of us were thrilled to be in the West, in a land where outdoor activities are far more common than going to the mall. Being surrounded by such glorious nature was healing on many levels. We enjoyed living in a beautiful house on Cloister Place, an aptly named street where I holed myself up the summer after our first ski season in Colorado to write what would become *A Tour of the Heart*.

I meticulously organized each notepad, scrap of paper, map, card and brochure and began to chronicle our adventures in France. This, too, soothed me at a time when our country was still hurting from 9/11 and its aftermath. As a writer, I found it to be a challenging period for praising the riches of France, yet I hoped the animosity toward the French would subside. I took solace in getting our story on paper even though I wasn't sure what would become of it.

Pete embraced skiing, a sport he'd always loved, full-on. (He actually got into cycling as rehab for a bad ski accident.) I did too, albeit with considerably more caution. (Go figure.) Work-wise, Pete took a maintenance job at a resort to pay the bills.

We were for the most part happy in our love and life, partly because we occupied a living space—a house—that felt like ours. And the West seemed so right for us. I became pregnant but, sadly, had another miscarriage. That became a big preoccupation of mine, and we visited specialists in Denver to find out what was going on. They said the same as the doctors in Paris, which was that they could find no explanation why this kept happening. This proved harder for me to hear than if they had discovered a problem.

After a year and a half in Pagosa, Pete and I moved to Telluride, Colorado, a much more happening mountain town. We were both taken by its striking scenery, excellent skiing and rich cultural offerings. T-ride also has a great local feel, a lot of sophistication and a sort of anything-goes attitude. You can be anything or anyone you want in Telluride, something Pete and I always appreciated very much.

We first lived in a high mountain enclave in a rented log cabin at an elevation of almost 10,000 feet. The winds often howl incessantly there and avalanches slide practically to residents' back doors. So for the first time in my life, I learned to make a proper fire.

That first winter in Telluride proved to be life-changing for me. I did the unthinkable and became a ski instructor. I'm entering my ninth season at Telluride Ski & Snowboard School, an elite club of sorts, one of the best ski schools in the country. I think I've done well there because I'm a good teacher as well as a fun "tour guide." What I lack in physical ability and strength, I make up for in communication and enthusiasm. On a personal level, I challenge myself both physically and mentally in this position and with skiing in general, much the same way I did on the bike over a decade ago.

Teaching kids skiing has also helped me to fill the void I felt from not having children. I can't remember how many miscarriages I had—it was all so traumatic. I blocked a lot of it out. Maybe six. I never thought I'd get over the sadness and disappointment of not having a child. But suddenly one day, that ache disappeared. My experience with children on the hill is surely largely responsible for that. I know I'm making a difference; ski memories—or vacation memories for that matter—are among the best in the world. I also teach adults and enjoy imparting women with a fun, can-do attitude on the slopes. Our chairlift rides are often peppered with tales of relationships. It seems as though most women—no matter the age— like to make a sport of attempting to figure men out.

I backed off from writing after moving to Telluride. I think I felt burned out and was more inclined to embrace a different lifestyle, one that involved more time outside and less at my desk. My travels to France slowed, too. Whenever I had the itch to take off it was to a wonderful destination in the West.

Pete embraced life in Telluride with all the gusto of a King of the Mountains climber. He worked many years in a ski and bike shop which helped him to further his passions. He's remained an avid cyclist and regularly tackles ascents that rival those of the Alps. His love for Telluride's steeps and deeps carries him through every winter with a huge, wide grin.

Our romantic relationship ended in the fall of 2004. As much as it was heartbreaking, it unraveled with love. There was no messiness about the break-up. We still cared deeply about each other but it seemed like too much of a struggle to make it work. Today we're dear friends. We occasionally see each other in Telluride and often talk on the phone. Sometimes he feels like a brother to me, but passing him on the road when he's on his bike can still bring me to tears.

I know we both cherish the memories of the trips to France we took together. For me, they encapsulated transformative moments I'll never forget. Maybe it's because of all the note taking and that I wrote about our adventures and encounters. Yes, that's part of it. But still, how could I ever forget "pushing Bessie," climbing Ventoux and attending the final stage of the Tour de France together on the Champs-Elysées. As I look back, I realize those trips—and the metamorphosis that occurred during my cycling days—served as the bridge between my fancy life in France and my more down-to-earth existence in Colorado.

For Pete, I know he remembers our travels with great fondness and affection; he recognizes that he did some extraordinary things in some remarkable places. He also had a devoted tour guide that tried her darnedest to share her love of France with him. (I think I succeeded.)

And, of course, there's our love. I'll never forget how much I loved Pete as we careened through France. Feelings like that thankfully remain locked in time although I think this book helps to bring them alive.

As for Bella, Pete sold my beloved bike for me on eBay, a couple years after moving to Telluride. I needed the money; *hélas*, a writer's life is not always an easy one. It was just collecting dust in a garage, anyway. I do miss her, though. How I loved her sleek frame and her brilliant, Robin's-Egg-blue glossy color. The terrain in and around Telluride is too steep for my enjoyment, plus the lack of good shoulders on the roads frightens me. I haven't done any real road riding in ages. I miss that freewheelin' freedom, although I guess I've replaced it with other activities such as hiking, swimming and skiing. I do look forward to the day when I can get back out on a road bike, hopefully on a back country *route de France*.

I ramped up my writing four years ago when I started my blog, BonjourColorado.com. In it, I feature stories on travel, shopping, beauty, food & wine and more from Paris to Telluride (and lots of destinations in between). The theme of self empowerment through sports is explored in many of my stories, something I'm still trying to build on in my life, whether I'm skiing a double black diamond or camping alongside a river. (I still love my luxury hotels, though.) And yes, as you can imagine, I love playing off of my two personas: that of French sophisticate and Rocky Mountain girl.

I've also done Travel Fun, a talk radio show on travel here in Telluride, for almost nine years. Through that program, I've enjoyed getting other people to share their travels and adventures and then I post those interviews on my blog.

As for love, my two adorable cats, Leo and Clara, remain my most faithful companions. Both love to cozy up with me in my one-bedroom, slopeside apartment. Oh, and I invite Steve to come around as much as he wants. We've been together almost four years although we don't live together—maybe partly because he has two cats, too. It was my chubby cat, Clara, that brought us together. He's the General Manager of a big lodge across the ski run from me in Telluride. He loves to travel, delights in fine meals at home and out and is smitten with me and many of my rituals, including sipping tea in my fussy apartment at five o'clock. (Although I do make him crazy sometimes.) He's Italian, so we love sharing the European way of life as well. We enjoy skiing and swimming together and our attraction to each other is electric. He's also a big jock that's known to blow me off on powder days. And he'll plan a surf trip for himself before he'll carve out the time for a romantic vacation for us any day. So, as you can see, there's still much to work out.

I'm not sure how he'll deal with *A Tour of the Heart*. Maybe I'll get more romantic getaways with him as a result. Who knows? Love can be so strange sometimes.

This story needed to be told, though. My heart has been bursting with it for more than a decade. To me, it shows the power of love and travel, something that's always best experienced *à deux*.

Acknowledgements

So many people have helped to shape *A Tour of the Heart* over the span of more than a decade, it's hard to remember everyone. I ask for forgiveness in advance if I don't cite you specifically by name or even worse, if I forget you altogether. Know that to everyone that has made a contribution to this book, I am extremely grateful.

Thank you to all the Comités Regionnaux de Tourisme, Comités Départementaux de Tourisme and Offices de Tourisme in France that helped me with the research phase of this book. I was warmly welcomed throughout France, thanks largely to your outstanding efforts toward the discovery of your region, department and town. Without your careful consideration of my project I know I would not have found so many wonderful nooks and crannies of France. Also, meeting so many tourism representatives along the way enhanced my experience tenfold.

Certain travels were also facilitated by the French Government Tourist Office and Marion Forestier in particular. Thank you for your assistance and introductions, *un must* in France.

I'm very appreciative toward Guy Geslin from Renault Eurodrive for having hooked me up with a car during the first trip to France. Guy, you have always been supportive of my work, something I'll never forget.

Thanks to Relais & Châteaux I was able to experience some of the most sumptuous properties of France. I'm grateful for your help with all, since somehow camping around France didn't quite fit the storyline. Thank you especially to Brenda Homick for having made so many arrangements for me.

Two great lodging moments on my second trip to France occur in Concorde Hotel properties. Thank you for your assistance and for having such a superior-quality brand.

Rail Europe helped out with train travel, something I love and enjoy all over Europe, especially in France. And to think that in certain parts of France, such as Alsace, you can hop on the train with your bike. *C'est merveilleux!*

Thank you to American Airlines for having made possible my first trip to France with Pete. You also made it easy for us to bring our beautiful bikes as baggage, something that I especially appreciated, since our adventures wouldn't have been the same without my beautiful Bella.

I will always recognize Kimberley Cameron as being a pivotal person with my manuscript moving forward as a book. Thank you, Kimberley, for encouraging me with my writing and also for suggesting such a wonderful title.

My dear friend, Jane Fitzgerald Nishimura, has always nurtured my work and especially this book. Jane, I appreciate all the input you've provided, mostly because I think you're so damned smart. Thank you for always thinking about how you can help me and then acting on it. I'm also grateful to Sheila Wald here in Telluride and Marilyn August, my long, lost friend in Paris. Both of you also read my manuscript, provided valuable feedback and facilitated certain introductions.

Thank you to all those who took the time to share a contact, provide a word of advice or supply me with information. Sometimes it worked, sometimes it didn't—I still appreciate every effort you made. Kate Betts and Martha McPhee, two New York-based writers, particularly come to mind. Thank you, Martha, for also taking the time to read part of my manuscript.

On the production end of things here in Telluride, thank you to Deb Dion Kees who carefully went over every word of my manuscript, most likely countless times. Deb, I so needed a person like you—not only for your skill and attention to detail, but also as a rudder that could steer me through this project at a time when there was no room for self-doubt. Thank you for all.

I'm thrilled with the artwork Chandler Thayer created for the book cover. Chandler, you captured the spirit of my book beautifully. Thank you for listening so attentively to my ideas and for translating them into such a lovely painting. I'm also grateful for the input you provided regarding the design of the book.

Thank you to Lauren Metzger for stepping in at the eleventh hour and producing such a delightful map. Lauren, I look forward to working with you on more maps for *A Tour of the Heart* which are to appear at www.atouroftheheart.com. Thank you also to Brian Torp for the photos you took of me—I'm sure they'll serve me well for publicity purposes.

Thank you to Jim Berkowitz for caring so much about my work and me, particularly my websites. Jim, know that I've appreciated your know-how and ideas over this past year. Many thanks also to Broox Best who has always happily made himself available to me for computer issues. Broox, thanks for helping me to be less eighteenth century.

I also want to acknowledge my KOTO family in Telluride. You've been a steady force in my life for nearly nine years and I love being a part of the KOTO clan. Thank you for just allowing me to "do my thing" all these years. Big hugs to Ben, Janice, Stephen and Suzanne.

Mary Dawn DeBraie, from Alpen Schatz, has consistently promoted my work and me to everyone within her wide sphere of contacts. Thank you for that, MD, for your friendship and also for encouraging me with *A Tour of the Heart*. It's wonderful, too, to have a friend in Telluride that shares such a love for finely made European goods.

I'm not sure this book would have happened without Mark Eversman. Mark, I couldn't have asked for a better mentor/cheerleader. We met over two decades ago when you were editor and publisher of *Paris Notes* and I'm happy our relationship has deepened. I feel lucky to have you in my life. Know that I appreciate all the information and input you share with me, even when we have one of our big 'ole go-arounds. We haven't always agreed but we have always cared. Thank you also, my dear Mark, for your delightful cover design and your input on the subtitle of the book and the jacket copy. Forever the editor, indeed!

Thank you to my friends in Telluride and beyond for buoying me up when I needed it most. Special thanks to Dave Brown, Darren Miller, Paula Marlatt, Rosa Lea Davis, Cristina Candido, Katie McHugh, John Gerona, Lindsay Brown and many of my pals at Telluride Ski & Snowboard School. You've all said just the right thing to me at the right time, something we all need to hear, especially when you're a freelance writer with a book project dancing in your head. I'm grateful to my dear friends Nancy Bacher, Rosemary Farnan Balog and Brigitte Nicolet for the relationship wisdom we've shared over the years. Such a research aid is invaluable, particularly when you're trying to sort out feelings for a love story. Brigitte, you lived much of my story with Pete firsthand— *merci pour tout*. Thank you also to Roz Strong for helping me to see life and relationships more clearly. *Merci* to Larry McGuinness for your friendship and for being a consistent colleague in the world of travel—primarily to France— over all these years.

I'm grateful for the love and support my family has shown over the years. I know my brothers have taught me tons about male / female relationships and as you can tell from reading this book, some of it I get, the rest I'm still sorting out. Thank you especially to Frankie and David and their wives, Wendy and Geri. Each of you has played a part in *A Tour of the Heart* whether you realize it or not. I'm sure it's not easy having a writer in the family, so thanks for sticking with me.

I want to acknowledge my 100-year-old Aunt Rose and my 92-year-old Aunt Ange. Both of you have always taken a big interest in my writing and for that and so much more I'm extremely grateful. I hope I have made you proud. I'm very proud of the two of you, especially when you tell me that reading still keeps you up at night.

And to my father, a wordsmith extraordinare, thank you for emphasizing the importance of correct speech and good writing from an early age. Thank you also for showing, through example, how to pick a decent restaurant when on the road! Thank you for nurturing my love of France and the French language. Thank you for making so much possible.

To my mother, who imparted me with the joy of travel and discovery from an early age, I will always credit you with having been a huge influence in my life. You've been a fine companion for me, on the road and just about everywhere else. You also were the first to read this story in its raw form. Thank you for believing in this project from the beginning.

Thank you to Leo and Clara, my sweet kitty cats. You've both been great about keeping me company throughout all the long hours at my desk. I'm grateful for this and so much more, particularly your unfailing love and affection. I promise some day we'll have a garden where you can sniff and play in safety.

Although I don't mention him much in this book, my ex-husband, Stéphane de Bourgies, is always with me in spirit whenever I'm in France or just feeling particularly French. Steph, you taught me so much about France, *toute la finesse* you seldom find in books. For that and so much more I'll always cherish our time together.

To Stefano Togni, *mi amore*, I feel so blessed to have found you. Steve, thank you for all your love and support. Thank you for believing in me with such pride and conviction. I'm grateful for your wisdom, pep talks, faith,, teatimes, hugs, olive oil and so much more. Thank you, thank you, thank you most of all for feeling confident enough in yourself and our love to be in favor of this story being told. You are indeed a rare find.

And what would this story have been without Peter Hazard? Pete, thank you for being willing to embark upon such an adventure with me. From the bottom of my heart, I thank you for all we shared. You believed in me from day one and I feel so fortunate that you've continued to be a fan of mine throughout these years. There's no doubt that in you, I found something more than a travel companion. You are a very fine man.

About the Author

MARIBETH CLEMENTE is the author of *The Chic Shopper's Guide to Paris, The Riches of Paris: A Shopping and Touring Guide* and *The Riches of France: A Shopping and Touring Guide to the French Provinces.* She lived eleven years in France and then moved to Colorado where she has lived for over a decade. Maribeth hosts a travel radio show, blogs on her website, www.bonjourcolorado.com, and writes for various travel publications and websites. For more related to *A Tour of the Heart,* including a travel guide to the regions she covers in this book, visit www.atouroftheheart.com.

Go to www.atouroftheheart.com

for the complete

downloadable travel guide

to

A Tour of the Heart

A Seductive Cycling Trip
Through France.

Visit www.bonjourcolorado.com

to read stories on

travel, beauty, shopping,

food & wine, skiing

and more from

France to the Rocky Mountains.

There you can also find out about

some of Maribeth's

recommendations for

online shopping

and other boutique discoveries.